Does History Make Sense?

Does History Make Sense?

Hegel on the Historical Shapes of Justice

TERRY PINKARD

Harvard University Press

Cambridge, Massachusetts
London, England
2017

Library of Congress Cataloging-in-Publication Data
Names: Pinkard, Terry P., author.
Title: Does history make sense? :
Hegel on the historical shapes of justice / Terry Pinkard.
Description: Cambridge, Massachusetts : Harvard University Press, 2017. |
Includes bibliographical references and index.
Identifiers: LCCN 2016043278 | ISBN 9780674971776
Subjects: LCSH: Hegel, Georg Wilhelm Friedrich, 1770–1831. |
History—Philosophy. | Justice (Philosophy)
Classification: LCC D16.8.P495 2017 | DDC 901—dc23
LC record available at https://lccn.loc.gov/2016043278

To Susan

৵

CONTENTS

Does History Make Sense?

For on the one hand, we have in history ingredients and natural conditions which are remote from the conceptual world—i.e. all kinds of human arbitrariness and external necessity. On the other hand, we set up against this the thought of a higher necessity, an eternal justice and love, the absolute and ultimate end which is truth in and for itself. In contrast to natural being, this second, opposite pole is based on abstract elements, on the freedom and necessity of the concept. This opposition contains many interesting features; it comes to our notice once again in the "Idea" of world history. Our present aim is to show how this opposition is resolved in and for itself in world-history.

—HEGEL, *Reason in History*

The subjecting of man to law is a problem in politics which I liken to that of the squaring of the circle in geometry. Solve this problem well, and the government based on your solution will be good and free from abuses. But until then you may rest assured that, wherever you think you are establishing the rule of law, it is men who will do the ruling.

—JEAN-JACQUES ROUSSEAU,
Considerations on the Government of Poland

Introduction

ꙮ

Famous as it is, Hegel's philosophy of history is nowadays mostly seen as itself having only "historical importance." Few doubt its influence (for good or ill), but it seems that nobody really believes it. In particular, the "progressivism" it supposedly espouses (as a version of what later came to be derisively termed the "Whig" interpretation of history) and its "teleological" approach to history finds few, if any, defenders in the faculties of philosophy and even fewer in the faculties of history.[1] Moreover, there has always been more than a deep suspicion among practicing historians that Hegel's philosophy of history occurs at such a high altitude that it simply has to be indifferent to the facts, so that it is in effect a kind of polish that you can spray onto any account of the real facts of history without having to take any of them into real consideration. That is also behind much of the suspicion that it is really just an insupportable "a priori" theory of history. For other scholars who work in the post-structuralist idiom, although Hegel's philosophy of history may be one of the great stories of essentialism about self-identity, nonetheless, as such a story, it can be of interest only as a cautionary tale about how easy it is to forget that everything is not only contingent but also that forgetfulness of this contingency goes hand in hand with repression and oppression. Hegel's dismissive accounts of non-European civilizations do not exactly help his case in that regard.

However, one part of Hegel's philosophy of history still has some currency, namely, the idea that he proposes a decisive break between the ancients and the moderns, and that "modernity" itself represents some basic fundamental break in human time. This thesis is, of course, not specific to Hegel, and others claim to find a similar view in Hobbes, Machiavelli, Descartes, Tocqueville, and so on. Perhaps at best, in Hegel's treatment something like the view that "modernity" represents some basic, nonreversible turn in human self-understanding nonetheless receives its most explicit formulation. Those who hold some version of this view of Hegel's thesis about "modernity" need not (and often do not) accept his other views about, for example, the necessity he supposedly finds in history.

The reception of Hegel's philosophy of history has also been plagued with a set of widespread and lazy interpretations. The laziest of these relies on the long-since discredited idea that his entire philosophy rests on some kind of movement of thesis-antithesis-synthesis and that history is just such a movement. Exactly what is gained by saying that Persia is the thesis, Greece is the antithesis, and Rome is the synthesis (or that Greece is the thesis, Rome is the antithesis, and Germany is the synthesis) has never been made clear, and the fact that Hegel did not say that means that there is little to be gained by attempting to clear it up.

An almost equally lazy reading takes Hegel to think of history as having a goal (freedom, realization of spirit, etc.), and that all moments of history have until around 1807 failed to reach that goal, however much they may have contributed little pieces to the puzzle about how to realize it, and, so the story goes, the goal has now been reached. This makes the philosophy easy to teach (take a period in history, show it failed to reach its goal by virtue of not being modern European, and, *voila,* one supposedly has Hegel's theory in hand), and it makes it easy to understand (history is just like any other goal-oriented activity in that it sometimes reaches its goal only through fits and starts). Such a view informed the recent rather vacuous debates about the "end" of history. Even the more sophisticated versions that go beyond this lazy interpretation—the ones that rely on metaphors such as the acorn developing into an oak according to an internal plan—suffer the same flaw. However easy they are to understand and to teach, they ultimately make Hegel's views both implausible in the extreme and empirically vacuous, however illustrative they might be said to be about the worldviews held by people of his generation.

There has also been a tendency, completely understandable and much more sophisticated, to treat Hegel's philosophy of history as if he thought history was a single, unitary "thing" or "development." Thus, people have looked to the rest of his system to get an idea about how this one "thing" developed teleologically, and the "acorn-oak" metaphor has suggested itself quite naturally as the best way to capture that sense. That interpretation, while lending itself to some very sophisticated interpretations of the rest of his system, is, however, false to what Hegel is seeking in his philosophy of history.[2] It rests ultimately on a flawed understanding of Hegel's *Logic*.

Is there anything to Hegel's philosophy of history other than its "historical" interest? I shall argue that there is, and it has to do with what Hegel means by saying that it is "freedom" taken as "infinite"—a statement which on its surface is anything but clear—and that this view follows from Hegel's social conception of subjectivity. Hegel's social and historical view of the nature of subjectivity, when properly articulated, shows (according to Hegel) that there is indeed an "infinite" end at work in history—that of securing justice—which in modern times has transformed itself into a concern with justice as freedom. Freedom was not the original goal of history, but it has become the principle of modern life.[3] This at first looks like it clashes with the way Hegel presents his story, namely, of how the long course of history is mostly a story of unjustified domination disguised under various cloaks of legitimacy and how the use of power to achieve various ends usually have little to do with justice.[4] However, behind that story of power and domination is a concern for justice, which in its most general sense involves an abstract conception of the proper, good ordering among people in a collective endeavor, whether that order be interpreted as conforming to a cosmic order that itself constitutes a set of ethical principles or a sense of playing by a set of rules that are themselves fair.[5] "Justice" itself makes rare appearances in Hegel's telling of world history, and, for the most part, history has not been a showplace of justice.[6] This does not mean that the struggle over recognition and justice is not the story behind the story.

Most crucially for Hegel, the philosophical comprehension of history is a comprehension of how historically the metaphysics of subjectivity itself—

and not merely our conception of the metaphysics of subjectivity—has changed.[7] This, as with the struggle over justice itself, has to do with the nature of the "infinite ends" of subjectivity at different points in history. Because of this, our "agency" actually changes its shape over time. (I will also stick, for the most part, to Hegel's terms, "subject" and "subjectivity," rather than use "agency" and "person."[8])

As these claims are phrased here, none of those statements are very clear at all, and on their surface, some of them even seem preposterous. Whatever clarity or plausibility is possible for them requires a more careful parsing of Hegel's own views.

However, so I shall also argue, there are also some crucial flaws in Hegel's own view of the historical development of modern life when we look at them from within the terms of Hegel's own views about subjectivity and history, and those flaws affect his own understanding of how necessity in history works. This does not mean that Hegel's views cannot, on its own terms, be reshaped and reworked. It does mean that they cannot stand on their own merits without such reworking.

My aim here is not primarily a study of how Hegel changed his mind over the years he lectured on the topic. That has already been done.[9] Nor is it here concerned with his relations to the other German idealist philosophies of history. That too has been admirably done.[10] Nor is it overtly concerned with how Hegel's philosophy of history connects with what is probably its most famous offshoot, Marx's theory of history. That is another book in itself. Here my interest has first of all to do with how Hegel's thought measures up to the standards he set for it and whether it succeeds on its own terms, not in terms we might bring to it from the outside. From that point of view, it is, as it were, a Hegelian commentary on Hegel's work. Second, it also has to do whether those standards, especially when seen in light of other ways of approaching the material, can be seen to have a basis in themselves.

As Hegel himself envisaged what he needed to say about this topic, he thought that it should start from considerations about the nature of intelligibility itself. His answer to that was his *Science of Logic*. After the *Logic*, which concludes with a conception of the intelligibility of subjectivity itself, Hegel took his system necessarily to move on to a more detailed condition of the intelligibility of nature and then of subjectivity as embedded in nature and then as gradually distinguishing itself from other entities in nature, only to come to an end when it finally comprehends its own nature. (These subjects of these latter conceptions constitute the other two volumes of his *Encyclopedia of the Philosophical Sciences,* the overall sketch of his system for use in his lectures in which he filled in the crucial details and elaborated on the all-too-abstractly presented arguments in those volumes.)

Hegel's project is not that of an investigation of something like "how we humans must think," at least in the sense of delineating some species-specific grasp of things that may or may not be as things are from the perspective of another species, nor is it a purely conceptual investigation indifferent to what the world is really like. It is, rather, a direct descendent of Kant's *Critiques* and, more especially, Fichte's *Wissenschaftslehre:* Fichte's "science of science" becomes in Hegel's *Science of Logic* a general account of explanatory adequacy, an account of accounts. It is more like what A. W. Moore and Robert Pippin have recently called "making sense of things" (as metaphysics) and "making sense of making sense" (as logic) taken together.[11]

However, as he also noted of his system, you can begin anywhere within it, and that is what I shall do here—starting in the middle, going back to the beginning, and then jumping to where Hegel himself begins his account of history: the "East." Readers, on the other hand, are invited to start where they would like, perhaps jumping ahead to the sections where Hegel's narrative of history begins or to the earlier section on what a history of modernity would look like.

I

Preliminaries

The Logic of Self-Conscious Animals

&c;

Substance and Subject

Here is one way of starting. We are natural animals, but there is a way in which we are different from other animals. One way of thinking about that is to claim or try to demonstrate that there is something very "un-animal" about the stuff out of which we are constituted. That is not Hegel's way. For him, there is a line that runs from nature to fully minded agents, but it is not a line that runs from the animal to the nonanimal but rather from animals with a certain type of self-relation to animals with a very different self-relation. Something like that thought is behind his summary statement in the *Phenomenology* that "everything hangs on apprehending and expressing the true not just as *substance* but also equally as *subject*."[1] Or, as we might alternately put it, if Hegel is right about the importance of that statement, then everything about what we say about Hegel hangs on what we take Hegel to mean by that assertion. Let us start with the view that Hegel's statement about substance and subject is the key to his idealism. At first, let us simply lay out some of the basic commitments and come back to their interpretation and defense later.

One of the oldest interpretations of Hegel's thought takes his idealism to consist rather straightforwardly in the claim that only spiritual (or perhaps mental) things are real, and that the supposedly nonspiritual world of interstellar gases, stars, and the more mundane supposedly nonspiritual world of rocks, plants, and animals is an unreal or untrue manifestation of that deeper spiritual reality—or, on another version of the same view, it holds that there must be some singular big Mind that constructs objects out of its own experiences but that those objects remain only spiritual constructions, even if they appear (untruly) as physical. This is the most common view of Hegel's idealism: It is supposed to be a monistic metaphysics of *Geist*, i.e., of "spirit" or "mind."[2] Mind is not a feature of nature so much as nature is supposed to be a manifestation of a more basic spiritual order of the world.

Although it is always tempting to assimilate Hegel's idealism to one of these other, more familiar forms of idealism, it is also misleading. One of Hegel's favorite analogies—which pops up in all the various places where he remarks that animals are true idealists—is in an indication that his is not an idealism that declares everything to be ultimately mental. Animals do not, he notes, take food to be untrue or merely one-sided phenomenal appearances of an underlying mental reality. Rather, as he puts it, they confront the things that show up to them as food and "without any further ado, they simply help themselves to them and devour them."[3] Animals do not, that is, construct the objects of their world out of their mental experiences. To animals with the requisite sensory apparatus, things "show up" as food because of the purposes the animal brings to bear on its environment by virtue of being the kind of animal it is. Lettuce shows up for rabbits as food because of the kind of creatures rabbits are, just as rabbits show up as food for foxes because of the kinds of creatures foxes are.[4] What "shows up" to an animal as salient in its world depends on the species interests it brings to bear on that world. Food can "show up" only to creatures with the proper organic makeup and the appropriate nervous systems, but nothing shows up to an iron spike. However—and it is here that Hegel's genuine idealism starts to come into view—for self-conscious creatures, very different things can "show up" in experience, for example, states, constitutions, divinities, artworks, and ethical requirements.[5]

We can put the first provisional formulation of Hegel's idealism in this way: It is a view that the way the world shows up for living creatures depends on the nature of the creature and that the world "shows up" for creatures with a capacity for self-consciousness in a way that it cannot for non-self-conscious creatures. Put in this way, it is not the thesis that the mind creates the world or that what is really fundamental or more basically real are mental things, nor is it the idea the world is inherently spiritual and not material, nor is it the idea that subjects "construct" (either socially or individually) these kinds of things, nor finally that subjects impose conceptual meaning on some kind of distinct and neutral sensible information. The world is not dependent on us for its existence or its structure, but what "shows up" as salient in our world is a function of our species interests as the beings we are.

There is a second way of stating Hegel's idealism that augments the first one, which has to do with the way things show up to thinking creatures. It holds that not only are there items which can only be entertained in thought—although the infinitely large and the infinitely small are not perceptible they are thinkable—there is also nothing in the world that is in principle unavailable for conceptual thought. There is no reason to think, for example, that there are items which can be felt or grasped in some deep emotional state but not thought. A corollary to this is that for Hegel's idealism, the world taken as a whole—the "totality" of such things—is only available to thought and not to intuition. We can think of the infinite, we can imagine it, but we cannot see it. Because of this capacity for comprehending the world that goes beyond the more direct deliverances of experience, things can show up for humans in a way that they cannot for non-self-conscious creatures. As such self-conscious creatures, we become capable of wondering whether the way things show up for us is the way things really are. This capacity for self-conscious thought—and, in Hegel's language, for entertaining the "universal"—is the determining feature of our species life. That also means that our species life is also characterized by a profound unease with itself, another corollary of Hegel's idealism but which requires a different argument. This is a feature of our type of self-relation, not an indication that we are made of different stuff than other natural things.

Nonetheless, even if Hegel's idealism is not, after all, a monistic metaphysics of spirituality, it is still metaphysics.[6] What kind?

Life's Purposes

Once again, it is best to begin by laying the view out before going into it in more detail. The way the world shows up for animals has to do with their own nature, but that does not mean that the world has been organized to show up as it does to animals. Nature as a whole means nothing, aims at nothing, and cannot organize itself into better or worse.[7] However, there is nonetheless a place for a kind of functional teleology in the structure of organisms.[8] Living creatures have functions that are basic to themselves as organisms, namely, survival of the individual and reproduction of the species, even though sometimes those requirements may conflict with each other. In terms of Hegel's overall idealism, there is no need to see the teleological structure of organisms as implying an overall teleological structure to nature itself. That animals act in terms of an "inner purpose" does not imply that that there is an overall purpose to nature as a whole (such that nature's organization would require an organizer) nor that they are aware of that purpose. It is, as Hegel says, a mistake to think that all such purposes must be conscious purposes or be the purposes that are at work paradigmatically in conscious action.[9]

These ends are not merely artifacts of our own species-bound way of describing nature. The concepts of disease and injury suggest that such explanations in terms of an animal's nature have a basis in a real feature of the world and are not merely features of our way of describing nature. An animal, unlike, say, a rock can have things go well or badly for it, even in the cases where the animal does not have the neurological apparatus to take note that something is going badly for it.[10] Disease is a way of things going badly for the animal: An animal is diseased when something external to the normal functioning of the organism interferes with it, and the animal is prevented from (or has difficulty with) living in the terms of the standards appropriate to its form of life (or, as Hegel would put it, when it is inadequate to its concept). To say that an animal is in a diseased state is thus not merely a subjective requirement on our part or just a way of talking. Or, again as Hegel phrases it: "The defect in a chair which has only three legs is in us; but in life, the defect is in life itself, and yet it is also sublated because life is aware of the limitation as defect."[11] Thus, for things to go well or badly for a creature does not require the existence of their being creatures with "wills." We humans do not bring all value into the world.

However, what is a disease for the particular animal may be a means of sustenance for the microbes that are causing the disease. This is yet another manifestation of what Hegel calls nature's impotence in this regard.[12] It would be pointless to romantically protest and blame nature for this, since nature cannot put itself into any better order. In fact, "better order" makes no real sense at all in the case of nature as a whole. Instead, in nature, a creature's ends are bound up with circumstances external to it, such that what counts as disease for the animal will be nutrition for the parasite, and predator and prey exist together.

Life is its own purpose, even if the emergence of life on earth itself fulfills no further purpose of nature itself. Hegel calls life a *Selbstzweck,* an end unto itself (as does Kant). The living creature is its own end even though the purpose of life is distributed among many different creatures who do not in an important way share that purpose with each other.[13]

Just as disease is a real feature of nature, reasons also have a place in the natural world. Some animals can be said to respond to reasons that are in the nature of things, given the species-nature they have. The mouse running from the cat is responding to a good reason right there before it. The cat coming after it shows up to the mouse as danger, as a good reason to get on the move speedily to somewhere else. Some animals, even those whom we may not ordinarily at first describe as particularly intelligent, may even maintain a certain flexibility about how they do this and thereby display at least a type of cognitive skill. Since for these animals there is a way that they take in the world in light of their natures, they can be said to be subjects in Hegel's sense.[14] They experience things, and they act accordingly. He thereby clearly sees a kind of continuum at work in the passages from life to animal life to human life, and that continuum has to do with the quality of the responsiveness to reasons such organisms confront. The human subject responds to its purposes as purposes.[15]

The difference between having reasons and being aware of reasons as reasons means that there is a rupture between all other forms of life and human life. Only the human form stands in the kind of self-relation that we find exemplified in exemplary fashion in self-consciousness.

Making Sense of Human Life

The difference between animal life and human animal life has to do with the kind of self-relation that human animal life has to itself. Humans, that is, are self-conscious primates, odd creatures in the natural order, not because they are made of different "stuff" nor because they can exercise some kind of nonnatural causation of their actions but because they are constituted by distinctive kind of self-relation. To get straight on this, it is still worth spending a little more time on an exposition of the concept of self-relating life before we look at how it might be defended against its competitors.

The human shape of life is self-conscious. Describing it like this, of course, suggests that it is a life that is always reflectively aware of itself, but on Hegel's conception, such reflective self-awareness is to be distinguished from another form of self-awareness that consists in moving within a world of involvements in which there is an awareness of what one is doing in terms of various "ought's," "musts," and "ought not's" without there necessarily being any separate act of reflection accompanying one's awareness. For example, as you are reading this sentence, you are aware that you are reading a sentence and not, say, swimming, cooking, gardening, or skydiving. If asked, for example, "What are you doing?," the answer is: "Reading a sentence or two." This is not a matter of having already been reflectively aware that you were reading the sentence as you were reading the sentence, as if you were reading the sentence and in a separate act thinking to yourself, "I am reading this sentence." (If it were, a vicious regress would immediately set itself in motion.) To use a Kantian idiom to refer to this kind of self-conscious life that although self-conscious need not be reflective in all its operations, we can call it an apperceptive life. To shift to a slightly more Hegelian idiom: To be an apperceptive life—a subject—is to know that one is this shape of life exactly by being the life that falls under the concept, and an apperceptive life falls under that concept just by bringing itself under that concept.[16] We are self-conscious animals by being the animals that bring ourselves under that concept of "self-conscious animal." Moreover, we are not disembodied somethings that, on looking more carefully at themselves, decide to bring themselves under a certain concept. We are the creatures we are by bringing ourselves under the concept.[17] We fall under the concept by our actualizing the concept in our own lives. Hegel refers to this in various places as the concept's giving itself its own reality.[18] The absolute identity of the two-in-one—of the I aware of me—is the apperceptive self. This conception of subjectivity's apperceptive self-relation comprises more or less the ground floor of Hegel's metaphysics of subjectivity.

Because this is an achievement on our part, we live (in one of Hegel's striking metaphors) as "an amphibious animal, because [we] now have to live in two worlds which contradict one another."[19] We are natural creatures subject to natural needs and forces, and we are "spiritual," normative creatures who live in a world of various normative demands, involvements, and contours.[20] This opposition is at the heart of human subjectivity, but it is an opposition at all only because apperceptive organisms bring such a division on themselves. However, that we are amphibians who live with this tension between our normative and natural lives does not mean that we are not creatures who, as it were, have our apperceptive lives merely glued onto our natural lives. In our self-consciousness, we become different natural creatures—rational animals—and not just animals with an added function of rationality grafted onto us. In Matthew Boyle's phrase, Hegel's conception of human subjectivity is not an "additive" but rather a "transformative" conception of the role of reason in our lives.[21] It is a life that essentially involves the capacity to have a thought of itself to be the life it is, and it is that life, which, when conscious of itself, can take itself to be pulled in different directions.

Because it is an opposition, it is all too easy to think that such an opposition must therefore represent some way in which mind and body are totally different, or that our reflective capacities are different operations from our more animal sensitivities and that they must therefore function as some kind of monitoring mechanism for those animal sensitivities. Rather, on the Hegelian account, we are rational *animals,* who because we are *rational* animals, put ourselves into potential opposition to ourselves. A "rational animal" is not a substance with a subject stuck onto it who monitors it. It is a subject which is a substance that knows it is that kind of substance by bringing itself under the category "subject."[22]

The "Idea" of Subjectivity

Laying out Hegel's view pushes us back to his own way of beginning. The full story of why he took himself to hold such a view of human subjectivity is to be found in his dense *Science of Logic,* which claims to present an account of intelligibility, both of what makes sense of things and a logic of when sense has been made. This is not the place to go into any kind of detailed exegesis of Hegel's *Logic,* so, rather than following Hegel's own meticulously dense exposition of it, we can instead speak of it in a much looser way, similar to the way he himself did in his more popular lectures on the topic.

Hegel divides his book in three sections comprised of three different kinds of logical structure. The first section has to do with those judgments we make of individuals by pointing them out ("That thing over there"), by classifying them ("That one is red"), by making generalizations about them ("American Robins live on average 1.7 years"), or by counting them ("There are seven robins in the garden"). Hegel calls the logic of these judgments about individuals and how those judgments relate to each other the logic of "being."

Second, there are those judgments, such as "The tie only looks green in the store but is blue in normal sunlight," and "Deficiency in vitamin D may cause cognitive impairment in older adults," in which we explain things by appeal to some underlying condition or structure that is not immediately apparent in the mere observation of them. Hegel calls the logic of these kinds of judgments about the relation between the "essence" of things and their appearances the logic of "essence."

These two "logics" of "being" and "essence" are how we make sense of "things" in the most general way. Indeed, they are the logic of traditional metaphysics, and Hegel takes himself to have shown how the classical philosophical problems of metaphysics are generated out of the apparent paradoxes that arise in trying to state them clearly. Stating them clearly brings out the opposed ways of resolving the issues raised in such general thought of things, and that in turn motivates a reworking of the way in which the problems need to be stated. (The details of that are a story for another time and are not really suited for this kind of very general overview.)

These two "logics" disclose that we also need a third way of making sense, namely, to make sense of making sense—or as we might alternatively put it, making sense of when we really have made sense. Examples of that are judgments such as "What you just said does not follow from your premises" or "This makes no sense within the current standards of physics." The question, "What is this and how many of them are there?" is typically answered in one way that makes sense of things, whereas "Why does it look that way?" or "Why did that happen?" are typically answered in another way. "How does that follow?" is typically answered in neither of those two ways. These kinds of judgments belong to what Hegel calls the logic of the "concept."

This third part of Hegel's *Logic* is thus not just that of making sense of "things." It also introduces a sense of the way in which there are better and worse ways of being—examples of worse ways of being include those of a bad argument, an inconsistent or incoherent theory, a badly constructed artifact that fails to realize its purpose, and even a bad act or a bad person. In Hegel's terms, the logics of "Being" and "Essence" do not introduce better or worse ways of being. That of "Concept" does. The full concept of being a subject emerges in that section, not merely as an entity that causes itself to act in light of its reasons or passions (that is the kind of account given in "Essence") but as an entity that acts and thinks in terms of norms, constitutive principles of thought, and evaluations—as a locus of various kinds of ought's, as it were.[23] A subject is to be explained as a subject by being the kind of thing that moves in a logical space. Its thoughts and actions are explained by reasons, which means that what is doing the explaining is also something known by the subject and does not play this role outside of being known by the subject.

As noted, Hegel does not present his *Logic* in the rather loose way just given here but as itself manifesting a rigorous set of steps all along its development. Each stage (Being, Essence, Concept) supposedly fails at what establishing for itself what counts as success at that stage, so that, for example, "Being"—with all of its accounts of what it is to point out, classify, count, and such—fails to secure its end of successfully exhausting the purpose of thinking about the world so that it requires another set of purposes, those of "Essence." It eventually reaches a point where, in good Kantian spirit but not by any means by the Kantian letter, reason (or "thinking") realizes that it is responsible for setting its own limits (which by its nature it has) and that it is therefore "absolute." How all that works is another story, but not one especially for this telling. What is crucial for this telling is that this loose account itself can make sense of his *Logic* in a much looser way than Hegel himself thought the *Logic* should ultimately make sense.

The *Logic* culminates in what Hegel, in the preferred terminology of German idealism, calls the "Idea" (usually capitalized in English translation to distinguish it—the German *Idee*—from the noncapitalized "idea," or *Vorstellung,* itself often also rendered as "representation").[24] In both the *Logic* and his other mature works, Hegel consistently defines the "Idea" as the unity of concept and objectivity and often as the unity of concept and reality, and this makes a difference to his overall conception of subjectivity as both agents and persons.[25]

In clarifying Hegel's use of his term of art, "Idea," there is what looks like merely a terminological point but which makes a substantive difference to how to understand Hegel's account. In using the very term "Idea," Hegel is putting a Kantian concept to work for his own related but nonetheless different purposes. Kant had used the term "Idea" to talk about those "ideas" (representations, as they are often called) with which we tried to comprehend the world as an unconditioned whole, in other words, tried to do traditional metaphysics.[26] Reason, in Kant's nominalization of the term, knows that in experiential knowledge it is limited by the deliverances of sensibility, and, as unconditionally knowing itself as experientially conditioned, it pushes itself to seek the unconditioned. This self-push is necessary to reason since it claims to know itself fully, including the very limits of what it can know. This "unconditioned" would be the "whole" that reason seeks to comprehend. However, since we finite creatures can have no direct experience of the whole, we can only entertain the whole in thought. Kant called the world as comprehended in such pure, nonexperiential thought the noumenal world (i.e., the world comprehended in pure "thought"), and, for better or worse, he argued that the noumenal world was composed of a realm of unknowable things in themselves (and thus, that traditional metaphysics, as the a priori study of what turns out to be unknowable, was impossible). For Kant, an "Idea" is the result of an attempt to think of all the conditioned and bounded objects of experience as part of an unconditioned whole, and this meant that such "Ideas" of the unconditioned were—however important they were and however much of a necessary regulatory role they might play in knowledge—merely creatures of thought and lacked objective reality. (Kant also took the necessary failures that accompany all efforts to comprehend the "unconditioned" in pure reason to be a demonstration that traditional metaphysics was impossible. That is another interesting and well-researched path to take, but not for here.)

The subtleties involved in Kant's conceptions of the phenomenal, the noumenal, things in themselves and the failures of traditional metaphysics are not the issue here. It is crucial to note that Hegel took the upshot of Kant's use of "Idea" to mean that although the objects of ordinary experience could not be grasped as unconditioned—he took Kant to be completely right about that—the activity of thinking could indeed grasp the uncondi-tioned, that is, the "infinite," or, as it appeared in his way of putting the issues, the "absolute," and this was intended as a counterweight to Kant's claim that the noumenal realm was composed of unknowable things in themselves. Like Wittgenstein later, Hegel argued that if setting the limits of thought meant that one claimed to be thinking literally of the unthink-able, then one would be thinking what could not be thought.[27]

In his own usage, Hegel contrasted the phenomenal world not, as Kant did, with the noumenal realm but rather with the "concept" (or, rather, he substituted "the concept" for Kant's conception of the noumenal). We are phenomenal creatures whose nature is also to be noumenal creatures, that is, to be oriented by our sense of how the whole not only adds up in all its part but how it has a distinct meaning on its own. In the Hegelian sense, an "Idea" is the unity of the phenomenal world as it is ordinarily comprehended in science and commonsense with that of the noumenal world—the "con-cept"—that is, with the world as comprehended in thought.

However, part of the force of Hegel's approach is to take Kant's stric-tures about the limits of experiential knowledge seriously. For Hegel, an "Idea" is the unity of the phenomenal and the noumenal worlds, and thus, the "Idea," as Hegel explicitly puts it in his *Science of Logic,* is the unity of con-cept and objectivity.[28] The concept is what Hegel calls the thought of the thing "in itself" *(an sich),* and the "Idea" is the unity of the concept (the "in itself") with the phenomenal *(erscheinende)* reality that expresses it. The unity of the phenomenal world is that of an infinitely extending background, not all of which can be grasped through perception or intuition. The phe-nomenal world is more fully conceptually comprehended in the unity of how the abstract thought of things is at one with and modified by the thought of how that more abstract thought is concretely embodied. The grasp of the "Idea" of mind and world has an infinity that can be grasped not, as it were, as one thing after another but in the self-contained bound-lessness of the conceptual itself.[29] It is also crucial to Hegel's conception of the unity of the phenomenal and the noumenal that our conception of the "in itself" (or of things in themselves) is conceptual and has a historical dynamic to itself, which is mediated by the way those thoughts are con-cretely embodied and developed.[30] Although nature can be grasped in its conceptual unity, much of phenomenal nature is not at one with our concept of it, and this means that nature in detail is only best studied through the empirical sciences. (Or, in Hegel's preferred terminology, nature's fundamental relation to the "Idea" is that of "externality."[31])

The edges of the sharp rift between the world as it is rationally comprehended in thought and the world as it presents itself to us in experience are supposed to be softened and unified in an adequate "Idea." Likewise, the subject as split between the noumenal subject (an agent acting on consciously entertained reasons) and the phenomenal subject (an agent acting according to the drives and impulses inherent to its species) is a division that is reunited in the subject's own activity. The subject is the phenomenal creature who, by embodying this kind of self-relation, constitutes herself as a noumenal creature. She does this by bringing herself under the concept of an apperceptive life. There is thus no inherent need in the "Idea" of the subject to separate the agent into two spheres, one sphere of which is causally efficacious (the phenomenal) with the other operating in the space of reasons. The phenomenal agent becomes the noumenal agent in taking up a self-conscious relation to the world.

The Hegelian distinction between the "concept" of a rational agent and the "Idea" of a rational life turns on the way in which the "Idea" of a rational life is known by the apperceptive animals that are the embodiment of the "Idea," that is, is known by those rational animals leading that kind of life. In the "Idea" of a rational animal, it is not just "rationality" in general to which an appeal is being made but to human rationality as such (not just to the "concept" but also its phenomenal reality). That means that the more austere concept of the living, knowing subject as it is introduced in the *Logic* is, as Hegel explicitly says, only the "possibility" of such a subject, not its actuality (not its full "Idea"), since a conception of its actuality requires in turn a conception of how it develops itself concretely historically and socially.[32] As Hegel pithily summed that up for his young students: "The individual exists as a determinate being, unlike man in general, who has no existence as such."[33] The "concepts" that are developed within the "Idea" are the necessary components of the "Idea" itself—the self-articulations of the absolute, as Hegel likes to put it.[34] They are the components of what a human subject must take itself to know if it is to know itself as a human subject and not merely as an abstracted rational subject. Whereas in both empiricist thought and in Kantian schemes, the relation of the general concept to the things falling under it is taken to consist in something like a rule being applied to external instances, in the case of the "Idea," so Hegel puts it, "the universal *particularizes* itself and is herein identity with itself."[35] But what does that mean?

These concepts as components of the "Idea" are not external rules to which content is given, nor are they merely "empirical" facts subsumed under a priori thoughts, nor are they the conditions of the very possibility of thought. They rather emerge as necessary components, or, in Hegel's term, "moments" for human agents to make sense of themselves as they develop their conceptions of mind and world over time. They emerge within the view of ourselves as rational humans, and as such also develop historically as things fall apart and regroup themselves.[36] In that way, they do not function completely as norms (which can always be transgressed), but become incorporated into what it has historically come to be constitutive of making sense of mind and world.[37]

This line of thought will lead in the following direction. As this conception is developed, what seem to be constitutive of some social status turn out, as the shape of life develops itself, instead to be normative. A ruler may take certain things to be constitutive of rulership, such that if he did not conform to them he would simply no longer be a ruler at all. (For example, he might think that he must deal with his enemies fiercely or simply fail at being a ruler.) As things develop, what had been a constitutive principle can become instead nonconstitutive, come instead to be a norm that can always be transgressed, and in that case, the ruler comes to see those same things as normative, the violation of which would not immediately cancel his status as ruler but which might undermine it or, for that matter, be largely irrelevant to it. (In the example given, the ruler might think failing to deal with his enemies fiercely is a shortcoming, but it hardly affects his status as king.) In Hegel's system, the distinction between the normative, which can always be transgressed, and the constitutive, which defines a status and where transgressing those principles means cancellation of the status, is fluid and shifting. How this works is best left to later in the exposition of what goes in on history.

In Hegel's rather novel formulation, these "Idea-concepts" form the basis of the intelligibility of the way we minded creatures relate to the world and ourselves. Yet these forms of intelligibility themselves move in history and take on new shapes in light of the tensions and oppositions they develop within themselves. They are the components of intelligibility itself, and they are also themselves historical achievements.

As Hegel acknowledges, showing how or whether that works requires in turn the attention to historical detail that would otherwise be out of place in a more traditional philosophical account. Such an account bypasses the more usual hard and fast philosophical distinction between purely conceptual (or, in the Kantian scheme, transcendental) concerns and those of empirical matters. The components of the "Idea" arise in history, but as humans reflect on those concepts, put them to use, and modify them in the course of their collective lives, they refashion them into overall schemes of intelligibility, sometimes in art, most often in religion, and finally in philosophy.[38]

As we might put it, the self-knowledge of such a subject is not merely the self-knowledge of a rational agent in general but of a material subject (a substance) whose powers include those of standing in an apperceptive relation to herself. It is thus "human" reason and not the generalized Kantian reason of a generalized rational being that is at issue.[39]

The Hegelian subject is a "thinking substance," the way in which substance becomes subject, that is, a material creature who possesses the capacity for a kind of self-relation that is otherwise not found in nature.[40] Our various acts of thinking are manifestations, and not just particular instantiations, of the power of human thought, which as rational thought, is ultimately bounded only by itself. In Hegel's words: "The determinateness of spirit is consequently that of *manifestation*. . . . Its possibility is thus immediately infinite absolute actuality."[41]

This is part of Hegel's naturalism, which is also part and parcel of his idealism.[42] The world shows up to us because of our nature, which is to become and to be apperceptive creatures for whom things show up differently than they do for nonapperceptive creatures. We are rational animals who have various powers that develop first in the shape of immediacy in infancy and then into a more reflective form as we develop.[43]

Spirit and Self-Consciousness

"Spirit" is Hegel's name for a species of living things, namely that of self-conscious human life. That he calls it "spirit" instead of simply "human

being" is intended to bring out the way in which self-consciousness transforms the very nature of that life itself.[44] Spirit is subjectivity, and a subject is
a subject by being the life that falls under the concept of subject, and it falls
under that concept by spontaneously bringing itself under that concept. In
doing so, its "possibility"—its thinking of itself—really is its actuality as a
subject exercising agency and establishing itself as a person. Now, to be
standing under concepts of subject and what is associated with that status
will amount to standing within what Hegel calls a "shape of life," that is, a
kind of concrete order of thoughts, an "Idea."[45] In such a shape of life, subjects seek authority for their beliefs and actions, which inevitably leads to
the confrontations over what the space of reasons actually requires. A self-
conscious primate, that is, is eventually compelled by her nature—which is
to locate herself within a space of reasons as given concrete shape within her
human shape of life—to become not merely self-conscious but reflectively
self-conscious, and this is initiated in the original struggle over such
authority.[46]

That this authority should consist solely in an appeal to anything like
the abstraction, "the space of reasons," is not where we start. That abstraction is a result, and, for all that, the result of a rather long historical development. The space of reasons, which Hegel details in the *Logic,* is but the
"realm of shadows" of the practices of trying to make sense of ourselves and
the world. The logic portrayed in the *Logic* is, as Hegel's image has it, only
the shadows cast by the more concrete world of historical subjects. As such
shadows, in their very provisionality they often seem to dissolve as we
reflect on them.[47] Had subjects but world enough and time, they would not
have to worry about how to settle such matters, since their discussion could
go on forever. However, they never have world enough and time. They are
finite creatures facing an infinite problem.

Hegel himself faces up to this problem in different ways. In the
Phenomenology of Spirit, he asserts early in the book: "Self-consciousness is
desire itself."[48] Since desire is the inward noting of a lack in the animal—for
example, hunger can indicate a lack of nutrition, drowsiness a lack of sleep—
Hegel is there claiming that self-consciousness exhibits the felt lack of something. Hegel's claim, to which we shall return, is that what it lacks, at least
at the stage in the argument where he says that, is some form of sustainable
authority. For it to have the authority that seems to lie in its very concept of

itself, it needs recognition from another who also has the legitimacy to recognize such authority—it needs what Rousseau, with his typical briskness, called an "authority of a different order, capable of constraining without violence and persuading without convincing"[49]

Spirit manifests itself in appearance analogously to the way an intention manifests itself in action.[50] An action, for example, as a series of individual bodily movements has a unity by virtue of the intention (that is, the thought) which the movements manifest. The individual steps taken to fulfill the intention are thus, as Hegel terms them, "moments" of the action as "manifesting" the intention.[51] (For example, my intention to go over and open the door is manifested in all the individual movements I make in turning, walking to the door, pulling the lever, etc.) "Manifestation" in Hegel's usage is thus a kind of expression. For subjects, it is the expression of a thought or a principle. The action expresses the thought that animates it, since it is only the thought (the intention) that holds the different bodily movements together in a unity. The action, as unified by the thought, is thus different from the deed (what the actor succeeds or fails in doing) so that the actor can be intending such and such without ever actually accomplishing such and such.[52] What I take myself to be doing and what I end up having done can obviously part ways. This distinction is not clearly marked in the ways English speakers use "act," "do," "action" and "deed." Hegel sometimes marks this distinction between what I take myself to be doing and what I am doing by noting one as "action" *(Handlung)* and the other as "deed" *(Tat)*, but that is in part a self-conscious regimentation of the words.[53]

To know what one is doing is to be claiming a certain authority over one's acts as to what they are as acts. If, for example, someone were to send you a text message—"What are you doing?"—you would reply that you are reading about Hegel, and you knew that without having to have reflected on it prior to receiving the message. Even if the text message asked something different, such as "How do you feel?" and the answer was: "I feel very sick," the report of the feeling of being sick still supposes that one is saying something meaningful. Both of you understand the sentence because you have the self-conscious capacity for such comprehension. Even what looks like a report on one's internal states assumes that the kind of self-ascription involved in an apperceptive life falling under the concept of "apperceptive life" by virtue of bringing itself under that concept.[54] Now, the statement, "I feel sick" may also be accompanied by all kinds of moaning and grimacing, and it is thus easy to think that the statement is just another (linguistic) way to go on moaning. It is more. When another says, "Oh, you're just putting that on to get sympathy," the reply, "No, you're wrong. I really do feel sick," is more than another groan. It is a statement of knowledge, a statement about how you know yourself to be.[55]

Self-consciousness thus is constituted by a self-presence that in knowing itself is distinguishing itself from itself while knowing that there is no real distinction present.[56] It is the act of assuming authority over things like belief not by inspecting one's internal mental states but by something more like taking on a commitment. Later in the *Phenomenology,* Hegel says that that "self-consciousness is essentially judgment."[57]

What is this self-presence? Why is it both desire and judgment?

Self-Consciousness and Its Other

Hegel gives an account of the way in which a kind of immediate self-consciousness living in a world of background involvements is pushed into a more reflective form by virtue of breakdowns in its own practices. To motivate this view, Hegel argued in the opening chapter of his *Phenomenology of Spirit* that a straightforward stance of experiencing things which takes itself to dispense with any such self-conscious involvement is ultimately self-undermining. What he calls "sense-certainty" is the act of pointing something out, for example in such statements as "That one, over there." In such "sense-certainty," what looks like transparent reference to objects—a way of "taking" objects that need not rely on any "meaning" but only some kind of meaning-free reference to them—undermines itself in the way that it has to take into account the speaker's or experiencer's position.[58] Hegel entertains the suggestion that this idea of a pure reference to objects can be made good in terms a purely perceptual encounter with objects (as distinct from a meaning-free, purely sensuous act of referring), but this ultimately fares no better. That kind of encounter also takes itself to grasp such objects in terms of a pure referring activity that is not mediated by meanings (but which nonetheless occurs against the background of a set of descriptions). In turn, making that move raises the ante about whether what we refer to as, for example, a "green" thing might be in reality a "red" thing, or that even perhaps when we call an act of gratitude a virtue, we are actually referring to a vice. Those doubts raise the even more unnerving possibility that even the whole world might be actually inverted on us, such that everything that appears up is really down, left is really right, green is really red, sweet is really sour, just is really unjust, and so forth. Behind even ordinary acts of referring, it turns out, there is a mode of our "taking" things one way or another and having to posit matters that are not immediately present in the sense-experience itself. Our apperceptive lives are already at work in what at first glance seem to be decidedly nonapperceptive activities.

Just as we are tempted to take our conscious lives as resting on the basis of some kind of meaning-free reference to objects, we are also tempted to take our self-conscious lives as our showing up for each other in what also looks like a completely transparent fashion and of our actions as guided by ultimate desires that cannot themselves be justified (that is, are not mediated by any further meanings). Each thinks of the other subject as a self-conscious other, as an immediate second-person to its first-personal reference. However, it is in each having the second-person as the object of their thought that each shows up as the second-person. That is, it is in my first-person grasping of "you" as your thinking second-personally of "me" that "you" grasp "me" second-personally, and it is thinking within that complex thought that we comprehend ourselves thereby as plural, as what Hegel calls "The I that is a We, and a We that is an I."[59] In such thoughts, in the actualized state of such self-knowledge, we do not swallow, as it were, the other person simply into our own viewpoint, but rather, as Hegel puts it, see the "other as other" while remaining at one with ourselves.[60] We comprehend each other, that is, as each occupying a place in a concrete space of reasons that is occupied by human creatures in the natural order. That space is also a space of authority, of taking on the burden of justifying ourselves to each other and even to ourselves, all carried out within the idea of a rational human life and not just a rational life abstracted away from its animality.

Absent any other considerations, the possibility for a fundamental conflict is thereby established. If for whatever contingent reason, one of the self-conscious creatures takes himself to be unconditionally authoritative over some set of claims and the other disputes this authority, and when for whatever contingent reason, that first subject takes this to matter so much to him that he is willing to stake his life on it (and thus willing to kill for it), there is and eventually must be a struggle for recognition. Obviously, if both sub-jects die in the struggle, this problem is not solved. However, if one kills the other, the problem is once again not solved (since there is nobody to give the desire recognition). If out of exhaustion both call off the struggle, the prob-lem is also not resolved, and the struggle for its resolution is merely post-poned. In this context, when there is a ground-level, fundamental dispute over what reason requires and a decision must be reached, there is nowhere else to go but for one of them simply to establish by fiat some relation of authority. That, in turn, takes them both out of the abstract space of reasons and into the real world of conflict. In such a struggle, the only solution, absent any other considerations, seems to be for one of them, out of the fear of death, succumbing to the claim to authority on the part of the other. One becomes the master, and the other becomes the slave subservient to the master.[61]

The irrational appeal to force on the master's part arises out of the impossibility, at this stage of abstraction, of settling the argument about authority, when one of them stakes a claim to such authority that cannot at first be shared (and is willing to stake his life on it). However, there are two deeper strata of difficulty with the result of the dialectic of master and slave.

First, if all authority is recognized authority, then an infinite regress is set into motion, since one subject will have authority only if his authority is recognized by another subject, who in turn must be therefore recognized by yet another subject with authority, ad infinitum. If there are only two of them in the struggle, neither can claim authority, since it seems either that the regress cannot even get started (because there is no authority to start it), or that it just circles back and forth between two subjects neither of whom could ever acquire the authority to recognize the other one. If there were any mediating institutions such that an appeal to reason itself might be workable, the problem would be solved, but at this level of abstraction—in which one is discussing the concept of self-consciousness itself, not a partic-ular institutionalized shape it must in fact assume—there are no such medi-ating institutions. If one of them simply has authority, then the regress does not get going. The struggle is over which one of them has it.

The second stratum of difficulty with the dialectic of master and slave goes to the heart of Hegel's theory of subjectivity. Although the dialectic of master and slave is often taken to be aiming at the establishment of some kind of intersubjectivity, Hegel's point in the discussion is slightly different. In the initial confrontation, there is no grand failure of intersubjectivity per se. At one level, the two combatants understand each other perfectly well. (They certainly share enough to be able to talk to each other, and each seems to understand the expression, "Submit or die!") For that matter, each may even understand himself as having some version of what we might loosely call "ethical" requirements on him or herself. (For example, one or both may see themselves as ethically required to assert the superiority of their own "people" over those of the other.) Each is a form of self-consciousness, rooted in a world fraught with ought.[62] Their struggle over who is to exercise the right to determine their own respective normative positions (such as who is to defer to the wishes of the other and who is to give orders) indicates that there already is a bit of a shared outlook on things—shared enough for both of them to engage in a struggle to the death. Their problem has to do with the way in which they relate to the order of thoughts under which they bring themselves as "subjects" in the first place.

Putting Hegel's discussion into a different context may help here. Michael Thompson has distinguished monadic from what he calls bipolar judgments (or what we might better call "dyadic" judgments).[63] This is not merely a surface distinction between judgments such as "He did something wrong" and "He did her wrong." The latter type of judgments are dyadic—one wronged a specific other—and the former are monadic in that they apply to a subject conceived as a single individual standing in a relation to an order of thoughts. As Thompson phrases it, in a monadic judgment, "the other agent is something in respect of which either agent might 'mess up' instrumentally. All of the normativity in the case derives from the agent's own ends, and is thus merely monadic."[64]

That the "normativity . . . derives from the agent's own ends" does not imply that monadically conceived agents must be conceived as necessarily brutally self-interested or as indifferent to the suffering of others. Their own ends may in fact include norms such as "do not knowingly inflict suffering on other self-conscious agents," but they are still just their own ends, monadically conceived, not specific duties to specific others. A system of law, for example, may specify all kinds of duties regarding others and declare that one has done wrong if one harms another in a specific way. What makes the action (legally) wrong in such a case is that it violates the legal norm under which the individual fell. A monadic order has more or less the structure of a game. In the monadic order, doing a wrongful or rightful action is just violating the rules—such as committing a foul or stepping outside the white lines—and only secondarily in having done something or another to an other. It is like having the moral referee blow the whistle on you for being offside or committing a foul.

As Thompson notes, like himself, both Aristotle and Aquinas seem to distinguish clearly between the kinds of monadic requirements imposed by such a legal system from those dyadic requirements imposed by a system of justice. To be sure, a legal system can also impose dyadic requirements, or it can achieve much the same end by a system of rights belonging to individuals but which are rights that can be monadically held. The point is that it need not do either, and yet it can still be a legal system. The distinction between the monadic and dyadic stances even appears typically in legal systems themselves in the matters of private law, such as contract (where one creates via legal rules a duty to a specific other and a corresponding right on the part of the other), and in matters of criminal law, where, as Thompson puts it, "the verdict of the jury, 'Guilty!', expresses a property of one agent, not a relation of agents. If another agent comes into the matter—if there is, as we say, a 'victim'—it is, so to speak, as raw material in respect of which one might do wrong."[65]

In the imaginative encounter of the individuals who constitute the dialectic of mastery and servitude, the encounter is staged as that between two concept-using agents who jointly bring each other under the concept of concept-user, which means that they see each other as self-conscious agents. Each is a self-conscious life who at first takes his normative requirements to be monadic in structure. His commitments are his own and are mediated by the order of thoughts under which he places himself in order to be a knowing subject at all. He tells himself, as it were, that he is obligated to infer Q from P or that the evidence requires him to believe X. These are duties he owes but not to any particular person. It is by continuing to see himself as a monadic subject gripped by normative requirements but owing them to nobody in particular that he confronts the other.

Now, it does not follow from the assumption of such agents grasping each other as self-conscious concept-users that they also thereby have a sense of justice vis-à-vis each other—that they see the other as having the kind of status that would be given expression in some kind of dyadic relation, as in, "I owe it to her not to do that." They may well have a concept such as, "It would be wrong for me to do that," but that is a different matter. One can think of them as analogous to agents belonging to two different legal systems confronting each other and each demanding of the other that the other recognize—bestow or acknowledge the binding status of—the former's own legal system as binding on himself. With each coming from two different metaphorical legal systems in a context in which each demands complete jurisdiction over the other, each is, as Hegel likes to say, an other to the other. Even though both legal systems might by chance share some of the same content—or, for that matter, they might by chance even have the same norm of not coercing other rational agents into compliance with one's own legal orders—any such sharing would be accidental. It is not necessary for it to be a "legal system" that it have such a norm prohibiting that kind of coercion at all, and in the absence of such a norm, there will be conflicts that will be, from the standpoint of each, legally irresolvable. In particular, if both agents assert the full normative status of their own "legal system"—remembering that this is an analogy—against the other, there will be no way to adjudicate the conflict except by either abandoning the conflict or by appeal to force.

To the extent that one of the agents decides in favor of demanding full recognition for himself and his order of thoughts on the part of the other, there is a struggle which can also escalate into a struggle over life and death. This will happen when one of the agents for some reason demands the jurisdiction of his own order of thoughts—his own, so to speak, legal system—and is willing to stake his own life on such a demand. He demands recognition from the other as authoritative. The other, moreover, understands the demand. Both share a human shape of life, and they both understand what each is demanding and equally the seriousness of the demand. Each understands the other to be saying "submit or die."

That at first creates the misleading appearance that they share an order of thoughts, that they seem to inhabit the same "legal system" or that they are really playing the same game. However, from within the demands made for recognition, what starts out as two "games" becomes deadly. Once one of them, for whatever reason—madness, rage, Alexandrian dreams of conquest—decides that the system within which he lives simply must be recognized by others not in that system, there is no way out of the conflict other than a struggle for recognition which quickly turns lethal. When out of fear of losing his life one submits to the domination of the other, a new relation, that of mastery and servitude, is instituted.

Although the struggle begins as each attempts to subjugate the other by bringing him into his own system of concepts, by virtue of engaging in the struggle, they have changed the context in which they operate. They were at first two individuals at odds with each other. Now they are two individuals whose subjectivity is part of a shared normative enterprise, except that this enterprise now involves servitude on the part of one, mastery and command on the part of the other. As part of a shared normative enterprise, they have also changed the shape of their respective self-relations and therefore their self-consciousness. Whereas before, they were part of two different enterprises, now they share an enterprise with a conceptual and existential conflict at its very core.

The master demands recognition from the other as master, but the master refuses to give in turn any such recognition to the other. The master demands recognition but refuses to give it. Logically viewed, the master demands a dyadic judgment from the servant, whereas he refuses to take up any such judgment for himself, relating himself only monadically to his own conception of what his order of thoughts requires. He also demands recognition from somebody who on the master's own terms does not have the authority to bestow such recognition.

What Hegel calls "eternal justice" thus can, within the terms set by the master, not become manifest here. However, the servant, by being taken up into the master's "legal system," eventually comes to grasp, however inchoately, that his own status as agent depends on his taking up the dyadic form for himself. He is an agent with status only in the eyes of the master, and he comes to understand that likewise the master is only the master in terms of such a dyadic relation. The servant thus comes to a correct comprehension of the relationship, whereas the master acquires powerful motives for understanding it falsely.[66] The servant comes to understand what he is doing and, as he does, to distance himself from his status as servant. The master, on the other hand, has powerful motivations for not understanding his deeds in a deep way at all.

Transparency of reference breaks down in both the observational cases and the cases of second-person reference. What seemed like a fully transparent reference to another subject (in the second-person) as standing in the same order of thoughts as oneself itself breaks down under the pressure of disputes about who or what really has authority to specify what that order really requires or what exactly is the order in which both are standing. What seemed like merely a brute desire for submission by the other is in fact a mediated desire for authority. That is the dialectic of mastery and servitude, and it provokes, as Hegel puts it in his later entries in his *Encyclopedia,* the formation of a common will which in turn systematically yields its place to a conception of "universal self-consciousness" (a term borrowed from Kant's *Critique of Pure Reason*[67]), that is, of reason itself as constituting the order of thoughts with all human subjects as its members. It provokes, that is, recognition of a "space of reasons" as authoritative. However, that is a result, not a presupposition—an achievement, not something always already in place. It is also in its concrete form not fixed once and for all.

"Eternal justice" is not coeval with "subjectivity," but it emerges as essential to the shape subjectivity takes in history. Out of mastery and servitude emerges a conception of a justice to which appeal can always be made, even if it often goes unheeded and often is repressed before it can ever find expression. How that actually works in historical development is yet to be shown.

Rational Animals

Although there is nowadays a familiar hierarchical picture of subjectivity as that of a subject reflectively endorsing certain desires and finding its freedom only in such a reflective endorsement, Hegel has many separate reasons for rejecting that picture as basic to self-consciousness. His most prominent reason is that it generates a kind of regress about the subject's own self-consciousness since it seems to require for self-consciousness a consciousness of consciousness, which in turn requires a consciousness of consciousness of consciousness, ad infinitum. Second, the concept of "reflectively identifying with one's desires" is simply too weak to do the job it is supposed to do.

Instead, Hegel himself speaks of free action as the subject's being "in" the action. For example, he says that, "If I put something into practice and give it a real existence, it must be right for me, I have to be 'in' the act and hope to obtain satisfaction through its accomplishment."[68] Interests are part of our second nature such that for people of different interests, the world may show up to them in different ways, and this has to do with who they are as the individuals they are (along with their particular talents, their other inclinations and oddities of personality). An interest in this case is not best conceived as an internal mental state but as something that itself manifests itself over a wide range of things and activities. This is part of Hegel's larger claim in his *Logic* that the "universal" must be manifested in the individual, and that the way this is manifested makes a difference to the content.[69] Reasons show up for us and become motivating only in the context of our animal, social, and political lives.[70] Because of our animal life, things matter to us, and because of our rational lives, other things show up as mattering. Thus, because we are rational animals, "laws and principles have no immediate life or binding force in themselves. The activity which puts them into operation and endows them with real existence has its source in the needs, impulses, inclinations, and passions of man."[71] Human subjectivity is not that of two different faculties or machines coordinating their efforts. It is the (sometimes conflicted) result of the way in which rational agents themselves are at work in the world.

Hegel's view is thus a kind of outlier version of what has come to be called "internalism" in moral psychology, namely, the view that there is a close, perhaps even necessary, connection between our reasons (as norms) and our motivational structure—so close that some internalists argue that unless the connection is already there, a reason lacking that connection cannot even count as a "normative," action-guiding reason at all.[72]

Hegel is perfectly aware that he has raised the stakes for whatever kind of "internalist" he is by taking this particular position on the issue. To the extent that interests can change over time as a function of the shape of life at stake (which includes that shape of life's material culture), there will be some reasons that either cannot develop or at least can have no binding force for those people. When a shape of life stops making sense to the people living within it, the immediate self-conscious unity of the shape of life tends to become more reflective, and as it becomes more clear that there may not be any sense to be made of the crumbling state of affairs, the shape of life may fall into dissolution. The people living in the ruins of that dissolution have to pick up the pieces, keep what still works, discard the rest, and create something new out of it. (Hegel's German term for that process is *Aufhebung* as both cancelling and preserving, and rendered in English by the term of art "sublation.") Out of that reshaping come new reasons that have "immediate life and binding force" for such people.[73]

In the scheme of Hegel's version of naturalism, a reason for action is thus the significance that something has for a certain organic creature given the possibilities of that creature. Self-conscious creatures socially institute a new realm of significance for themselves that goes beyond the possibilities set by self-maintenance and reproduction, that is, goes beyond the basic ends of nonrational life. Those new realms of significance include, for example, religious observance, different forms of governance, ethical obligations, and so forth. Or, as we might put it, what shows up as salient for an animal are the reasons and their context, and thus for rational animals, a host of other things can show up as salient for them that cannot show up for nonrational animals.

This shifts the ground away from a more familiar picture of reasons as competing with the passions or with animal inclinations. The various desires, drives, and inclinations of rational animals can get their grip on the more developed conceptuality of self-conscious subjects, not because the drives, desires, and inclinations are nonconceptual natural events that must be "synthesized" into maxims or regulated by some rational monitoring faculty but because they are already meaningful. They are ready for conceptual systematization in a scheme of practical reason because, as purposes of life, they are already ready to take on conceptual form. The inclinations can become incorporated into the will of a self-conscious agent as motives because they are already there as incentives for a living being, that is, as putative reasons.[74] If animals have reasons, then the so-called sharp break between the nonrational animals and the rational animals is not in fact so sharp. Both respond to reasons. Where the genuinely sharp break occurs is that between the self-conscious rational animals (who can see their purposes *as* purposes and thus entertain their reasons as reasons) and non-self-conscious animals.

Hegel takes Kant, among others who see the passions as in competition with the intellect, to have necessarily "dissembled" about the issue of the relation between the passions and reason. On that view, our hearts may pull us one way and our reason pull us in another, and moralists have often phrased the issue as the debate over which side should have predominance in human life. In at least one very familiar interpretation of Kant, he too sees the passions as providing one source of motivation and reason as providing an alternative source, with the two often being at odds with each other. Hegel thinks that Kant "dissembled" on that issue, since Kant also held something like what Henry Allison has called Kant's "incorporation thesis." For Kant, no sensible incentive can actually be a reason for action (or a motive) unless the subject makes it a reason for action (which sounds very much like reason "monitoring" or "regulating" some lower-level activity).[75] Even very early in his career, Hegel had argued against Kant's way of marking the distinction between concepts and intuitions by showing how Kant's official doctrine of the separation of the two was itself undermined by Kant's own arguments supporting the contrary conclusion.[76] (Hegel's arguments were most emphatically not that there is thus no difference between concept and intuition. It was that the two are distinguishable but not separable.)[77]

Consistent with that view, Hegel argued in his writings on practical philosophy that Kant's separation of sensible motive and rational maxim (or imperative) was itself undermined by Kant's own arguments. If it is true that no sensible incentive can become a motive unless it is made into a motive, then there is simply no way of prying apart incentive and motive in a self-conscious subject (in an analogous way that a self-conscious subject, in the terms of Kant's first *Critique,* also cannot be aware of an "unsynthesized" intuition). A self-conscious subject can be aware that something looks like a good reason for action—because, for example, it would be fun, pleasant, enriching, etc.—but even an awareness of a brute desire is not yet the formation of an intention, a "thought," to put that into action.[78]

Kant's view is a familiar one that appeals to just about anyone's experience, and it is easy to see why that what looks at first like the collision of two great forces meeting each other in one individual—passion coming at it from one side, reason coming at it from the other—in fact is, if one takes Kant's incorporation thesis as his real position, really a struggle of reason with itself. The battle between passion and reason is a battle within the individual about what he really has reason to do. The attempt to display reason's struggle with itself as reason's struggle with its passionate "other" is really only "shadowboxing," not a real conflict between different masters.[79] The issue is thus not: How do we manage to get reason to overcome passion? Nor is it: How to build up one force to crush the other? But: Is following my immediate wants in this case a better reason for action than, say, keeping faith with other commitments?

The amphibious character of human subjects as naturally responsive to reasons that show up for them given their natures, and who often experience conflicts between duty and desire or theory and life, is a feature of the way in which reason itself can be in conflict with itself within a rational animal's life. To the extent that, to follow Hegel's rather extravagant way of speaking, "reason" is the absolute (as authorizing its own boundaries, including those which limit its own claims), then the experience of certain types of basic conflict is an experience of the absolute's dissatisfaction with itself, the way in which entire shapes of life can be built out of fundamental oppositions within themselves. It is more or less distinctive to Hegel's conception that this kind of conflict is a key feature of reason itself and not merely of the myriad distinct empirical conditions in which reason functions. The inadequacies to be found within an authoritative set of reasons are inadequacies for the shape of life in which they function as basic.

When Hegel speaks, as he often does, of a will "immersed" or "sunken" into nature, he is speaking therefore of a will that takes some sets of desires or passions to automatically generate reasons. A natural will would be a will that equates, for example, "That is attractive" with "That is therefore reason enough for me to pursue it." In effect, what counts as a good reason will therefore be part of the order of thoughts to which a subject belongs—what concatenation of principle and passion institutionally and practically is the case. That this or that passion is reason enough to act in this or that way thus hangs together with an overall view that passion and principle hang together in a certain way. That certain things are particularly hard to resist—something noted by Aristotle as grounds for excusing some otherwise nonvirtuous actions[80]—is only a statement about how some things are so attractive (for example, money, power, sex) or unattractive (shame, extreme pain, severe loss of status,) such that it is very easy for people to rationalize rearranging their economy of reasons to accommodate their taking those incentives to be justified reasons. What will count as justifiable depends on the order of thoughts at work and the context in that order.

One of Hegel's key hypotheses about historical development is that it will display the development of the "natural" will into a "rational" will. That is, it will offer illustrations of how certain shapes of life effectively take on certain things as givens, which function, as it were, automatically as reasons. Such shapes of life have not yet developed the proper critical capacities to separate out such reasons-as-given-in-a-shape-of-life from real reasons. For that to work, there needs to be some reasons that at least present themselves to us as not bound to a particular set of social rules but present themselves as distinct from them, as principles of criticism that go beyond the mere givenness of a particular way some reasons are in fact taken to be authoritative. We must have an appeal to "something higher," as Hegel puts it, to get a grip on these principles of criticism. This "higher" viewpoint is attained first, he thinks, in religion and in art and only afterward, after such seemingly external principles have been developed, do they appear in philosophical thought.

The picture of us standing back and reflecting on what desires we are to identify with is thus in Hegel's view at best a derivative picture from the more basic view of us as self-conscious primates apperceptively but not necessarily reflectively working our way through the involvements within which we always and already immersed. We are pushed into reflection on those involvements when the deeper seated tensions and contradictions in them begin to manifest themselves in our lives and the tensions become more clear.

Hegel's internalism is thus an outlier in two ways. First, even though there has to be a link between reasons and passions for the reason to be a real reason for the subject, this concatenation of passion and principle is relative to the historical shape of life. Shapes of life themselves are displaced historically by other shapes, and, if Hegel can make his case, that displacement can be shown in parts to have a rational structure.[81]

Second, the individual is not a composite of passion and principle but a unity, even if a fragile one. The subject is a rational animal, and not just an animal that has had rationality added onto it. It is a subject who relates itself to itself as the rational creature it is, with it being such a creature by bringing itself under the concept of such a creature. The subject is thus not something like a Kantian rational agent who also happens to be embodied in a human shape. Rather, the subject is a rational animal by bringing itself under that concept, although this act need not itself be a reflective act. The subject actualizes herself in actualizing the thoughts of herself as falling under that concept (which does not imply that the subject is always articulate about what that concept or what it further entails). In bringing itself under the concept, it thus stands in a relation to itself mediated by the concrete shape of life in which the subject lives and which is socially and historically indexed, even if not all the passions themselves are so thoroughly socially indexed.

If Hegel is right about that conception of subjectivity, then the familiar conception that the subject is somehow lying behind the action and directing his actions by a faculty of the "will," as the circus director is directing all his performers, is, however tempting, also deeply misleading. It is the embodied subject, not his mental events, that is the cause of the action, and the subject itself is not a little homunculus inside the human person pulling the levers or directing the show. The faculty of the will is just thought taking an embodied shape. All such activities involve a way of being in the world that "consists in having the particular knowledge or kind of activities immediately to mind in any case that occurs, even, we may say, immediate in our very limbs, in an activity directed outwards."[82]

The key distinctions are thus between animal-absorbed activities (which are not fully actions), self-consciously absorbed activities, and reflectively self-conscious activities. As Hegel puts it, although no new content is added when we move from being self-consciously absorbed in, say, a perceptual judgment (in Hegel's terms, in our being in-itself a rational animal) to being reflectively self-conscious about the same judgment (when we are a rational animal for-itself), the resulting difference in form is of crucial importance. Hegel's reworking of Kant's incorporation thesis is not the view that somehow the passions lose their force in moving people to action, nor that they are dissolved into the more bloodless ideas of impartially weighing reasons against each other. It does, however, claim that the passions stand in a different relation to the subject than they do to a non-self-conscious animal. The incorporation thesis brings, as he puts it, the "form of being-for-itself"—that is, the form of self-consciousness—to the passions, and this makes all the difference, since, as Hegel puts it, "the great difference that matters in world history is what has to do with this difference."[83] Animals act on desire. The human animal, in acting on a desire, acts with the form of self-consciousness, which means that in acting on that desire, he makes himself into "the kind of person who acts on that desire," and the justification for being that kind of person has to do with the specific shape of life. Because of the "form of self-consciousness," even at the level of acting on desire, we are already implicated in a collective enterprise.

Hegel consistently identifies freedom across his writings as a matter of being at one with oneself, or being "with oneself" (to give his German formulations of *bei sich selbst* a literal translation). Freedom is thus a form of self-unity, indeed, of self-consciousness. It is easy to misread Hegel on this point as arguing that freedom is some form of "identification" with the objects or principles of willing in terms of seeing them as "mine." That is far too narcissistic as an interpretation as if the major function of freedom was to make everything "my own." In a passage often stressed by commentators, Hegel says that "we already possess this freedom . . . in friendship and love."[84] The more narcissistic interpretation has to take passages like that to mean that "I" somehow incorporate the other into my own goals and projects for that specific other's needs and interests to serve as effective motivators for me. However, Hegel means it in a far more social sense: In such relationships, I find a purpose that I could not have on my own. That conception of freedom is heavily indebted to Rousseau's and Kant's conceptions of freedom as being both sovereign and subject in a community: I am both author of and subject to the principles that make up a community free of domination and in which each is thus "sovereign" (as constituting the principles) and subject (as subject to the legislation offered by the other). In Hegel's own terms, as "sovereign," I have an indeterminate and thus at best merely a purely reflective will, but as "subject," I acquire a wider set of purposes. Indeed, so Hegel argues, only his more dialectical conception is the adequate way to understand that relation between being equally sovereign and subject.[85] All other social unities that involve domination and irrationality are, to that extent, distortions and failures to live up to the concept of true freedom.

In each case, Hegel argues that there is a developmental story to be told about how we realize this power of self-conscious thought in action. Freedom is a matter of how one's order of thoughts determines one's actions. We act freely when our bodily movements are adequate expressions of the thoughts that form the unity of those movements. For this reason, Hegel concludes that freedom is the capacity to make what truly matters effective in one's life, and, in modern times, that more or less comes down to acting on our own reasons rather than on vague feelings of guidance from nature, the gods, or those who claim to rule us by natural right.

Since acting on reasons requires that the reason, the explanation of the action, be known by the actor, I act truly freely when it is my thoughts alone that take embodiment in the process that constitutes the action. To the extent that my actions are realizations of something like completely unconscious reasons, I am not free (or not at least fully free). To the extent that my conscious thoughts are not the final court of appeal, I am not free. Likewise, as he points out time and again, I am also not free with regard to empirical matters since, in those cases, it is the facts that determine what I am to think, not me, and that pretense to be the "absolute" in those matters is either pathetic or downright dangerous.[86] Nor am I free when I am under the compulsion of some basic need (food, sleep, water, etc.).[87] Nor am I free when I take my thoughts to be under the guidance of another person, or something else that is external to my own thought (as in the idea of "Thy will be done" said by a vassal to his master).[88] I am free when I can make what genuinely matters into something actual, and that means that I can be deprived of freedom by other people and by circumstances beyond my control. As a slave, I am not free. As a person for whom it matters that he or she be able to take care of their children, I am not free when social circumstances or unwarranted power deprive me of that ability.

The actor is free when she is at one with herself, that is, the action is up to her, she can make some sense of those thoughts, she can understand them as her conscious thoughts even when those thoughts may not be entirely clear to her, and she has the power to make what matters in light of those reasons effective in the world.[89] Since the actor is only free when she acts on reasons that are intelligible and not just "given," it is only in modern times that we have been in the position to say that "all are free," that in principle each such rational animal has the capacity to actualize the power of such free-standing thought, and it would only be in rational social conditions— where each is in principle (that is, in his or her "concept") equally sovereign and subject—that this true conception could be actualized. Freedom in this Hegelian sense is not an all-or-nothing affair, as it might look if one took it to be an issue of some kind of uncaused causation at work in free willing. It involves a relation to self in which the grounds one gives for one's actions are themselves justifiable, in which they "make sense" (in an extended sense of making sense that includes art and religion). Freedom is thus a way of way of being at one with oneself such that the life one leads is not rent by reasons that seem not to be real reasons. In pre-modern times, in which the great majority of people are under normative compulsion to take their thoughts to be guided by the gods or their betters and where there is no institutional way out of that arrangement, at most only "some are free." Freedom thus ultimately rests on our relations to others, not on some power to step outside of the natural causal realm. It rests on the "form of self-consciousness."

2

Building an Idealist Conception of History

∞

The Historical Manifestation of Infinite Ends

What Hegel calls "philosophical history" takes its subject matter, as he puts it, to be "the spirit which is eternally present to itself and for which there is no past."[1] This is, as he notes, something that looks itself like a contradiction: "How can what is outside history, since it is not subject to change, still have a history?"[2] The answer is that spirit—or what will amount to the same thing, social human mindedness—is that which is both the same thing in its development and yet whose development is so path dependent that it could not be what it becomes without having traversed that path.[3] How is that supposed to work itself out?

To stand in an order of thoughts is to have a place within a shape of life in which ethical principle and individual psychology are linked by the mediation of various institutions and practices. This link between individual psychology and principle is neither completely contingent nor is it quite what would nowadays be expressed as exhibiting anything like an analytic conceptual connection. It is, for example, not a matter of complete contingency that a principle, such as the early modern principle of putting honor before all else, and the particular psychology of the individual for whom "honor" is such a binding ideal, takes on the shapes it indeed assumed. Attacks on honor are, in that context, reasons that motivate. Nor is it merely a contingent matter that for the psychology of a late-modern individual, for whom something like the rule of law and negotiation are of prime importance, it is not merely an accident that he would be less likely to think that honor required him to avenge himself even beyond the bounds of law. And neither is it exactly a synthetic a priori link, a condition of all possible experience. It has more to do with Hegel's difficult logic of "the concept"—in which, "as existing for itself, the universal *particularizes* itself and is therein identity with itself."[4] For subjects who are trying to comprehend the world and themselves what is truly real (or "actual") is the unity of concept and objectivity, which Hegel calls the "Idea." Nor does Hegel hold (and does not even have to take a stance on the idea) that human desires are infinitely malleable. As subjects, we are self-conscious primates, and we have the organic desires of such primates. Moreover, he also accepts Aristotle's conception of there being certain facts about the human condition that every person must confront: Fear, anger, desire for status (wealth and honor), pleasure, pain, etc. These are not completely socially constructed matters, however much they are socially inflected. We know them by virtue of being the rational animals we are, by knowing, that is, the shape of life in which we live. Orders of thoughts are thus not mere collections of principles. They involve a unity of norm and practice, principle and psychology, and a picture of how that whole fits together. These unities of psychology and principle involve, in Hegel's own terminology, an "Idea" or even several "Ideas," a more concrete conception of how our basic concepts are actualized in the phenomenal world.

Orders of thoughts are, when practical, concrete constellations of passions, principles, and practices that fit into one order.[5] For such orders of thoughts, the issue is always more than whether that order is consistent, that is, more than merely the issue of whether the principles do not contradict each other. It has to do with whether the order itself generates a kind of moral psychology that can be successfully lived or put into practice or with whether the principles generate passions that in turn undermine the authority of the principles. The "Idea" can be at odds with itself in that it can manifest a world that supposedly contains a kind of necessity—for example, the way the ancient world thought of the economic necessity of slavery—and the way that world had to be normatively understood—with slavery as a deeply problematical concept from the ethical point of view even for the ancient world. In those cases, the principles and norms turn out to be at odds with a comprehension of how the world necessarily has to work. For example, in the case of slavery, many people, in the ancient forms of slavery up to the particularly brutal modern institutions of slavery, had trouble justifying the existence of slavery itself, and yet they could not see how it could be economically, that is, practically, avoided. This was, however, not just a disagreement between reason and the world. It was a disagreement of reason with itself.[6]

Written history—in distinction from the historical events themselves—is thus an account of such orders of thoughts, of the ways in which "laws and principles," or more generally, ideas and orientations, combine with human psychology and the surrounding material culture to generate the events that happen. Part of this view is that certain constellations of principle are bound up more to particular shapes of psychology than are others. (For example, the psychology, and thus also the virtues, of a medieval prince will not be those of a nineteenth-century bookkeeper.) Hegel's question was whether there was anything like a logic to these orders, all taken as "manifestations" of spirit. To answer that question, one would have to ask whether there was any unity to the manifestations, any uniting sense to them.[7]

This is the same as asking whether there is a purpose, an end—a *Zweck*—to these various orders of thoughts, such that if there were such an end, then they could be evaluated in terms of how well they manifest that end and how well they embody it. Moreover, if there is such an end, it would be an "infinite" end. A finite end is one that can be achieved by doing something specific. All ordinary wants are about finite ends. One might want to see a certain movie, and when one has seen it, the end goes away. One might want a drink of water because one is thirsty, and, having had the drink, one's want for a drink of water goes away. Finite ends can arise again and again, and there can in principle be an infinite number of them, with the limits being set only by the contingent limits of human life. (One might want more consumer goods than one's neighbor, he might want more than you, and the list would grow in principle to infinity. One is thirsty, drinks, and no longer is thirsty, and then one gets thirsty again.)

An infinite end, on the other hand, would be not something that can be achieved in any one action but which can only be manifested by various actions. (Happiness, on something like Aristotle's conception of it, might be one such infinite end, such that many different actions can be manifestations of it.) The end of drinking a glass of water, on the other hand, is fully exhausted by drinking the glass of water. Finite ends may simply add up, but infinite ends are never exhausted by the actions that manifest them. Finite ends—such as drinking the water—expire, but infinite ends have no intrinsic limit. They require a continual sustaining activity for them to be effective. Justice, for example, is not something that a collective enterprise can establish and then tick off the list of things still needing to be done. It must be realized over and over again. An infinite end has no limit at which it has finally been accomplished.[8] One comprehends such an infinite end not when one has added up all the actions that manifest it but when one has comprehended the principle that is at work in the way those actions manifest it. To revert a bit more into Hegel's own terminology: In human action directed in terms of an "Idea"—as a comprehensive understanding of how our "concepts" and "objectivity" work together—an "infinite" concept can be realized in finite actions (as when one acts justly or virtuously). The conception of what it ultimately means to lead a human life is an infinite end.[9]

For there to be such an infinite end in history, it need not be the specific purpose of any particular set of subjects but only of the collectivity taking itself as such a collectivity, as thinking of themselves as a "we" and not just "all of us." Now, in a great number of places, Hegel states that the final end of history is that of freedom, but that is merely the shorthand he adopted in his lectures both for his students (not always as attentive as they were supposed to be) and for the general public attending his lectures.[10] Hegel's shorthand can certainly suggest that all major events in history are aimed at producing a definite end, freedom. However, if that were the case, then freedom would be a finite end, and it is certainly unclear that it could have such absolute importance in that role. After all, as one of many goods, freedom is certainly high on anybody's list, but so is stability, and, for that matter, so are a whole list of other worthy goods (security, prosperity, piety, and so on). Moreover, if freedom were such a finite end, then if we achieved it, we would be done with history. That would be the "end of history"—there would be no more history, just an endless repetition of what would be needed to keep freedom (whatever that would be) in place. To be sure, Hegel has more often than not been credited with that conception, but such a conception would distort his own insistence that freedom is "infinite." If history involves such an infinite end, then history would end only when there were no more people.

Here is one way to think of it. The infinite "end" of history is more like health than it is like learning a determinate skill. One may achieve various levels of health (one may get sick and recover, or one can get sick and never recover), but health is not something you achieve and then cross it off the list as you move on to other things. Nor is health something that is always there at the front of one's mind when one acts. All those who argue for an "end in the sense of completion" to history confuse infinite with finite ends, including all those who think or thought history ended in either 1806 or 1989.

What Hegel suggests is that there is a deeper need out of which the need for freedom arises so as to become a necessary component of the deeper need. He characterizes this deeper need by a theologically loaded term "reconciliation." Reconciliation in this sense is what is achieved when people have come to terms with the world and each other. To put it broadly: Reconciliation is a matter of making sense of things, where "making sense" is to be understood in a capacious, rather than more narrow, sense. (One can in principle make sense of things in a variety of ways, in the practices of art, religion, theory, or by trying to fit components into a rational plan, and so forth.) True reconciliation has to do with seeing the human world as resting on acceptable reasons, or, again, to put it as loosely as possible, as having a rationale to it. Reconciliation is thus also an infinite end. Reconciliation is thereby tied closely to another concept that Hegel does not often use (except in his early, pre-*Phenomenology* writings), namely, that of legitimation. Hegel's ultimate thesis is that history manifests a human need for such reconciliation—a need for making sense—and, so he argues, it turns out that something like an order of thoughts about "justice as based on freedom"— as the proper unity of principle and psychology—is the only order that can possess the proper legitimation, and that this comes about very late in the development of shapes of life by way of the very determinate failures of earlier and other orders of thoughts.

This desire for reconciliation which history manifests at all points (although it does not manifest it in all, or, for that matter, even very many, of its events) is not a desire that is rooted in some deep biological basis in humanity. If it were, it would only serve as a finite end, like that of hunger or even perhaps of something like glory, honor, or status. It is a desire that follows from the nature of self-consciousness itself.[11] One of the major points of Hegel's discussion of the origins of mastery and servitude is to show how an unreflective consciousness can be forced to make the step to a reflective consciousness when the giving and asking for reasons transforms itself instead into a life-and-death struggle. Once such authority has been seized by force and implicates others into itself, there is the possibility of its being once again deauthorized. Once there is a distinction between ruler and ruled, the issue of the justice and the legitimacy of such rulership arises. If in order to be real, *wirklich*, effective authority, such authority must be recognized authority, then the lack of legitimacy of any hierarchy of ruler and ruled always remains an open possibility. It is not implausible to say that running throughout human history therefore is a desire to make sense of things which itself engenders in finite humans a desire for justice. Justice, reconciliation, legitimation—all these are components of the infinite end of *Geist* making sense of itself. None of them is a means to some other end. Nor are they mere givens or brute desires that we just happen to have. They are connected with the nature of self-consciousness and with the concrete way we thereby inhabit the human space of reasons.[12]

A crucial part of Hegel's philosophy of history has to do with how the need to make sense of things leads to a conception of justice, which as history develops, transforms itself into a conception of the necessity of freedom. The infinite end at work in history is that of self-comprehension and therefore that of justice, and, in our time, that demand for justice has become a demand for freedom. For that transformation to have taken place, humans had to transform their understanding of themselves. At the heart of historical movement is a deep issue about the nature of human subjectivity itself, both as individual subjects and as collective actors. The struggle over recognition is the ongoing thread in history that is the basis of justice as an infinite end in historical movement. The struggle over authority that is at the basis of the dialectic of mastery and servitude has crystallized into various institutions and practices—the "universal self-consciousness" of which Hegel speaks—that anchor the authority that percolates out of it in practice (or, we might say, which attempts to anchor it while often failing to do so in either the short or the long term). The infinite end of justice is a collectively pursued end that forms itself out of the myriad ways in which authority in social and political life is both accepted and resisted by individual subjects. Out of the struggles over such authorization, the standard of "eternal justice" takes shape as a proper ordering of human relations that is intrinsically dyadic. What constitutes the "proper order" among people turns out to be the slow moving "Idea" around which history turns.

Spirit thus has an extended temporal shape. We are what we are by being the creatures that bring ourselves under the concept of thoughts—by being moments of an order of thoughts—and that order extends thickly backwards and forwards. Likewise, each of us is a moment in the larger temporal order, looking back to our ancestors and forward to our successors.

This remains part of Hegel's own kind of modified Aristotelian naturalism. The animal acts in light of the demands of its genus. Much of what, for example, rabbits do is what they do because they are rabbits. They act in accordance with their genus, they act intelligently, perhaps set plans of a sort, even do something like make choices, but they do not do it self-consciously. Humans act in accordance with their genus, but those actions are self-conscious. The genus of rational animals is, as Hegel puts it, the genus that is aware of itself as a genus.[13] The lion hunts, and the human may likewise also hunt. However, human subjects also desire a reconciled world, one that makes sense to them and in which they have some justifiable standing. They are what they are by falling under an order of thoughts, which they fall under by virtue of bringing themselves under it. That order of thoughts, in turn, is concretely a social space whose "shadows" are the more abstract conceptions found within the *Science of Logic*.[14]

That this is who we are—"self-interpreting animals," in Charles Taylor's famous phrase—is, for Hegel, something that we have only recently—really, only since Kant—actually understood. And that, so Hegel argues, is the difference that makes the difference.[15]

What Is a Philosophical History of Modernity?

Here are three questions Hegel had to put to himself. First, can we make any sense of there being any kind of infinite end at work in history? Hegel's argument is that there is such an end and that this end takes on different manifestations as history goes forward in time. That of course remains to be shown, and furthermore, it must cohere with history as we can know it, not as we wish it might have been. Second, is there any way by which we could mark progress in the way that end has been actualized over historical time, that is, whether we are manifesting that end in any better way? It is, after all, not an a priori condition of possible experience that there be such progress. Third, in the process of attempting to answer the question about progress, we must ask whether there is or could be any "logic" to the movement that would legitimate judgments about such progress or whether any such claim to progress is really nothing more than a self-celebration of one's own current age.

A comparison with both Kant's sketch of a philosophy of history and with the second-century historian, Polybius, can perhaps put these questions into greater relief.[16]

Kant structured his sketch of a philosophy of history around both what he thought he had demonstrated about the moral desirability of a cosmopolitan world order and how he had shown that it is at least plausible that such an order will eventually come about, namely, by exploiting our "unsocial sociability" in a way so that our various natural antagonisms will drive us, even more or less against almost all our own intentions, into such a cosmopolitan order. If that is the case, then Kant takes the next question to be: How will history judge us? More specifically: How would future historians writing in an achieved cosmopolitan world order treat us historically? Even more specifically, how would they judge our own actions and efforts in terms of how we either promoted such an order or hindered its arrival (an arrival which is in any event necessary)?[17] Even more specifically: How will history judge me?

Kant in effect asks the question of how it is that a cosmopolitan world order (and thus a partially reconciled world) could and will come about by looking at it from the standpoint of a hypothetical future. Looking at our world from the hypothetical standpoint of a relatively distant future cosmopolitan historian writing about us, we can ask about what in our present circumstances (circa 1784 when Kant wrote his essay) was promoting the cosmopolitan world that eventually came about and what, on the other hand, was standing in its way. For Kant, a philosophical history is one written from the standpoint of such a hypothetical future.[18]

But why should one write history from the standpoint of the future? Hegel's view, in contrast to those of Kant, was that we need not look to the future to write such a history. We need look simply to the here and now.

Why? After the French Revolution, "modernity" was in full swing, and what we need to ask was whether this was necessary as a result of any historical "logic" or whether it itself was only a contingent "appearance"—whether "modernity" is, as it were, only a minor character making its appearance on the world stage and therefore something likely also to soon make its exit, or whether it represented some major new status that was "absolute" for our time. In contrast to this, we might also ask a very different question and wonder whether instead of progress, "modernity" represents perhaps a more brutal fall from grace, a regress in human life rather than progress. (That was certainly how at the time many conservative aristocrats experienced it.)

By 1820, Hegel had published his summary statement of the shape of the modern world, which consisted of a political and social order structured around rights, moral duties, and social goods. That order integrated within itself the rights to life, liberty, and property, and it was populated by moral subjects who took themselves to have binding duties based on universalizable reasons. It anchored itself in the institutional goods that were part of the lives led within the bourgeois family, the emerging civil society of the nineteenth century, and a constitutional, monarchical state with a representative government. The remaining issue was whether this modernity is indeed reconciliatory, or whether it only represented one more disappointment on a road leading to who knows where. We could thus ask: How did we get here and what may we conclude from that? Was it progress?

Hegel merged some themes found within that kind of uptake of Kant's philosophy of history with the account given by the Greek historian, Polybius, written in the second century BC, about the rise and world dominance of Rome. Like Hegel, Polybius also wrote from the standpoint of the here and now. Polybius' aim was to explain to his contemporaries (and, most importantly, to his fellow Greeks) how it was that world history had recently revealed where it was going and how that had turned out to be the Roman dominance of first their Mediterranean world and then eventually of the whole world. His history was intended to show what was essential to that world-historical event and why it is was also irreversible in any short-term way.[19]

Rome had succeeded predominantly because of its unique virtues and its religion. This is not an ephemeral matter, so Polybius argued, and non-Roman peoples are simply going to have to face up to this fact. Rome's triumph was, moreover, not just that of a local conquest but was of world-historical importance for the reason simply that Rome had made it de facto world-historical. The other candidate for exercising that kind of power—specifically Persia, the other great empire whose borders were near the Mediterranean world and which had staked claims to that world—had on Polybius' account essentially played out its hand, and, as Polybius seemed implicitly to think, was in the process of fading out of the picture. By taking over its world in the way it did, Rome had turned what otherwise might have been merely local history into world history.

In effect, Hegel was arguing a similar point. European modernity was where things had ended up, and the foreseeable future was, so he thought, ineluctably going to be a version of European modernity. The great civilizations of the rest of the world were destined either to fall under its dominance or to atrophy. Whereas Polybius was in effect telling his fellow Greeks to get used to this state of affairs both because this is the end to which history had led them and because there was a partial justification for it, Hegel was, in effect, putting himself forward as a modern Polybius but with a much more robust theoretical underpinning than Polybius himself could have possibly imagined.

Polybius actually gave two different kinds of reasons for Rome's triumph. On the one hand, Rome had triumphed and would continue to do so because of the strengths of its institutions and practices (with its religion as a core part of them), but, on the other hand, as he also stressed, it had also been a matter of "chance" (or "fortune") that had led to Rome's rapid rise and triumph. Looking back on the Roman conquest from a couple of thousand years later, Hegel concluded that Polybius's account of Rome's triumph was merely that of supersession: Rome replaced the other powers vying for dominance of the Mediterranean world. It did this not only by its superior virtues but also by its hard-headed understanding of the relation between power and violence. It had presented the world of its time with a *fait accompli* such that it would now be impossible to revert to the days before its rule. As Hegel saw it, although Polybius' account of Roman superiority left it open that Rome would one day be itself superseded by some other power—such is the nature of *Fortuna*—Polybius' account did not have an understanding of how Rome might have been not the supersession but the sublation—the *Aufhebung*—of what came before.

Hegel's question for his own day was a version of what was left open in Polybius's account: Was it merely a matter of blind fortune that European modernity had triumphed (such that there was no necessity to its achievement), or was there something about European institutions and practices that meant it was destined to serve as the model of progress for other civilizations? Was there a logic? From our contemporary perspective, all one has to do is state Hegel's questions to elicit what is our typical response, which is: Yes, it was contingent, and no, there was no logic. For Hegel to make even part of his case successfully to us, there are a fair number of hurdles in his way.

Hegel's well-known shorthand for his philosophy of history was that it progresses from ancient despotism (where only one—the emperor—is thought to be free) to the aristocratic societies of the ancient world (where only some were thought to be free) and from there to the modern idea which commits itself to the proposition that all are in principle free. This shows, so Hegel thought, that there was something about European practice that made this conception of universal freedom into a reality and that there was something about the practices of other civilizations that made it impossible for them to reach this conclusion until they had thoroughly transformed themselves.

What was it about European practices and institutions that not merely allowed for that development but also put a pressure on themselves to actualize it? In answering that question, Hegel's own classicism and his own blinders led him awry and ultimately, in many instances, into a distortion of his own views on the right shape of order of thoughts. But that does not mean that he failed utterly to make his case.

3

Hegel's False Start

Non-Europeans as Failed Europeans

〜

Reflective Distance as the Condition of Freedom

That Hegel is guilty of what we call "Orientalism" is nowadays a truism. He sees in "Orientals" the dangers to which a contemporary European shape of life might succumb. In part, it was this idea of such a "danger" that led him to see all "Oriental" shapes of life as essentially stalled and failed versions of the progress that the European shape of life had at the heart of its own development. His was, of course, not the first attempt at showing this. Adam Smith and Montesquieu had already argued for similar views about the role of the East in world history.[1] However, there was more to his dismissal of them than simply a psychological aversion on his part. He fused his deeper accounts of the nature of subjectivity with a distorted picture of the "East" to produce his account of the "Orientals." His failed attempts at integrating the "Oriental" world into his philosophy of history nonetheless still sheds much light on what he was trying to accomplish and how, if he were to admit those failures, he could nonetheless rework his views to keep much of his outlook intact while at the same time shedding his Orientalism. This requires us to reinterpret Hegel by means of Hegel and to see where that takes us.

In his 1807 *Phenomenology,* Hegel had given an account of how it was that our collective sense of what counted in absolute terms for "Europeans" required a philosophical history of European life. This was because (or so the *Phenomenology* was supposed to show) no account of what counted as logical reasoning, as ethical reasoning and behavior, or even as art and religion could make do without an account of how it was that we had been driven to those conceptions by very specific failures of such accounts in the past, such that the failures themselves provoked the move to a new order and also provided the conditions and material by which the new order emerged out of failure.[2] The explanation of the place of subjectivity in their collective lives—that is, what it was that put them into the position of being able to make sense of things in general—could not do without an account of why it came to seem unavoidable to include such things. However, the *Phenomenology* had only given that account for Europe (albeit with some passing and very cursory references to Persian, Egyptian, and Judaic religions), and Hegel realized that, by his own principles, he had to make his full case in light of world history and not just the story of how the Eurasian peninsula developed from Hellenic Athens to nineteenth-century Europe.

Hegel's lectures on the philosophy of history begin with a discussion of what he takes to be the origins of world history in the East, and they take up the bulk of the collected text of the lectures on world history. Clearly, Hegel thought that he had an important point to drive home here. Yet it is in these discussions that Hegel's account is most off the mark, and their rather uninformed dismissal of non-European ways of life undermines whatever validity they might have as genuine accounts of non-European peoples.

In the *Phenomenology*, Hegel's references to non-European ways of life were almost entirely couched in terms of his discussion of the Egyptians and, to some extent, of the Persians. When it came to the Egyptians, he seems to have taken the greater bulk of his knowledge from his reading of Herodotus. He later tried to update his knowledge about ancient Egypt and India with more modern sources, but he stuck by the overall picture he had originally formed of them. When in his lectures on world history in the 1820s, he refers to Africa, China, India, and Persia, he displays a tendency to interpret everything about them in a limited and even hostile way. In the case of Africans, Hegel, like many people even today, seemed to have been blind to the variety of cultures alive there, such that he interpreted them as one homogeneous mass living in a geographically homogeneous area.[3]

Pointing out how just how far from reality are Hegel's characterizations of Africans, Chinese, and other peoples is a bit too easy, a bit too much of an exercise of the proverbial shooting fish in a barrel.[4] That neither excuses Hegel nor exonerates him, but once one has moved beyond the pros and cons of Hegel-apologetics, it is more fruitful to ask what the philosophical views were behind his dismissive and admittedly Eurocentric view of the world and to ask if those views inevitably lead to such a dismissive outlook.[5]

First on the list of why Hegel saw Africans and "Orientals" as failed Europeans is Hegel's own deeply held classicism. It certainly informs his metaphysics of subjectivity, and it pervades his discussion of the arts. It also leads him to take Herodotus and Thucydides as among his great models for the writing of history. In doing so, he also took up Herodotus' basic theme of Greek freedom triumphing over eastern (and therefore Asiatic) despotism and made that into one of the key themes of his own account. Thus, in good "orientalist" fashion, Hegel uses Herodotus' idea of the Greek / Persian conflict and the Greek victory as the triumph of freedom over despotism, and equally as the triumph of hard won valor over the laxness and indolence brought on by Eastern luxury. Hegel generalizes Herodotus' invention of that trope for his own understanding of European history since Herodotus' time. On the basis of that classical view, the "East" thereby ends up standing for all the things that Hegel is arguing against in his own day. For him, it seemed crucial therefore that the Asiatic, despotic conception of life be understood as a defeated conception, as something which history has now passed by. Asiatic despotism can no longer be on the menu of rational choice, and any modern European despotism would have to be judged as going against the general progressive movement of modernity.

However, if that were Hegel's only motivation, then he would be dissembling about what he is doing. His misreading of the non-Europeans goes deeper than that and has to do with his most basic characterization of subjectivity itself, and it has to do with the relation between nature and mindedness itself.[6] Nor can Hegel simply be let off the hook by invoking the lack of literature on the subject in his own day. His failure goes deeper and is not just a matter of there not being enough books on Africa, China, and India for him to have consulted.[7]

The first issue comes back to Hegel's own complex form of "internalism" in ethics. Something can count as a reason for somebody only if he or she is in possession of the appropriate "psychology" to take it as a reason. For Hegel, the passions and the principles come, as it were, in a package. The general "shape" given to a way of life in terms of the way it combines appeal to principle with very specific practices brings together a kind of second-nature informed by its practices with the kinds of principles that make sense to itself. Although what will at ground level count as a reason for any person will be a function of his time (that is, of the shape of life of which he is a member), those shapes of life themselves develop and with them the space of reasons itself also develops.

Not unsurprisingly, Hegel thinks that in non-European ways of life, in effect, people will function as quasi-children. They can be taught right and wrong, good and bad, good and evil, and they can deliberate about those matters with some sophistication, but they can only reason about it by applying the existing rules. Hegel's view is not that such people are irrational. It is that they are completely or almost completely absorbed in their natural and social worlds and have not yet worked their way of that immersion. Thus, although they may have developed many useful skills and even a level of high craftsmanship in the arts, their stance toward their own ethical life lacks the proper critical distance. That Hegel thinks he finds this confirmed in the ethnographic literature he cites both says a lot about what prior views he brought to the issue and a lot about the views of his own time. (For example, he relied a good bit on English accounts of India, which meant that his views were formed around the reports of those reporting on what they regarded as a backward and subjugated populace.)

If we keep in mind that such peoples in Hegel's treatment of them (Africans, Chinese, Indians) are myths, it is worth asking what Hegel found deficient in them. First, what is characteristic of such people is, as noted, an absorption in the world. For spirit to be "immersed," or "sunken," into nature is for there to be a complete absorption on the part of self-conscious subjects in their world. Their reasoning has to operate against the background of an uncritical acceptance that there simply is a way things are to be done and that all inquiry has to stop there. They thus typically form themselves into traditional societies, where everything is to be done exactly as it has supposedly been done in the past. Even if this is in fact false, and they actually shift their existing norms for behavior over time, such a shift has to go unnoticed by them or to be regarded as merely contingent change. They have to think that what they are doing is what is natural and as such is the way things have always been done.

They are only "rule followers," not fully engaged subjects. They do not, Hegel says, have genuine historical narratives because they either do not think the laws and principles they are following are worth writing down, or if they are writing them down, they are only recording existing practice, which, for them, has always been that way. This also meant that there would be no need to separate mythical time (the "once upon a time . . ." of all legends) from real historical time. Thus, for Hegel, these people stand "outside" of history not in the sense that spirit is not "manifesting" itself in their activities, nor that they lack self-consciousness, but in the sense that they contribute nothing to progress in history since they themselves can have no conception of progress—except perhaps in limited technical areas, where such progress may even go unnoticed (such as a move from Stone Age to Bronze Age techniques, which, shortly after they are introduced, immediately come to be seen as simply the way things have always been done).

Second, because of the failure to develop such a basic reflective practice, such peoples therefore essentially lack the element of individual self-sufficiency. For Hegel, in the "African" and "Oriental" shapes of life, subjects are self-conscious but not so in a way that develops robust rules of criticism for its practices. (He is dead wrong about Africans and "Orientals," but that is another matter.) It is only when there is a shape of life that has become especially reflective about itself and is therefore pushed to see that what it often takes as a given, as beyond deliberation, may in fact be subject to doubt, that it also looks for a history. Only then does it look to see if it is doing something more than just carrying on in the same way. On Hegel's view of things, this truly reflective stance only first comes on the scene with the ancient Greeks. What distinguishes them from all earlier shapes of life is that the individual and his or her (mostly his) own subjectivity appears as having a force and validity all its own. It is this—and this alone, he says, at one point—which distinguishes Greeks and the European moderns from the "Africans" and "Orientals."[8]

The overall distinction is clear enough: Prior to the Greeks, people were simply absorbed in both nature and in social life, and there was no place for individuality. After the Greeks, the distinction between absorption and reflective self-consciousness came to the foreground, and an entirely new set of metaphysical problems appeared in the lives of those peoples (or per-haps even appeared as genuinely "metaphysical" problems for the first time). Hegel's additional belief that this overall conceptual distinction fits the actual distinction between modern Europeans and Africans and "Orientals" is not as happy a match.

China as the Embodiment of Political Atheism

Hegel has a particular problem on his very own terms fitting China into this picture. Whereas he seemed to take his more or less full ignorance about Africans to license him to dismiss them and move on, his limited knowledge of China showed him that the Chinese possessed a long and celebrated empire, that they had what certainly looked like grand cultural achieve-ments, and that they had had, and still had, an equally long and great tradi-tion of historical writing. In fact, increasingly in the eighteenth century, the Chinese were beginning to be highly regarded by some Europeans even as an alternative model of civilization, something from whom Europeans had to learn from rather than a matter in which the Chinese needed instructing by Europeans. After all, Europeans spent staggering sums to import Chinese luxury goods, whereas the Chinese could not find virtually anything in Europe that for them was worth importing. Famously, Voltaire even held the Chinese up as the great counterexample to all those who claimed that a great civilization could not exist without an established church.

Hegel's response to this was to claim that Chinese history shows that China is in fact an unchanging civilization.[9] (It was not an unchanging civi-lization, but that was a common view in Hegel's day and, in the West, even until recently.) Moreover, on Hegel's view, it was not only unchanging, it was essentially stalled within a version of unreflective self-consciousness (which, given the evidence, is an astonishing thing to say about China). The great importance of the Confucian virtue of filial piety in the little bit of Chinese thought with which he was acquainted convinced him that the Chinese regarded the state in the same terms that they regarded the family. (Hegel was not alone in holding that view, and it is part of classic Confucianism to regard the relation between prince and subject as bearing similarities to that between parent—particularly the father—and child.) For him, that meant that the Chinese could only think of ethical requirements as on a par with the kinds of familial requirements that, within the shape of life itself, feel natural.

Although Hegel himself did not think that familial requirements are in fact merely natural requirements, he did think that they were based in natural facts about human sexuality, aging, coming to maturity, and the like. They were ways of responding to, shaping, and coping with the problems that surface in those features of human life, much in the way Aristotle thought of the virtues as responding to basic human characteristics, such as fear, love of honor, or the desire for wealth. Nonetheless, in Hegel's view, in modern European life, familial obligations are something distinct from other political and social relations.

Thus, echoing Kant's charge against his fellow Europeans that, without enlightenment, they remain in a state of dependent tutelage, Hegel claims that the Chinese too are held in a permanent stage of tutelage since they conceive their relation to the state in the terms appropriate for a child's relation to the parents.[10] From that, it follows that all requirements for them have to function in their political psychology as mere social requirements with no deeper moral basis for them at hand. They simply have to be taken as required commands, a bit in the way a child has to take much of what her parents tell her to be simple commands to be obeyed. In a critique that prefigures in certain ways the manner in which later European mandarins accused their own cultures, Hegel warns that the Chinese population consists in what, after Hegel's time, came to be called the "masses"—indifferent to politics, culturally mediocre, and not merely subject to despotic rule but actually welcoming to it. Thus, "in China," Hegel says, "the distinction between slavery and freedom is not great, since all are equal before the emperor, that is, all are equally degraded. No honor being present, and no one having a particular right in respect of others, the consciousness of debasement predominates, which itself easily passes over into a consciousness of depravity."[11]

Whereas for Voltaire, China had looked like an alternative to the degeneracies of Western absolutism, for Hegel, it was instead almost a paradigm example of where Europe should not be headed. Hegel sided more with Montesquieu on the issue of China, namely, as an essentially despotic shape of life. That Hegel's "China" is simply not China should not be confused with his argument about what would be deficient in a shape of life that might embody the constellation of psychology and principle that character-izes Hegel's mythical "China." Such a legalistic regime could only base itself in something approaching a positivist conception of law, more or less along the lines of the British jurisprudential thinker John Austin's nineteenth-century conception of law as command issued by a sovereign followed by the credible threat of force to back it up. (Austin's work appeared in English shortly after Hegel's death.) In such a regime, the more modern, Kantian-inspired idea of respecting people as ends in themselves would not be possi-ble. Genuine respect for people as ends in themselves can only come about when there is a both a consciousness of principles that go beyond mere com-mands of a superior or the dictates of de facto social rules.[12] Because the Chinese supposedly have no higher set of principles than those contained in their own practices, and the law ultimately rests on a sovereign command unmediated by any other higher principles, Chinese political life is thus really, as Hegel calls it, "political atheism."[13]

Even if his treatment of China shows nothing deeply real about China, at least his treatment of China brings his own views into sharper relief. Against those who argued that Hegel's own conception of institutionalized ethical life—*Sittlichkeit*—only amounted to an endorsement of whatever it was that a given time-slice of society held to be required, to be part of the "rules," Hegel retorted that "there can be nothing more ethical *(sittlicher)* than the Chinese empire."[14] Obviously, on Hegel's own understanding, insti-tutionalized ethical life, *Sittlichkeit,* cannot be enough on its own.[15] Without incorporating both idea of rights and the standpoint of "morality" into itself—both of which function so as to provide and abstract and independent stance on ethical life—ethical life *(Sittlichkeit)* degenerates into mere custom *(Sitte).* Likewise, to draw a contrast with those who argued that Hegel's own portrayal of the modern European state was too all enveloping and suffocat-ing, he countered with the contrast that "China is nothing but a state," which has no room for difference within itself.[16] That this is not China in any real sense is, of course, more than just a grave mark against Hegel's portrayal, but the argument he makes is a deeper one against, first, a more assertive kind of legal positivism and absolutism; second, against an identification of morality with de facto social rules; and, third, expressing a deep hostility to any political regime attempting to regulate and control the inner life.[17] If morality is identified with social rules, then such social rules dialectically turn out to be devoid of morality, and social rules devoid of morality turn out to be social rules that have no place for individual difference within themselves. A human habitat constituted entirely by de facto social rules is no fit habitat for rational subjects, nor is a regime that legislates what the subject is supposed to feel inwardly a fit habitat for self-respecting subjects.

In effect, Hegel charges that the Chinese shape of life has not allowed "negativity" to be at work there. That is, it has not promoted the way in which a given set of problems often requires the drawing of distinctions and separation of spheres if the problems are to be solved or tamed. In theory, that requires positing new concepts and constellations of concepts, but in practice, it means carving out new spheres of authority in social life. It was not that the Chinese and Chinese philosophy did not recognize contradictions and try to resolve them. It was that it only did that in a nonphilosophical manner. When "the Chinese" encounter contradictions, they do as we ordinarily do at the empirical level of discourse: They realize that they have to discard one of the contradictory commitments or reframe the commitments so as to make what looked like a contradiction into a set of compatible commitments. No deep epistemology or metaphysics is required for that kind of activity. Hegel thinks that this is as far as the Chinese got, which is why he tends to view philosophers such as Confucius as simple moralists trying to get the de facto social principles all in the right order rather than probing deeper for their truth.[18]

Hegel's indictments against China can instead be posed as a kind of hypothetical: What would a social world that identified the moral with the de facto socially acceptable look like? One could identify morality with given social rules, but doing so would overlook an important difference which is not necessarily visible when seen from within a shape of life that operates in terms of identifying the two. What he finds particularly disturbing, so he thinks, about the Chinese example is that its incipiently positivist attitude to law and morality only goes in one direction: Those at the top of the commanding pyramid need pay no attention to any rights on the part of those down the scale who are being commanded since those at the bottom simply have no rights. Thus, so he argues, the system tends be that of irrational domination of many by some, or even of all by one.[19]

It seems that a good bit of his evidence for Chinese servility and political malfunction came largely from French and British commentary on the contemporary decrepitude of what turned out in some areas of China to be the initial stages of a crisis and eventual breakdown of the Qing dynasty (although the full breakdown occurred much after Hegel's death). Hegel seems to have confused some evidence of the weakening state of a particular period in Chinese history (the late period of the Qing dynasty) with Chinese civilization in general. He seemed to be making an inference to the effect that since everyone he knew agreed that China is an unchanging civilization, the particular, historical difficulties having to do with the Qing dynasty in the early nineteenth century must therefore be manifestations of a deeper defect in Chinese civilization itself. There is little acknowledgement on his part of how during, for example, the Song dynasty (960–1279) China managed to create a vibrant, market society long before the Europeans had dreamed of such a thing.[20] Hegel also seemed to have identified the Qing's official statements about the nature of its rule with the realities of rule in Chinese life. The Qing emperors liked to present their rulership as centralized, with the emperor issuing commands that were then seamlessly carried out by all the prefects below. In reality, it was far from seamless and involved much give and take—"politics" in the ordinary sense—among officials, citizens, and peasants up and down the local and social hierarchies.[21]

Putting it that way might seem too easily to exonerate Hegel, in effect, dismissing his disregard for the Chinese by arguing that, after all, since it is not China that he is describing but only "China," that is, his own fantasy about it, we can simply ignore his descriptions of the "Chinese" as having anything to do with the Chinese. However, dismissive attitudes cannot themselves be simply dismissed just because they are mistaken. Hegel's not so implicit claim to the Chinese was: Until you cease being Chinese and become European-style moderns, you will go nowhere.

Nonetheless, the argument about what kind of political psychology goes with what concatenation of principles is important, and it also shows how, on Hegel's own terms, one might demand a reconsideration of large parts of his own canonical philosophy of history once one has dismissed his descriptions of China. Part of what he took to be the force of his account was that China (and India, et al., with Africa being fully excluded) was not a counter-model for the problems facing European modernity. China, and the other non-European ways of life of which he speaks, were not alternatives to European modernity essentially because they had stalled in their development, and his explanation for the stall had to do with the way he took them to not have developed a kind of collective reflective self-consciousness about what ultimately mattered to them. Hegel's view was that in European culture, the tension in the way that Europeans use those concepts had become explicit and available to self-reflection. Within the non-European civilizations, so Hegel thought, there was no real possibility of bringing those reflective tensions to the surface.

It was thus important to Hegel to argue that the much-vaunted Chinese philosophy was not in fact really philosophy at all but something more along the lines of unsystematic thoughts on religion and life. If the Chinese really had a philosophy, they would have developed a reflective stance to their shape of life, a mode of standing outside of the social rules and critiquing them. Chinese philosophers did in fact do that, but Hegel did not see it in the texts he consulted, and it does seem that he did not consult many of those texts very deeply, if at all.[22] He overlooks the obvious counterexamples, such as the Neo-Confucian movement with its development of the "principle of heaven" as a reflective standard to govern all regimes in China, independently of the particular sovereign.[23] Now, perhaps he can be partially excused for ignoring other various schools of Chinese thought since, after all, there were not that many texts available for him, but he also overlooked the rather obvious way in which, for example, Confucian teaching stressed that the man of virtue has to be self-sufficient and that he acquires this self-sufficiency by way of a focus on the "higher" elements of living well, as well as having overlooked the Confucian insistence that "harmony" in a society requires difference and dissonance within itself (for which Confucius used the metaphor of musical harmony). He does, however, at least give some credit to Chinese moralists, comparing them to some philosophical positions taken in Western antiquity, since "the idea of an abstract subject, the wise man, is the high point of such doctrines with both the Chinese and the Stoic moralists."[24] However, that is only a muted acknowledgement on his part since this "high point" was in his view not really so very high at all. Roman stoicism was itself only another product of a "legalistic" shape of life. The negativity that comes with European philosophy and science, with its drawing out the distinctions necessary to a shape of life taking freedom as its watchword, was supposedly absent.[25] On his account, "Chinese" life could only develop the concept of a "monadic" subject for whom duties and requirements come only from the

legal system and are addressed to individuals who fulfill their duties in obedience to those laws, but without any sense of individualism to provide an
element of "negativity" to that obedience to social and familial duty. To the
extent that one could show Hegel that classical Chinese thought and political
practice had more in them than such monadic conceptions, then on his own
terms, Hegel would have to rethink that part of his philosophy of history.

India as Europe's Self-Created Mirror of European Dreaminess

When Hegel turns to India, he remarks that like China, it is unchanging,
essentially stalled in its development, but he also notes that it has for centuries been an object of longing by Europeans. What he says about it reveals
his whole program for interpreting Indian life: "It has always been the land
for which people long, and it still appears to us as a realm of wonder, as an
enchanted world."[26] That it is seen as an "enchanted world" is central to his
view that India also provides no counter-model for enlightened—and thus
disenchanted—Europeans.[27]

Amartya Sen has noted that European treatments of India have tended
to embody three ideal types: magisterial (as was the attitude of the British
ruling their colony), curatorial (classifying its differences more or less in the
way a traditional butterfly collector might describe his collection), and exoticist (which, as Sen says, looks for the wondrous in Indian life). Although
Hegel himself would have almost certainly have put himself in the "curatorial" camp if he had been forced to choose among those three categories, he
actually belongs, as Sen thinks he does, more in the exoticist camp, except
that for Hegel, India's wonders are not to be extolled.[28] His sources for Indian
thought also are, for the most part, British sources, which tend to reinforce
both his "curatorial" and "exorcist" impulses.[29] What Hegel wanted to argue
about India was that it embodied the all-too-wistful focus for so many
Europeans who were projecting their own dreaminess onto it as a counterweight to their own prosaic life. The loss of an "enchanted" world in
European life was, for Hegel, a mark of progress, even it was also a loss.
Although such a disenchanted view might from one point of view be emo-
tionally unsatisfying, coming to terms with a "disenchanted" nature was
part of the cost of a modern life. In effect, Hegel wanted to argue that India
was basically a "dreamy" way of life onto which Europeans easily projected

their own nostalgic and melancholic dreaminess.[30] However, his view was not that Europeans were merely projecting their own dissatisfactions onto Indian reality. It was that Indian reality was a fertile ground for Europeans to engage in such a dreaminess about their own dissatisfactions.

Thus, so Hegel claimed, what at first seems "enchanted," even as a "garden of love"—which is exactly what one would expect from a life that seeks to return to the "enchanted" world—turns out to be, when measured against modern conceptions of human dignity and freedom, entirely deficient.[31] For Hegel, if the exoticist-seeking Europeans looked to India for a mirror of what they have lost, then the mirror only reflected back to them how deficient their own dreamy state was. For Hegel, Romantic, nostalgic Europeans were only looking at their own emptiness reflected back to them in the form of Indian emptiness and taking it, oddly enough, as a confirmation of their own potential fullness.

Whereas the Chinese are absorbed in the world and therefore are "prosaic" (unimaginative and incapable of thinking outside of what is given to them), the Indians, on the other hand, are unfocussed and dreamy and, because they are not absorbed enough, are therefore "poetic." Whereas China is unimaginative, India is all imagination. China cannot develop the necessary set of theoretical and practical distinctions to be free and modern, whereas India develops all the distinctions arbitrarily and simply spins in the void. The Chinese have no real conception of divinity and thus no way to distinguish the "is" (the given social world) from the "ought" (which only the higher status of divinity can at first impart to people). The Indians, on the other hand, do indeed have a "higher" conception of divinity, but their conception of the "higher" element is essentially empty. It is the "one" of all things and nothing more. Moreover, since they see everything as divine and see everything as in constant change, there can be no conception of progress for them. Once seen in that light, the practical difference between Chinese and Indian despotism collapses, and, in practice, China and India therefore work out to the same thing: Tyranny. (Or so goes Hegel's view.)

Although he thought the "Chinese" failed utterly to develop a conception of reason as apart from given social practice, the Indians (on Hegel's mature account of them) had indeed worked out a version of reflective thought that can be properly called "philosophical," even though the only philosophical results they could reach were essentially empty. Hegel more or less stuck to this view, although he had to revise it as more came to be known about Indian philosophy in the last ten or so years of his life and greater claims were made for its originality.[32] In 1827, he published a review of Wilhelm von Humboldt's recent work on Indian philosophy, but he there reiterated, although in greater detail, his basic and long held view that in the last analysis, Indian philosophy could not really advance to the level of genuine "philosophy" (that is, not to the level of ancient Greek and post-Greek philosophy) since the contradictions that Indian philosophy turns up do not lead to any real resolution but only to an empty, formal thought of the "one," for the reason that "what is highest in Indian consciousness, the abstract essence, Brahman, is in itself void of determination, for which consequently there can be only a determination external to the unity, merely an external, natural determination. In this breakdown of the universal and the concrete, both are devoid of spirit—the former being empty unity, the latter being the unfree multiplicity; the person, deteriorating into this state, is bound only to a natural law of life."[33] Indeed, Humboldt's stress on "absorption"— *Vertiefung,* Humboldt's translation of "yoga"—as the basic principle of Indian thought and life only reinforced Hegel's overall view.[34] Indian emptiness cannot lead to progress but only to unending tyranny, the rule of those who have the power to impose their wills and find no ethical reason hindering them that they have to explain away.[35]

What is driving Hegel to see things this way is thus a concatenation of his basic philosophical views—in particular, about how the ability to critically distance ourselves from all forms of givenness, whether it be social or natural, rests on a capacity that must be developed and which has a very specific history—and his own early nineteenth-century, European-influenced interpretations of both shapes of life. The charge of "political atheism" is particularly potent for him, since if it were true that Chinese philosophy and practice had in fact developed all those modes of critical reflection, then the necessity of religion—in particular, the necessity of Protestant Christianity—for the development of a free, modern state would not seem to be so necessary. He realized what was at stake was an adequate conception of what it would mean both theoretically and practically for individuals and collectivities to be in a position to be free and how coming to be in that position was a matter of history and development, not something written in the stars or in Platonic heaven. He thought that China and India, because of the most basic commitments of their shape of life, were unable to progress further and still retain any of the things that made them the shapes of life they were.

What the "Indians" and more particularly the "Chinese" show is that the picture of the dialectic as inexorably moving from breakdown to breakdown itself breaks down. Part of the problem he sees in "China" is what some of his contemporaries praised in it: It is an ancient, unchanging civilization. It thus does not break down under its own weight. From that, Hegel concluded that its path to progress must therefore come from a confrontation with something outside of itself. To put it in Hegel's own preferred jargon, "China" cannot generate its own negativity, so its negation must come from something both external to it and indifferent to it (in the sense that there is no deeper connection of meaning between the confrontation between China and its supposed "other"). This confrontation, of course, is taken by Hegel to be that between China (along with India) and the West (specifically, northern Europe).[36] Hegel did not entertain the idea, mostly because his knowledge of non-European history was so limited, that Chinese civilization was in fact responding to internal pressures of the modern world in its own way, and the Qing empire of Hegel's day was dealing with many of the same tensions that the others nations in that period were dealing. Nor did he understand the forces at work in India that were confronting it as it too was trying to find its way in what was a period of global and not just European transformation and that, for example, Indian cotton textile production was one of the provocations of the English industrial revolution in textiles.[37] If he had realized that, it would also have forced him to alter his narrative in a rather dramatic way. He also did not see that the confrontation with European modernity would propel both a revived and a new sense of national identity for Chinese, Japanese, Indians, et al., which would be formed out of the same kinds of pressures that were driving Europeans.

Nonetheless, in Hegel's own narrative, not merely Chinese and Indians are condemned to be failed Europeans. Persians and Egyptians are likewise condemned, but in a subtly different way.

Persians and Egyptians as Failed Greeks

Setting up his agenda in that way provided Hegel the means to resuscitate the classical Greek conception of Persia as Greece's opponent while also seeing Persia as both more progressive than China or India and still as a rightly defeated and vanished empire. Since both China and India had remained as identifiable countries in Hegel's time and were potentially on offer as alternatives to European modernity—or at least as having some unique contribution to make to its further development—he thought he had provided an argument that showed why neither of them could really be taken that way. That argument depends, as we have seen, on whether his descriptions of them are correct, since if they are not the way he took them to be, he cannot be said to have much of an argument that they cannot develop in their own way to a condition of freedom, nor that they have nothing to offer European modernity.

His arguments about the "Orientals" thus were intended to show that, within their own terms, they not only could not think their way out of the problems, they also could not even see them as problems, as something requiring a solution.[38] For him, the classical category of "oriental despotism" even had to be taken by the "Orientals" themselves not as something wrongful but as a necessary, although perhaps woeful, fact about the world.

In effect, he took that as underwriting the correctness of the classical Greek conception of their enemies, the Persians. On the one hand, the element of "negativity" makes its appearance with the Persians, although in a thoroughly inadequate way. (The religion of "light" allows the contrast with its "determinate negative," that of "darkness," and this an abstract, although readily inadequate and unsatisfying way to begin to think through the difference between the normative and the natural.) On the other hand, the Persians, like all the "Orientals," are prone to take their success as an excuse to wallow in luxury and become effeminate. They could exhibit great valor as fighters (which, so Hegel notes, is true of all barbarians), but they could not ultimately construct an empire that could last nor could they produce any philosophy of great note. Their philosophy was at best just their religion restated.

Likewise, the ancient Egyptians could build on the "negativity" worked out so insufficiently by the Persians, but they could only build it up to the level of an enigma. Hegel accepts Herodotus' idea that it was the Egyptians who first considered the idea that the soul might be different from the body and was immortal.[39] However, for the Egyptians, spirit and nature, along with the normative and the natural, were both united yet still at odds with each other, and since they could not get beyond that statement of it (made in their art, since they had no real philosophy, on Hegel's account), their shape of life rested on an acknowledged basic unintelligibility. For them, nature was identical with spirit, and yet spirit was different from and at odds with nature, and, left at that, such a comprehension of the world makes all within it unintelligible. It meant that their art always seemed to be expressing a great mystery that could not be unraveled, and once one stops inquiry at the unintelligibility of the world, there is no further progress to be made. The form of subjectivity that takes itself to be fully natural, to be simply that of "rule-following" (where the normative is equated with social rules), to be all imaginative wandering in empty thoughts, and so on—all the features of the "African" and "Oriental" worlds—culminates in this dead-end. At best, there can be change but no progress, no deep sense of "change for the better." It is a form of subjectivity that ultimately is unsatisfactory since in its final "Egyptian" form, it ultimately drives itself into an unintelligibility about itself.

Here was Hegel's verdict: The Persians and Egyptians, while going beyond the political atheism of the Chinese and the ineffective dreaminess of the Indians, had to stop short at the unintelligibility of their world. They developed their own comprehension of subjectivity such that they got an inkling of the metaphysical antinomies at work in thinking about "the unconditioned" that were the result of their own development, but they did not go beyond that thought. The concept of subjectivity under which they brought themselves was thus doomed to unintelligibility, and, in the long run, they could make no sense to themselves.

Ultimately, so Hegel argued, the European shape of life built itself out of the ruins of the "East," and in gathering up the rubble from the "East's" ruins, it developed a different self-comprehension of subjectivity. For Hegel, with his limited sense of the non-European world, the "East" therefore does not necessarily vanish but remains only as a self-perpetuating ruin, unable to make progress on its own terms.[40] However, by developing the sense of contradiction at work in the initial thoughts about reason and nature, the Persians and Egyptians introduced an element of reflection within themselves, and this, so Hegel thought, played a not-insignificant role in their subsequent breakdown.

Sometimes Hegel is partially excused for holding these views about non-Europeans as if it was all a matter of misreading empirical data, or as if, given the biased literature of his day, he cannot be blamed for drawing false conclusions from such bad sources. It is said that, after all, in his time, there simply was not that much available to him about these other ways of life, other than a few already slanted travelers' reports and the like (even though, if that were the case, he should have had the good sense to take such reports with a larger grain of salt).[41] Yet on his own terms, Hegel's mistake is not per se with his conception of subjectivity nor with his conception of freedom, but rather with his idea that entire civilizations in effect never move on to the right type of reflective subjectivity.

In the last analysis, Hegel's rather negative characterization of non-European shapes of life turns out to be less about them (despite what Hegel himself actually thought it was about) and more about the problems inherent in any collective enterprise that either takes something like the "moral" to be equivalent to "actually existing social rules" or which takes its own collective project to be simply unintelligible and thus available only the mystical. Even though that may be a fundamental mischaracterization of the non-European shapes of life Hegel discusses, both options were live in Hegel's time for European life itself. In effect, Hegel was saying: See where this leads you?

4

Europe's Logic

Greece: Slavery as the Condition of Self-Sufficiency

Hegel's world history thus really gains its focus when he switches to Greece, which is not much of a surprise. Greece is where the story really starts for him, since it is where the kind of reflective self-consciousness that propels a philosophical history (in his sense) first plants its feet firmly on the ground and where he is simply better informed than he was about Africa, China, India, Persia, or Egypt. It also means that despite its claims to be a philosophical "world history," the rest of the lecture series is about Europe, since like Polybius's Rome, modern Europe (for Hegel) is the defining element of the modern order. It also means that from that point on, Hegel's story is entirely European, which as a history of modernity, he thinks is only proper (but which is not the whole story of modernity, even in his own time, although it would have been hard for him to have known that.)[1]

Like others before and since, Hegel regarded the emergence of classical Greece as something of a wonder—the idea of "Greek miracle" so often cited—and although it was unprecedented, it was not without precedent. On his account, the ancient pre-Greek world, paradigmatically in Egypt, had foundered on its own unintelligibility. Greek life, however, gave the ancient world the more developed form of self-consciousness, the reflective distance it had otherwise lacked. The Greek world now rested on making sense of what it meant to be a sense-making agent.[2]

Hegel does note how the Greek world grew out of the turbulence of the ancient world and the collapse of what we now call the "Bronze Age" of civilization in that part of the Mediterranean.[3] It seems that what brought this about was not some, or even a few, identifiable causes but what Eric Cline has suggested might be a "perfect storm" of climate change, earthquakes, foreign invasion, internal rebellion, the cutting of trade routes, disease, the eruption of volcanoes, and mass migration.[4] The collapse of the ancient civilizations of the Mediterranean meant that the earlier organization whereby only "one was free"—a sacred ruler who embodied all power in himself—itself collapsed and lost its hold.[5] The effect was to force the reduced population of the early ancestors of classical Greece into living in closely knit units that were severed from the ancient organization wherein only "one" was free. The Greek miracle, as it were, was its creation of the polis, a new form of social and political organization in history in which the ability to defend the community united with an ancient conception of justice into a new kind of unity that broke with the past and thereby combined the advantages of the emotional closeness and solidarity of traditional tribal life with the reflective and economic advantages of an urban life.[6]

Hegel's classicism shows up most clearly—but again hardly as a surprise—in his treatment of ancient Greece in the lectures on the philosophy of history. His own views on Greece are informed by and large by a mixture of Herodotus and Thucydides, all restructured so as to present his own account of why the ancient Greeks both present a certain highpoint in civilization and why, as good as it was, it could not endure. From Herodotus, he takes over the narrative that it was the Greek decision to preserve Greek freedom that heroically led them to defeat the Persians, and, also like Herodotus, he sees this not merely as one battle among many but as the world-historical decisive confrontation of Greek freedom against Asiatic despotism (That idea from Herodotus became a theme with a long afterlife in European thought.) From Thucydides, he takes over the narrative of the glory of Periclean Athens as both dazzling and fundamentally doomed, as yielding to a fate that seemed to be directing it from without. The defeat of the Persians serves for Hegel as one of the key manifestations of the path-dependency of history. At that point, as Hegel puts it, "world history's interests hung in the balance."[7] If the Persians had defeated the Greeks, then the philosophical sense Hegel makes of history would probably not have been possible. Everything would have been different.

However, Hegel thought that the basis of Thucydides' explanation of the decline and collapse of Athens was, although overall in the right direction, wrong in one fundamental way in its diagnosis. For Thucydides, the diagnosis lay in a characteristic of Greek *hubris,* an overreach against one's limits and thus an overstepping of the boundaries of the virtues on the part of the Athenians that led Athens to move from self-confidence to aggression, and caused Sparta, among the other Greek city-states, to fear the extension of Athenian power and ultimately to face down Athens and defeat it. As Thucydides suggests, the overreach that characterized Athens is written into human nature such that one can expect the same kind of thing to happen again with regard to some future and otherwise successful state.

However, what for Hegel was missing in Thucydides' account was that Athens and the whole Greek system of democratic city-states were doomed from the outset because of the constellation of principle and passion that necessarily attends the organization of such city-states. It was not hubris and the decay of virtue, but a deep contradiction at work in that constellation of passion and principle that was to constitute the fate of Athens, the outcome of which was that Greek life ended up with a deep unintelligibility about itself. It was not that Hegel disputed Thucydides' suggestion that something like the Athenian overreaching lay in human nature (nor did he dispute that it would most likely happen again in history). However, it was essential to understanding the logic of historical development that such a conviction did not rule out the idea that we could nonetheless be making progress in our interpretations about what it meant to be a self-conscious subject.

On Hegel's account, what compels our attention to the Greek shape of life was at the heart of its dissolution. In his negatively mythical versions of Chinese, Indian, Persian, and Egyptian shapes of life, individual subjects were more or less either fully absorbed into their natural and social worlds such that they could not get an adequately critical distance on their own practices or were so abstractly disconnected from their social worlds that getting an adequately critical grip on them was also not possible.[8] In such a positive order of things—where the basic rules are simply "given"—there would be lots of room for the intellect to make changes and adjust principles, but there is no room for any more radical, rational reflection, and each subject remained fully dependent on his or her involvement in the whole (even for what looks like the exception, namely of those dominant individuals who in rulership laid down the law for others but were subject to no law governing themselves). In contrast, the Greek shape made real the formation of an individual who could plausibly claim to be fully self-sufficient. The concept of the individual in Greek life, which specified the aspirations around which the real individuals of that life ideally modeled themselves, was that of a self-sufficient individual, or, as Aristotle at one place characterizes the virtuous man, a "law unto himself."[9]

It is the place where, in Hegel's words, "beautiful individuality" shows up. The Greek shape of subjectivity, in its origin, bases itself on the conviction that the goods pursued by subjectivity are objective and part of nature. The gods themselves are part of the world, not located in some "beyond" outside of time and space. Yet, in distinction from Hegel's imagined "Orientals," the Greeks also had a place for self-conscious subjectivity as occupying a status that can put itself above, as it were, all the goods that are presented to it as reasons for belief, feeling, or action. The Greeks never resolved the obvious tension between those conceptions, however heroically their artists gave expression to it and however systematically their philosophers drew the implications. As Hegel sums it up: "Rather, spirit as the in-between between of both extremes is the concrete abstraction. . . . Between the sensuousness of the person as such and his mindedness in the form of thought, of abstraction, is the particular subject the middle-term and that makes the Greek character into beautiful individuality, which is brought forth by spirit in its reshaping of what is natural into spirit's own expression."[10]

The Greek subject in his ideal form as such a self-sufficient virtuous individual thus achieved a kind of self-distancing that is not possible in a fully absorbed life. He could place himself a distance from the social and natural world that otherwise constitutes everything such subjects are, and, in the Greek case, for a very short period, this type of individual lived in harmony with the social world. As Hegel succinctly summarized that view: "The Greeks in their immediate actuality lived in the happy middle between both self-conscious subjective freedom and the ethical substance."[11] That "happy middle" also included the self-sufficient individual whose social space was nonetheless essentially dyadic (as a citizen of the polis).

However, what held Greek life together was not originally a fully worked out conceptual comprehension but something more like an aesthetic unity. In the Hegelian conception, in every genuine work of art, there is an aspiration to bring together certain basic tensions not simply in terms of cataloging them and laying them out side by side but rather as holding them together so that a kind of harmony emerges in the work itself, the experience of which falls under the concept of "beauty" (but which is "aesthetic" and not natural beauty). Greek political life, which leads to the Athenian ideal of a commitment to democratic participation by citizens under conditions of equality, embodied such an ideal of aesthetic beauty. The political order did not exist on the basis of externally compelling people to participate. Each citizen freely joined the deliberative body. To the extent that individuals came together to deliberate about what to do as a collective, they could each be assured that no matter how deeply the passions went pro and contra certain policies, each citizen was deliberating with the interests of the city-state (especially in Athens) in mind. Differences of opinion were about how best to serve Athens' interests, and not about different interests themselves. Outside of that common commitment to the good of Athens, individuals could thus develop their own idiosyncrasies and talents more or less as they pleased. As Thomas Hobbes rendered Pericles's speech to his fellow Athenians, Pericles boasted: "And we live not only free in the administration of the state, but also one with another void of jealousy touching each other's daily course of life; not offended at any man for following his own humour, nor casting on any man censorious looks, which though they be no punishment, yet they grieve."

The model for Athens was that each citizen was to be self-sufficient and could be confident of having his views heard and debated. The whole functioned organically in a way analogous to that in which the organs of animal function worked together to produce and sustain the whole without any particular "organ" having such a unity as its aim. If each citizen did his part, then even though great passions could be provoked and great disputes might arise, the social whole would spontaneously harmonize. Full equality was maintained among self-sufficient citizens, but its beauty did not consist in equality in which real difference did not emerge. (This was what he thought

the "mass" society of equals in "China" was all about.) What made it beautiful was the element of negativity, the very distinctness of the citizens, the
way they distinguished themselves from each other in their actions and thus
the way their whole personality necessarily showed up in public life. As
Hegel put it, "the democratic [constitution] is what was suited for the Greek
spirit, for living, self-sufficient individuality. In that city, each could be present with his whole particularity in order to actively co-contribute."[12] It was
therefore a world in which the unifying principle was not really so much of
a principle but something more akin to the sensible intuition of beauty. Art
had its home there, since the artist could express the truth of Athenian life
in a sensuous work and have it be complete, requiring nothing outside of
itself. In Greece's golden age, no philosophical commentary would be
required for a Greek to comprehend the truth that was being offered up in
aesthetic form. He lived that truth in his political life in the polis, and he saw
and heard it in the work of art.[13]

But that was its problem. Women and slaves were excluded from all this,
and this exclusion was not accidental to the nature of the Greek polis. To be
a citizen, a man had to be self-sufficient, a law unto himself. The individual
self-sufficiency of the member of the polis required that the dirty work of his
everyday life had to be done by others so that he was free from manual labor
or even craftwork. As Aristotle phrases it, "it is the mark of a free man not
to live at another's beck and call," and a craftsman or laborer has to take
orders from somebody else.[14] The beauty of Greek life, its achievement in
the arts and in philosophy, thus came at a high price: slavery (and the oppression of women, although that was by no means Hegel's main concern).

The Greek, democratic model differed from the so-called Asiatic despotic model (on the accounts given by Herodotus and Thucydides) in that it
defended freedom (at least in the figure it assumed within the Greek shape
of life), and individual citizens were dependent on themselves, not on the
arbitrary wills of others. As long as such citizens exercised their virtues, no
despot could take power from them—except for the fact, more or less unac-
knowledged, that Greek male citizens were in effect despots within their
own circle (which also meant that those circles outside of the despotic rule
of men had to be excluded from political life).

A second sense of self-sufficiency for the ancient Greek subject is that he
has no need to consult anything other than his own self to determine his

actions. The exemplary model of freedom in this shape of life was the myth-ical Greek hero. The Greek hero is an aesthetic creation: He is portrayed as completely self-sufficient in that he acts without principle, but he also does what he takes himself to be required to do.[15] As Hegel likes to put it, although he founds cities based on law, he lives by the laws of no city. Passion and principle unite in his person because in essence, as a founder of cities, there is in his case no real difference between passion and principle. Acting on his passion is his principle, and when a hero acts in such a way, he is justified. He is not unreflective, but he does not have to reflectively identify himself with his desires (of whatever rank he gives them), nor does he have to reflectively justify what he does, since the hero is entitled by virtue of who he is to do what it is he needs to do. He is thus the very model of what it would mean to be a law unto oneself.

The hero is necessarily also a fictional character, a kind of cultural ideal who, if he were real, would resemble a sociopath.[16] Yet the subject who does what he needs to do and is justified in doing so remains a powerful picture of freedom, and in the sensible portrayals that art gives—in poetry, paint-ing, or sculpture—this kind of freedom offers up the richest possibilities for aesthetic portrayal. It gives rise to a kind of art which cannot, Hegel says, be surpassed—in the sense that no better sensuous and intuitive presentation of freedom can be given.

However, the hero does not instantiate any general principle. He simply acts and does what he has to do. Being a human—or the son or daughter of a human and a god—he acts as any human would in founding a new politi-cal order, but being a hero, he does this in a way that no contingent human could do. The hero, as a law unto himself, is autonomous. What the aes-thetic presentation of the hero obscures, however, is that such full auton-omy as an ideal seems to make sense ultimately only in a social order that is also in essence based on domination of others—in other words, the slave society that was ancient Greece.

Its downfall lay partly in the way that it could not make sense of itself—it could not exist without slavery but slavery ultimately was problematic for that shape of life. For example, since slaves could be manumitted, what was the real difference between a slave and an ex-slave? Aristotle gave slavery an unconvincing justification with his idea that some people are "natural slaves," since they supposedly cannot rule themselves and therefore require masters, but after him, most Greeks simply gave up trying to defend it without virtually anybody seriously suggesting that they abandon it. For them, as for the rest of the ancient world, slavery was an institution that hardly seemed justified, but nobody in power thought they could do without it. At its heart, classical Greece had a tension within itself that gradually grew into a tension emerging as a self-conscious contradiction. Eventually, the various attempts at avoiding the contradiction by redefining terms, arguing for "natural slaves," or more closely specifying the duties between slaveholder and slave were seen as inadequate, and the contradiction now appeared not as the temporary failure of those thinking about it to get out of it but as a kind of insoluble unintelligibility at the heart of things.

Linked to the tension between the necessity and the indefensibility of slavery was the way in which classical Greek life demanded as its key value a kind of self-sufficient individuality, which, when it fully developed itself in actual practice was actually completely at odds with the system that nurtured it. It was only as a citizen that somebody could be self-sufficient, a law unto himself, but to be a citizen, he had to be recognized by other citizens with the requisite authority to recognize his own authority over himself, and for him to be recognized as having self-sufficiency in that sense, he also had to be free from dirty work and mundane matters. Thus, the world in which citizens think of themselves in terms of the aspirations to self-sufficiency in this one-sided way necessarily sustained itself as a slave society even if it could not ultimately make sense of doing so.[17] Its unintelligibility to itself made it, so Hegel thought, in the long run unable to sustain the passionate normative allegiance that had earlier fueled the defeat of the Persians. Nonetheless, out of its experience of slavery, it developed the concept of freedom, and out of the Greek experience, the opposition of freedom/slavery became a defining concept for what happened after it.

As it first emerged in Greece, freedom was conceived as a negative phenomenon: To be free was not to be a slave. Rather, freedom, as a new component of a shape of life, was to be in a social order where one exercised authority over one's own life, and freedom was what the name for what slave lost when he or she became enslaved. However, out of its negative definition, its positive sense developed on its own: Freedom was about self-direction in one's own life, which in turn depended entirely on one's entitlement to the principled status of "citizen" in a polis.[18] A person outside the polis could not exercise human freedom. Living outside of any polis, he could only be, as Aristotle noted, either a beast (and thus not free at all, since he could not participate in practices of recognition) or a god (and thus a creature whose authority was completely self-derived, a status which could only be mythical). Freedom was thus not an inherently human possession. It was a status that only a few members of a social class possessed. Free people could make what really matters effective in their lives and in their world. Unfree people could not, and if there really were "natural slaves," as Aristotle entertained the idea, there were some people who simply could not have the capacity to make what matters truly effective. Their status was somewhere between children and animals.

On Hegel's view, nonetheless, the art of classical pre-Socratic Greece was never to be surpassed, since as a shape of life held together in a fundamentally aesthetic way, its modes of ultimate intelligibility to itself were fundamentally aesthetic.[19] The way in which citizens were called to respond and justify themselves to each other was anchored in the sense that each acting in their required but nonetheless spontaneous ways would lead the social whole to spontaneously harmonize such that a political work of beauty would be the result. The giving and asking for reasons by Greek citizens was rooted in an aesthetic-religious condition, not fundamentally a more narrowly conceptual comprehension because, as a spontaneously produced harmony, it needed no concept to guide it (to put it in the way Kant characterized aesthetic judgment). Yet it also conceived of itself as acting under a sense of "eternal" justice, out of a necessity that lay in the very nature of things aesthetically portrayed, and which could only be accessible through the reflective capacities developed by the Greek shape of mindedness itself.

Yet, since this aesthetic ideal contained the archetype of self-sufficiency for each citizen, it was also fundamentally at odds with itself. The tensions between the Greek idea of justice as a kind of necessity born out of what spontaneous harmony requires and the necessity of an ideal of beautiful individuality that is required of such an aesthetic conception itself comes to its most nearly full presentation, so Hegel famously thought, in Sophocles's *Antigone,* where the central character demanding recognition for himself is not in fact a "himself" at all but Antigone, the daughter of Oedipus, who self-consciously disobeys the command from her uncle, Creon, not to perform the religiously required burial rites on her dead brother's corpse. Antigone embodies almost all the contradictions in Greek life within herself. As a daughter of a ruling family, she demands full recognition, which is fully at odds with the status of women in that shape of life. Her uncle, Creon, has the unlimited right to issue commands for the good of the community, and he has clearly spoken. Whatever she does—obey Creon or disobey Creon—is, on the terms of the polis itself, equally right and wrong. Even worse, whatever she does violates the bedrock principle that she is not to make up her own mind about where her practical requirements lie, since there is no stance outside of the polis and its spontaneous harmony that could function as a standard for her to make up her own mind. Antigone comes to an end because of these contradictions. She is the heroine of the play because she basically *is* Greece as it has unfolded itself in time.[20]

Tragedies such as *Antigone* brought the Greek public face to face with the deeper contradictions at work in their collective life. The eternal laws of justice, as embedded in the divine organic order, are themselves necessary to produce spontaneously the kind of beauty in which the upending of the natural organic order of things is put aright by some form of punishment in keeping with those eternal laws of justice.[21] However, when the laws are carried out by fragile humans, they will not always be consistent with each other, since in a world of conflicting gods making unconditional but conflicting demands on human allegiance, there will always be a world of tragic human conflict—tragic because the conflicts are internal to the shape of life itself and are not merely conflicts with the religion of another shape of life. A tragedy such as *Antigone* makes those conflicts doubly problematic since the tragedy presented a kind of failed reconciliation. It exhibited a world where Antigone's doom must happen as a result of the divine order of things—since the basic structure of that world has been thrown out of kilter, it must be set aright again, and that entails Antigone's suffering—and yet it implicitly provoked, without having explicitly to raise the issue itself, the doubt as to whether that order made any sense. If it is senseless, Antigone's suffering is also senseless.

For the Greek democratic political ideal to be real, citizens had to assume that debate in the public arena was conducted in a way such that each citizen firmly had the good of the polis as his basic, unyielding commitment.[22] That commitment itself was beyond deliberation, and commitment to the agreed-upon policies had to be equally stringent. Tragedies like *Antigone* raised the thoroughly disturbing thought that the gods might be such that they could make even the best of such deliberations ineffective since all human deliberation might result in policies that contravene the divine order. If that were the case, then even the most ordinary citizen would have to be able to think for himself about which law—the "divine" or the "human" law, or even which among many "divine" laws—he was required to follow. That left citizens at odds with themselves and potentially at odds with each other. In such a world, the move from a fundamentally religious and aesthetic comprehension of things to a more secular and rational comprehension suddenly came on the agenda, and that meant that tragedy was to be replaced by philosophy. If the world was to make sense (and for us to be reconciled to it), it had to make sense rationally. That required a new and more alienated form of self-relation which developed out of the breakdown of the initial Greek conception of subjectivity. It provoked the Greeks to move from tragedy as an aesthetic way of understanding themselves to philosophy as a search for a conceptual and not aesthetic comprehension of things. Greek life moved from the tragic view of the world to the philosophical.

Despite its beauty and its cultural achievements, this was not a system that could ultimately make sense of itself. The good fortune it enjoyed in defeating the Persians could not be expected to last forever (and it was overreaching to think it could). To keep its democratic equality real, it also had to remain small, which made it ultimately indefensible against larger, stronger powers (first against Macedon and later more definitively against Rome). More to the point, the very ideal of self-sufficiency itself could last only as long as such putatively self-sufficient individuals could maintain the ideal that required each of them to put Athens' good before his own good. The very activities of separating oneself from the social whole that was the core of Greek democracy meant that eventually people would put their own interests ahead of the social whole, and when they did, the sophists were ready and waiting to sell them the skills they needed to get their private way in public debates. Small wonder, Hegel noted, that this beautiful system in its full bloom only lasted about sixty years.

The rise of Alexander, who always carries the epithet, "the great," came after the classical Greek shape of life had ceased to exercise its authority as it had done in the past. While it is probably true that Alexander—Aristotle's student—was indeed a charismatic individual who could inspire others to organize and even more others to carry out his will, he was also the end of the story. The empire that resulted from his conquests (achieved with extraordinary brutality) was what we call a conquest state—it subjugated independent peoples under its own rule and used plunder to finance itself. Typically with conquest states, when the elements of plunder are no longer there, the conquest state quickly vanishes, and so it was with Alexander's great "empire," which fell apart immediately on his death. Like so many others of his own time and afterward, Hegel more or less bought into the idea that by virtue of such conquests and his allegedly noble character, Alexander really deserved his epithet, "the great," and Hegel dismissed those who criticized Alexander's harsh methods and mercurial personality. He seems to have accepted Pliny the Elder's story that Alexander had his conquered peoples send his beloved teacher, Aristotle, specimens from the East (in particular, an elephant or details about elephants), thus enabling Aristotle to write his history of animals. (The story has been disputed.[23]) But even on Hegel's own account, Alexander's greatness came about only in the interim of the breakdown of an older shape of life and its replacement by a new shape which was growing at the same time.[24]

Because of the necessity of the ideal of self-sufficiency, the polis had to be small enough to enable face to face interaction. This made the Greek polis too small to defend itself, and when another, well-organized powerful empire showed up at its door, it no longer had the power, motivational or otherwise, to resist.[25] Classical Greece's long, slow breakdown and final, stunning submission to Roman rule finally came as no surprise. Its successors had to discard what did not work in that shape of life and had to fashion a new understanding out of the new reality on the ground (the rise to world domination by Rome). In terms of a more Hegelian metaphor, it was time for spirit to move on.

Roman Dominance and the Cultivation of Inwardness

In Hegel's philosophy of history, the move from one period to another is characterized as that of "determinate negation." The failure of a way of life is expressed in the way in which it fails to sustain allegiance to itself, and in the dissolution of such a way of life, those living during its dissolution have to pick up the pieces that still seem to work, discard what is no longer of use or value, and fashion some new whole out of what remains, almost always without any overall plan for what they are doing. The succeeding shape of life is different, but it is not the "abstract negation" of what succeeded it. That is, its own shape is not just that it is "not" the same as its predecessor. Rather, it has the shape it does by virtue of the way it tries to make good on the failures of its predecessors and the way it sees itself as dealing with the failures and successes of its predecessor. It is "not" its predecessor in a very determinate way.

The passage from Greece to Rome is illustrative of this. It is not a dialectical generation of Rome out of Greece—Greece does not "produce" Rome—and thus it differs from the way Hegel otherwise proceeds in most of his other work. The *Logic,* for example, claims to generate the kinds of claims that go on in "Essence" out of the necessities of making sense of "Being." So Hegel's claim goes, the very intelligibility of the ways in which we describe, count, and classify objects requires us to look at the way things are described as appearances or as causal products of something else, and the answers to the questions "What caused that?" or "Why does it appear that way?" are not a matter just of describing, classifying, or counting. Rome does not, however, appear as a logical derivation from Greece. Rome had an independent—and from the standpoint of Hegel's *Logic,* arbitrary—founding (which it mostly mythologized), and it construed itself as bound by the acts those founders carried out in the founding.[26] It is just not that we (or some cosmic spirit) have to make sense of Greece by coming up with a new category, "Rome." (That would be a claim so wildly implausible one would wonder why anyone would want attribute it to Hegel.) Rome's own founding, and its relationship to Greek civilization, also depended quite obviously on the nonlogical fact that both operated in a Mediterranean sphere.

Nonetheless, Rome succeeded Greece by incorporating the workable elements of Greek life into itself and necessarily changing those elements in doing so. On Hegel's view, the Greeks had a more natural unity whereas the unity of the Roman world was so clearly man-made. The significance of this in terms of Hegel's principle was that the Greeks embodied a kind of metaphysics that viewed the world as fundamentally possessing a kind of order to itself such that if people followed out the requirements of their stations in society, the whole would spontaneously harmonize with itself. The early Greeks did not have to have much of any kind of theoretical account of how the elements of the whole cohered with each other. It was enough that the spontaneous harmony produced something of beauty. (As it were, the early Greeks no more needed a theoretical account of the unity of the elements of their life than a painter needs a theory of the unity of the different colors with which she is painting. What counts is how they all add up to a beautiful whole, not what concept the whole manifests.) This meant, however, that political unity—what Hegel calls the formation into a state[27]—required a mutual recognition among citizens about who was and who was not a citizen, and in the Greek context, that carried over into some relatively natural way of identifying people (in Greece, such as being born in Athens to an Athenian man and woman, and so forth). Some social requirements were thus taken to be rooted in natural but nonetheless normative or principled facts about life. This also implied that the only political unities that could be established were small ones, and that ultimately meant that the Greek city-states could not defend themselves against larger powers (or that despite their early successes, their luck was bound to run out, as it did when they encountered Rome).

The Roman Empire, on the other hand, was clearly a constructed entity.[28] There was no ethnic unity to those peoples who fell under Roman rule. What instead united Rome was a clear understanding of how to use power to dominate others. The Greek city-states could not form a single political unity, even though they could from time to time establish successful alliances with each other. There therefore had to be very different political psychologies at work in Greece and Rome. In essence, Rome was a political unit that required itself to be always at war since there was no other real basis for holding it together, and that produced a very different psychology. If Greece was about the dynamism of full participatory democracy—putting aside for a moment the positions of women and slaves—Rome was about the use of power and violence to achieve one's ends. Greek psychology exhibited the virtues of courage that came out of loyalty to the good of the polis. On Hegel's reading, Roman political psychology had at its root the courage and valor more appropriate to a band of thieves.[29] It was the value of those who valued domination above all else, and the kinds of family relationships and sets of virtues to which it gave rise. (Hegel seems to have accepted at face value Polybius's view that Rome had world domination in view from its beginning. However, Rome's emergence as an imperial power is arguably much more contingent than either Polybius or Hegel takes it to be.[30])

Like Alexander's empire, Rome too was at first a conquest state essentially organized around constant expansion of its power and control. Like Alexander's conquest state, its economy was basically that of plunder, and Rome had to face up to the problem of collapse when it could no longer expand. With its characteristic pragmatism, Rome transformed itself into a tributary state, which typically established links with local elites, set up bureaucracies, or set up subjects to collect the taxes and to stabilize such tax collection and other demands of empire.[31]

Rome thus put into place a different set of principles than those which governed Greek life in that it brought people into a functioning political unit who otherwise did not share the same ethnicity, religion, local commitments, family life, and so forth. Greek life fundamentally depended on relatively small communities—the so-called city-state—in which face-to-face contact was part of the glue that held things together. Rome both permitted and required a larger social unity to function.

Rome, although not by design, fashioned itself into a multi-ethnic political unit, even though in its founding narratives, Rome itself still presented itself in ethnic terms: In its stories of itself, the Roman people were said to have thrown off the rule of Etruscan kings—in other words, rule by another "people"—and to have replaced it with their own rule over themselves.[32] Yet at the same time, more or less throughout its history, Rome also thought of its core members as "citizens," not as subjects, and it eventually extended Roman citizenship to a wide variety of people living within the empire. In the process, Romans managed to move away from thinking of "we" as members of an ethnic group to "we" as citizens of something else.

In the wake of its success at domination and conquering, Rome began to legitimate its dominion by thinking of itself as having a universal mission, that of being the model of what we would now call a "classical" civilization in the Mediterranean.[33] Since in its own eyes, its success had to lay somehow in its being pleasing to the gods—in taking its success as lying in the very nature of things, not in mere chance—it saw its own conception of *humanitas* as the proper model to which barbarians could aspire. However, the ideal of *humanitas* was too abstract to give any real orientation to life under

Roman power except for that of imitating what was going on in the capitol. Rome was no so much a paragon as it was something that demanded to be imitated or held itself out for imitation simply because it was so powerful.

In effect, the Romans took themselves to be rulers because they were meant to rule and believed authority within at first the Republic and then the Empire was there because it was supposed to be there. They had no deeper conception of the nature of that authority, and the uncomfortable reality of it was, on Hegel's terms, that its conception of authority as it was practiced actually amounted to that simply of domination and accounts constructed after the fact to legitimate it. Its conception of authority vacillated from mythical accounts of great and virtuous founding figures in the past (somewhat resembling in that way Greek heroes) to accounts of contemporary authorities whose "authority" was really only that of power backed up by force. In that way, the move from "Republic" to "Empire" did not involve any great change in Roman political psychology. The sense of public life that had animated early Roman history had already begun to unravel under the pressure of its having no basis for itself except that of war-like conquering activity, and once that sense had more or less thoroughly dissolved, the Republic gave way to the Empire, which nonetheless continued to speak of itself in the Roman after-the-fact way as a continuation of the Republic. Since Rome's own self-understanding was that of keeping faith with its founding, it invented myths for itself about how the great innovation that marked the shift from Republic to Empire was in fact no innovation at all but only a way of continuing the same way of doing things.

Such a conception of authority meant that Roman philosophy had to remain fundamentally abstract since their political life, rich and detailed as it was, was also fundamentally abstract in its outline.[34] There are no fundamental sets of principles holding the whole thing together. Instead, there was only, at best, the original virtue of Roman patriotism which itself dissolved under the opposing pressures of the Roman shape of life itself. The various detailed virtues that Romans could cite as constituting the essence of the Roman life were themselves abstractly conceived and put to different use as the demands of power shifted. The psychology that held Rome together could not survive the pressures that becoming a conquest state put upon it, but becoming a tributary state only intensified its need for further domination.

The Greeks had held themselves together out of allegiance to something like an aesthetic religion, articulated into a variety of different gods. They took themselves to be bound to very specific requirements that were written into the nature of things, with the justification resting on the conviction that if everybody carried out the requirements of their social position, the whole would spontaneously harmonize into a work of beauty. Rome had no such belief in the inevitable beauty of its rule, and it had no developed working out of what the principles of such rule should be. It simply did what it thought it had to do to maintain its rule. Yet this did not mark a retrogression of any sort. Unfavorably as Rome looked to classicist temperaments such as Hegel's when they were compared to the Greeks, the Romans made innovations that surpassed those of the more idealized Greeks. If the Greeks were about beauty—"poetry"—it was with the Romans, Hegel says, that the world learned to speak prose. The Romans built roads, laid down laws in books, constructed engineering marvels, and crafted the instruments of a sober, pragmatic (and even a sort of multicultural) rule.[35] They were open and admiring of the achievements of past cultures, especially those of the Greeks, whom they conquered, and they moved to incorporate what they saw as effective in Greek life into their own way of life. They picked up the pieces of other civilizations as they subjected these peoples to Roman rule and used what was useful to them.

In effect, Hegel thought the history of Rome was an ongoing struggle among different classes and groups. In one of its main origin myths, it saw its own beginnings as a people oppressed by foreign (perhaps Etruscan) kings which a set of aristocratic families managed to force out and thereby to create a republic of citizens governed by those aristocrats. In that particular origin story, Roman political and social authority thus ideally rested on a myth of a liberation movement driven by a united "people" led by its best members. That unity lasted until the pressures latent in it began to appear, and thus there followed a period of struggle between the plebeians and the aristocrats over power and status, including struggles over whom could hold high office. (That story itself also had highly mythologized core to itself.[36]) After the plebeians had won some place for themselves, the Roman state gradually dissolved into a struggle that its thinkers liked to style, following the idea that they were keeping with their founding, as going on between private interest and public virtue but which more realistically involved all kinds of important constituencies attempting to grab some of the power and wealth for themselves and their clients. Faced with this, the Roman shape of life had no way to understand it except as a continuous decline of virtue on the part of people and thus to tell stories about a golden period when the good of the state and sacrifice for the good of Rome was supposed to have been uppermost in people's psychologies—that is, the golden age when those now struggling for recognition had not had the temerity to do so.

The great pragmatism of the Romans enabled them to survive various crises and create the energy for more conquest out of them. Nonetheless, since the deeper principle of Roman life and which therefore informed its psychology was that of domination *(Herrschaft)* pure and simple, legitimacy continued to be underwritten by gaining and then exercising domination over others.[37] The principle holding people together beyond that, so Hegel argued, could therefore only be that of property, family history, military standing, prestige, etc., that is, a set of socially sanctioned entitlements to various things (including entitlements to other people as one's slaves). That in turn meant that subjects were fundamentally granted effective social recognition only, as it were, as office-holders. One's status as a subject was defined by the de facto rules that bestowed domination of land and people (or that likewise could be employed to deny an entitlement to oneself, as was the case with slaves). That for large stretches of Roman history, various personages were also recognized through various practices as exemplary men of virtue, heroes of battle, and so forth does not, or so Hegel thought, undermine the more basic idea that there is no real basis for any recognition in Roman life than as an office holder. There was nothing deeper to Roman subjectivity than its being a place-holder in a normative social space. The only true social reality was thus the relation of power masquerading under the form of authority, of one will struggling against another, and the Roman shape of life therefore was at its basis one long ongoing struggle for recognition.

Metaphysically, for the Romans, there was nothing more to subjectivity than socially defined entitlements and commitments. Thus, when they turned to the idea of what authority Augustus and later emperors might claim, they resorted to the idea that somehow his authority was "patrimonial," that he was in effect the natural head of the household for all of Rome and its territories. That put a stop, however ill conceived, to the regress that otherwise seemed to follow from Augustus's claim to imperial (commanding) authority.

That the Empire supplanted the Republic was not an accident. The principle of domination in effect ensured that eventually, in the right circumstances, somebody would make a play for power and succeed. Even if later Roman thinkers may have thought the Republic's collapse was brought about because of matters such as a decline of virtue, it was in fact a consequence of the principle of Roman life itself.

If nothing else, the limited freedom of Roman property-holders was defined against the background of the unfreedom of the vast group of slaves and other people on the lower points of the hierarchy. Even more than with the Greeks, the concept of freedom for Romans was determined negatively. Its sense, what it meant, as it had meant for the Greeks when they first formulated it, was that it was "not" something else. Freedom was what slaves and all those dominated lacked.

Hegel characterizes the move from the defeat of the Persians by the Greeks, and the establishment of the Greek spirit as the leading edge of historical progress as the way in which, as Hegel puts it, "spirit takes its leave of nature."[38] It would seem therefore that if Greek life was still bound to the idea of the cosmos as providing authoritative reasons within itself (in terms of natural, divine harmonies producing a thing of beauty), Rome would have offered the more successful alternative of spirit's bidding nature adieu—or at least Rome would have been just one step away from it—but Hegel does not draw that conclusion. The fact that each will was in contest with every other will, and the fact that some had more power than others forced them to the conclusion that there had to be a kind of "fate" to the course of things that escapes all efforts on the part of subjects to direct it or even to comprehend it. Roman subjectivity took its shape and its filling by its participation in a public sphere, and it was only actual in that sphere.

However, because of its own logic, Roman life over the ages effectively emptied subjects' lives of any kind of meaning to be found in the public sphere, and Romans were thus provoked into inventing a new form of inwardness *(Innerlichkeit),* where their subjectivity was at least felt still to be at work.[39]

With that, the passage from the ancient world which, on Hegel's rendering, is a vastly different concatenation of meanings from our own, began. Many of his contemporaries thought that there was more continuity between the ancient world and his own such that we could call for a return to "Roman" or "Greek" virtue. On Hegel's view, such calls simply failed to see the chasm that separated Hegel's world from that of the ancients: "In this respect, there is nothing so shallow as the constant appeals to Greek and Roman precedents we hear so often. . . . Nothing could be more different than the character of those nations and that of our times."[40]

For the late Romans, the chief concern shifted into that of cultivating their inner self. Although the world around such a Roman might have been going in a contingent direction indifferent to any of one's aspirations or needs, the inward world of thoughts and senses were thought to remain under his own direction. This new form of inwardness was first expressed in the philosophies of stoicism, skepticism, and Epicureanism.[41] For the Romans, the subject's essential purpose turned out to be not only its own purposelessness but also its sustaining itself in finding its own essential meaning in that purposelessness, in the calm acceptance of fate and making it part of one's volition.[42] In that way, Romans managed to shift the conception of freedom away from its negativity—its not being slavery—into a more positive matter of the individual "will" and its purported strength or weakness in accomplishing what it commands. In doing so, Rome was also just one step away from nihilism, and when it fell apart, although many were indeed distressed, the world's heart was not "broken," as Hegel said it had been with the eclipse of Greece.[43] It was merely a sad passing.

History's Watershed: Rome to Christianity

Now, it is not exactly unknown that Hegel thought it was Christianity that stepped into this unsustainable shape of life and offered a way out of it that shuffled off the elements of Roman imperial life that could no longer really work and replaced them with a view that the truth was indeed both "within" us (as subjective) and, at the same time, universal and timeless (as the Greek philosophers had thought).[44] So it would seem that Roman life, having both emptied itself out and universalized itself as the mission of bringing *humanitas* to the barbarians, and Christianity, in having given a purpose back to Romans that was consistent with this universalization, would have seemed to offer the kind of solution that fit the Hegelian scheme. However, this would have meant that the collapse of the empire was something contingent. After all, on Hegel's terms, why could Roman life not have carried out reforms and gradually mutated itself into something livable and sustainable? In any case, the empire did Christianize itself under Constantine, and for centuries, Western Christians continued to think of themselves as "Roman."

Why then did Hegel not draw the conclusion that Rome could have, but for contingent reasons did not, continued to function as a going concern? It seems that he thought that this kind of universalization of Roman political psychology was itself unsustainable precisely because it had to deny something which it itself had developed as fundamental to its shape of subjectivity. What it denied was something like the necessity of having a bounded social space that provided its members with a fundamental orientation in life—that is, a social space in which determinate goods are available to people which are made up of the elements of a common way of doing things and institutions transmitting that into practical knowledge of the world. Such goods are the elements that make a satisfying life—a life in which certain things of importance are within the real powers of real subjects to achieve and are not merely possibilities available only in daydreams. Those goods can only be formed and sustained in bounded communities where a certain base level of solidarity can be sustained, and that, so Hegel thought, can only persist in smaller, more determinate communities. Roman universalism had no way of recognizing the authority of such communities within its own mode of self-comprehension and thus had no way of comprehending those goods. For the Romans, as Hegel puts it, "different peoples did not yet count as legitimate, the states were not yet reciprocally recognized as essentially existing."[45] At the time of the Romans, the only workable conception of community had to be that of an ethnic community, an ethnic people (a *Volk*) as the Greeks supposedly had. There was no way in which Rome could successfully project its universalizing movement into one overarching ethnic community.

Roman life was therefore parasitic on other communities sustaining those more determinate, community-bounded goods despite Roman domination, and once the facts on the ground of Roman domination began to change, there was nothing left to hold the whole together. Success at being a Roman subject—at occupying something like a legal status, an "office" in a social space—became impossible as it became impossible to be a Roman. If the Greek polis had been too small to defend itself, the Roman Empire was too big to govern itself with the resources Rome had at its disposal, since its size made it depend on the virtue of those ruling in its name in the far-flung provinces. Roman psychology, based on domination, could not sustain that type of virtue forever since it rested on Rome continuing its domination. Holding it together would require a different form of universalism that recognized the equal standing of individuals and, as Hegel came to think, the equal respect for different communal identities can only exist in some kind of mutual recognition among nation-states, and not in a pluralistic political state (or at least not ideally in such a state, or at least not in that time in history). Roman life had no resources within itself to develop such a view.

This deficiency in Roman life, however, was itself rooted in a deeper problem. Roman life had to be based on an idea that subjectivity consisted in nothing more than occupying a social space in which one undertook socially defined commitments and received socially defined entitlements. It in effect "thinned" out the "thicker" Greek conception of subjectivity as consisting in a way of securing a kind of excellence in life that constituted an "infinite end," that of Greek Eudaimonia, of flourishing in terms of natural standards of excellence. However, this thinned-out Roman conception of subjectivity actually marked a way in which progress might be made. Rome in effect brought the sociality of subjectivity into full view for the first time and laid the practical groundwork for the way in which our conceptions of subjectivity historically had to, at least at first, bid nature adieu as a first step toward reintegrating a conception of subjectivity back into the natural world. But if Roman subjectivity lacked a conception of the normative status of subjectivity apart from its location in social space, how exactly is that a lack? And how is it a lack internal to the development of Roman subjectivity itself?

The passage from a Greek conception to the Roman conception is illustrative of, and crucial to, Hegel's idea that the metaphysics of subjectivity itself, and not just our conception of the metaphysics of subjectivity, develops in historical time. The abstract "concept" of subjectivity is that of a self-ascribing subject moving in a principled and normative logical space.[46] The "Idea" of subjectivity, taken in the abstract, is that status possessed by self-conscious rational animals, a status which thereby requires recognition from other subjects. On that conception, there can be still only the thinnest invariant moral or normative core of the "Idea" of subjectivity. The various conceptions of subjectivity are thus expressions and articulations of deeper sense of the kind of subjectivity at work in our practices.[47] There is something to the core of a self-conscious human life seeking to realize its purposes and comprehending its "purposes as purposes" that like all other animals seeks to repulse attacks on itself and the like, but it takes a community of recognition to turn that into a determinate set of action-informing principles. More modern principles, such as that of the "dignity" of individual subjects, could only emerge out of the struggles for recognition and, most importantly, emerge out of the ways in which a shape of life failing to incorporate those principles into itself leads to its failure as a whole in making sense of itself, to its breakdown as the subjects operating in terms of such conceptions—in bringing themselves under "that" determinate concept—could not achieve the purposes they took to be essential to the historical shape subjectivity had taken at that point.[48]

This kind of movement follows the outlines of Hegel's *Logic:* there is an initial, "speculative" concept with a meaning to it that forms the "in itself" *(Ansich)* of the subjects in question—what it means to be that kind of being, its "concept"—and as it becomes articulated and worked out ("posited," *gesetzt* in Hegel's terms), the tensions within that conception become more apparent. That "positing" in turn prods a reworking of the practices and the terms by which subjects attempt to make sense of their practices. In those situations, how to put the practices into the proper conceptual or linguistic form is itself a matter of contestation, since one way of doing so will rule certain things in and other things out that another articulation would not.

Hegel's peculiar "internalism" about reasons and motivations comes home to roost in such an overall view. Following Aristotle, Hegel holds that there will be certain parts of the human condition that will be always be at issue for people: how to deal with emotions such as fear and anger, how to deal with the desire for status, how to deal with wealth and the desire for more of it, the facts of aging and infancy, and so forth. Those set the bounds of what can count as a reason for such self-conscious organisms. If success comes about by acting in light of reasons, then when our own subjectivity is conflicted—such that the reasons for us are inherently at a deep enough level in conflict with themselves—that form of subjectivity cannot succeed in its purposes. It comes to be increasingly and explicitly at odds with itself and others, and the process of dissolution easily sets in as its shape of life no longer makes sense to it.

Roman life and practice puts on display the historical development of a conception of subjectivity that makes social structures of recognition into the constitutive aspects of subjectivity. What made this impossible to live with was that it put such a strain on the emotional and intellectual capacities of people so that it ultimately made it impossible to be those people. For the Roman shape of life, being a subject was simply being a member of the Roman legal order with all of its complicated divisions among local laws, imperial laws, and the like. There was no further essence, as it were, to subjectivity. Subjectivity just was acting in terms of the normative order of legal right. If subjectivity is a position in a legal order, then it depends on the relations of power that keep that legal order—especially an imperial legal order—in force. One's very subjectivity is thus fragile and dependent in the deepest sense on who, as it were, is giving the orders. The reflective move prompted by the failures of a scheme of purely social recognition—of individuality as merely that of an office-holder—disclosed a new set of reasons having to do with the cultivation of inwardness as a sphere where one's subjectivity was still at work and not failing, as it seemed to be doing in the wind-down of Roman rule.

Early Roman Christianity only apparently filled the void that Roman life brought with itself. The Greeks had at first lived in a world that seemed to make aesthetic and religious sense, but that had proven to be unsustainable. The Roman world offered a different account, but as its own internal tensions began to be more and more apparent, the sense it had given to things and which had successfully ruled for hundreds of years began to unravel. Early Christianity substituted a claim that although things might not seem to make sense now, their sense would indeed in time be made known unto us, and until then we must exhibit "faith" that all of this will become clear. The senseless Roman world will one day reveal its sense to us, and until then, we only see through a glass darkly and sustain the hope that it will become disclosed to us.

Christianity also brought the principle that "all are free" to the forefront. In the idea that God does not play favorites but loves each equally,

Christianity began to supply the content for such inwardness—that is, it provided an account that specified the goods by which an individual could comprehend his or her own life as itself being of worth in more than just the terms of whatever "office" they were recognized as holding. Moreover, it offered an account of how their own subjectivity was at work in that life, such that their worth was not a matter of unpredictable "fate" but a matter that fell within the requirements of their own subjectivity as abstracted away from the given Roman legal order and subject to a more comprehensive, divine order.

The original Roman sense of freedom had been negative—one was free if one was not a slave. The Christian alternative folded itself more deeply into the idea that subjectivity was an office in a social space—that of being a "Roman" with the privileges that came with it—and worked out at first abstractly that it was something having to do with the individual's own inwardness and self-direction. In the Christian world order, the subject could be his or her own person—could be in Hegel's terms, *bei sich*—if he or she was willing to repent of sin and thus to free him- or herself from the slavery to those passions and inclinations that were at odds with the subjective core of subjectivity to be found in religious faith. From the Christian point of view, even the masters of Rome had turned out to be slaves to such passions, and it was the "truth" that was embodied in the Christian message that would set all, master and slave alike, free.

Although Rome was the incubator of such a sense of freedom, it could not make that principle a reality in people's lives and remain truly Roman. The true standing that individual subjects had could not come from each other but only from the one king of kings, the Christian God himself. Paul formulated this Christian idea in his well-known pronouncement in Galatians 3:28 that, in Christ, there was neither master nor slave, neither male nor female, neither Jew nor gentile. Each Christian now occupied not so much a worldly "office" as a metaphorical place in the divine family.[49] Each was a son or daughter of God and therefore, in the divine order, a brother or sister to each other. The position of being a child of God in turn required one to carry out the father's wishes, and that called for an act of interpretation, since the father was no longer issuing clear directives himself but, after his earthly appearance through the "son," He only issued directives and wishes via his human intermediaries. Who had the authority to interpret those directives became the key issue of life, not who was in control of the Roman center of power. However, the comprehension of ethical requirements as divine directives from a monotheistic but still personal God opened up the possibility of a fully monadic, as opposed to dyadic, understanding of the ethical order. In that move, the concept of morality as distinguished from ethical life—or at least the concept "in itself," *an sich,* of morality as the monadic relation of an individual to a rational moral order—showed up as a possibility awaiting further development. It involves measuring oneself in terms of one's justification before God, and it therefore calls for the individual to take a deeper, inward turn. One's immediate relation is to the divine order of the rules established by God. In Christianity, however, there is also the relation to others as being part of the divine family, as standing as brother or sister to others. This created a tension that itself had to be developed in historical terms.

Being a son or daughter of God, each was now called to figure out what really was required of them as individuals to make those principles real, at work, *wirklich,* in their lives. This added a positive, subjective sense of self-direction. Christianity thus seemed to displace the Roman idea of freedom which could only be obtained negatively. Roman freedom consisted in having others dependent on oneself but being free of such dependence on others. Christianity substituted, at first, an idea that all of us were free in relation to each other since all of us were dependent on a heavenly master, who, like a Roman father, had powers of life and death over us and the authority to command, but who, unlike a Roman father, loved us all. (Or, as Milton was later to put it, "but Man over men / He made not Lord; such title to himself / Reserving, human left from human free.")

The heavenly kingdom was a just order, and in that system of justice, all of us were, by accepting Christian faith, now freed from slavery of a certain type. Articulated in that way, however, the statement of the faith had little institutional import in Roman life, and thus, Roman life in its original form could not determine what that freedom might look like in practice. But what was this freedom? Christian freedom, after all, at first certainly did not exclude subordination, secular slavery, or serfdom.

This Christian alternative became an actual reason for individuals only with the breakdown of Roman life. The relation of the individual to the moral order instead of the embedding of the individual in ethical life became the prime object of reflection. Once that possibility of moral life became a real possibility, it was now also possible to project it retrospectively back across time and understand the earlier failures of shapes of life as having failed for not having made that possibility actual. On the new conception, each could be free, at one with themselves in actions that ultimately made sense, even if the whole world sometimes seemed allied against them. In its failures, Roman life had generated out of the weight of its own deficiencies a revised version of the more positive, Greek version of freedom as self-direction. However, why then was Roman universalism together with Christian inwardness not enough? Why did Hegel think that history *necessarily* passed from the Roman world to the "German" world?

"Germans," Germans, and Europe

Polybius had seen that suddenly with the rise of Roman power, there was now a new topic for history, namely, "universal history," which is animated by an idea of the purpose toward which the world had been moving. Hegel took that a step further and asked what had happened since the fall of Rome. That is also equivalent to asking if a new form of psychology, of the link between "principles" and "passions" had arisen. The solution was to look at how the "universal *particularizes* itself and is herein identity with itself" in new circumstances. Was there a new shape of subjectivity that had to be developed for this to take root?

To this end, Hegel turned to the emerging sciences of ethnicity in his day particularly as they had been abstractly elaborated by G. R. Treviranus and J. F. Blumenbach. His thoughts on the matter are both straightforward (and, in that sense, clear) and also a bit uncharacteristically muddled. He more or less accepted Blumenbach's typology of the races as an established empirical fact, and he concluded that for each racial type, there was a corresponding psychology that accompanied it, which he then extended into the concept of an organic "people" (or "nation"). Nonetheless, what holds a "people" together are the "principles" to which it is committed, not its ethnic makeup, but, so he also held, the ethnic makeup of a people partially shapes the kinds of principles and collections of principles to which they can become committed. He says, for example, that "spirit in history is an individual which is both universal in nature and at the same time determinate: In short, it is a 'people' *(Volk)* in general, and the spirit with which we are concerned is the spirit of the people *(Volksgeist)*."⁵⁰ Moreover, this kind of ethnic difference is not accidental but conceptual. The various ethnicities *(Völker)* can be comprehended in terms of the kind of unity of "universal" and "particular" is at work. That is, they can be comprehended in terms of how close their own mindedness is to their natural dispositions—or, in other words, how much degree of self-determination is and can be manifested in each of them. Although Hegel at least toyed with the idea that there may be a "logic" to ethnic difference, Hegel's conception of ethnicity actually resembles the much more recent concept coined by the ethnographer, A. D. Smith, of an "ethnie." In Smith's accounts of the rise of nationalism, an "ethnie" is a group sharing common myths and memories, whose members enjoy a kind of cultural intimacy with each other. An "ethnie" is thus not primarily a racial concept.⁵¹

Now, on the one hand and in one sense, this is not at odds with Hegel's more general view. On his view, it will be the case that there will be different psychologies at work in different kinds of orders of thoughts. A seafaring commercial people may well generate a correspondingly different psychology than a land-locked agricultural people. However, the nineteenth-century temptation to take the empirical facts in what can only be described as a racialist direction was always on hand to tempt Hegel, and he did not always resist that temptation. Since Hegel's views on subjectivity neither imply a racialist attitude nor necessarily support it, if it were just left at that, there would have been nothing in his overall view that would have ruled out his expunging such racialist ideas in his writings.⁵² In principle, Hegel would only have needed to be confronted with the distance between his statements and what the evidence supports to have felt the necessity to change his mind. However, Hegel did not do that and took his ethnic views one step further. Each "ethnie," or so he sometimes seemed to claim at various points, could by virtue of its natural makeup only take on certain types of principles, that is, could only develop a certain type of order of thoughts. The tie between psychology and principle is tight enough, so Hegel thought, that if it were the case that some groups of people naturally had psychological dispositions of a certain sort, it would be at least ultimately unlikely that they could develop orders of thoughts that more closely fit what the demands of reason would require. Moreover, so Hegel claimed, an examination of the various peoples of the world leads us to exactly that conclusion. The philosophy of history is a history of such peoples and the kinds of orders of thoughts to which they gave rise.[53]

Yet, on the other hand, Hegel quite explicitly argued against the idea that ethnic difference in any way licensed any kind of natural subordination of one people to another: "Descent affords no ground for entitling or denying entitlement to freedom and dominion to human beings. Man is in himself rational. Therein lies the possibility of equal rights for all men and the nullity of any rigid distinction between races which have rights and those which have none."[54] However, he still held that this was compatible with his conception of ethnic "peoples" ("ethnies") and of some of those "peoples" living at less progressive stages in history.

The question which animates his philosophy of history—his modified version of the Polybius question—has to do with how is it that Europe has managed to achieve "modernity" and to make a non-question-begging claim to be the universal standard-bearer for humanity. His answer turns out to be at odds with some of the fundaments of his theory. In particular, his stated views on how "spirit" develops in terms of a logic of dissolution and succession are completely at odds with his views about ethnicity determining the ultimate shape of principle, while, on the other hand, his views about how Europe comes to be such that it forms the avant-garde of historical development depends on his views about the relation between "ethnies" and principle.

Polybius argued that it was the superiority of Roman religion and its public virtues that made it almost inevitable that Rome should rise to prominence in the world. Hegel's question is how it is that, if that is true, Rome itself should have finally gone under and been succeeded by what eventually came to be modern "Europe" as a collection of independent nation-states.

The answer to how it is that "Europe" succeeded Rome turns out to involve the "ethnies" of the people who ended up sacking Rome and establishing their own dominant culture, and these were the *"Germanen"* (not the *Deutsche,* the Germans). In claiming this, Hegel was drawing on a widely held view—widely held even for centuries—that the tribes who lived beyond the Roman borders, and who supposedly refused and fought off Roman domination and eventually overwhelmed Rome, were barbarians called the *"Germanen,"* who brought their own ethnic culture to bear on Roman civilization and changed it forever. These *Germanen* were originally described by Caesar, who grouped all the tribes resisting Roman rule east of the Rhine under that rubric. Later, Tacitus wrote a celebrated essay on them around 98 AD. In Tacitus's account, although they were admittedly a crude people, they displayed a set of otherwise admirable virtues: They were devoted to freedom (of a crude, stubborn kind), were virtuous, were fiercely loyal to the very end to each other, simple in their tastes, were "like unto no other tribe," manifested exemplary courage in battle, and had always lived in their ancestral lands. These *Germanen* later became accepted among wide swaths of the German intelligentsia from the Renaissance to the twentieth century as the genuine ancestors and models for "who" the Germans (the *Deutsche*) really were.

Unfortunately for all those who believed in Tacitus's *Germanen* as Germans, all of this was for the most part a myth.[55] Tacitus's essay on the *Germanen* was in effect a political tract meant to criticize the contemporary state of Roman life. In it, he compared the current Romans—corrupted, as he saw it, by luxury and power—to an idealized and mythical tribe who, although unsophisticated and barbaric, at least manifested the virtues so conspicuously lacking in the Rome of his day. Tacitus in fact most likely never actually observed the whole of the people whom he called the *Germanen*. He more or less made them up. However, much later—sometime in the Renaissance—Tacitus's book was picked up by Germans who took over and modified themes from it with the belief that the book revealed the "true nature" of the German people. (The most disastrous of these became the idea that since they were "like unto no other tribe," they were racially pure, even though Tacitus's reference to them in that regard was simply a well-used trope in ancient writing.[56]) Those mythical *Germanen* even appear in Montesquieu's *Spirit of the Laws* in their Tacitean form, where Montesquieu suggests that perhaps the French themselves (or at least the French aristocracy and royalty) are descendants of those virtuous, freedom-loving *Germanen,* like unto nobody but themselves. Unfortunately for all the people who relied on the text, there simply never were any *"Germanen"* in the sense that Tacitus describes. The tribes described as *Germanen* were in fact a collection of many different tribes, not one pure ethnic unit.[57] The *Germanen* were not the "Germans."

What was it about them that made the bearers of the new order of thoughts? To answer that, Hegel falls back on Tacitus's myth. The ancient *Germanen* had, so Tacitus claimed, an inherent love of freedom, and Hegel endorses this: "The ancient Germans were famed for their love of freedom. The Romans formed a correct idea of them in this particular from the first. Freedom in Germany *(Deutschland)* has been the motto down to the most recent times."[58]

Nonetheless, despite having bought into the myth about the "German" love of freedom, Hegel was not completely taken in by the myth as it had taken shape up to his own day. For him, those *"Germanen"* were not Rousseauian noble savages (and, for that matter, even Rousseau did not use the *Germanen* as his model), and they were not particularly to be admired. They were, in Hegel's various descriptions, barbaric, dull, narrow, ignorant, and inane. What they had going for them was, besides their love of freedom, their commitment to living according to the virtue of *Gemütlichkeit*—a kind of easy-going, unhurried way of life coupled with a love of coziness. On Hegel's view, this otherwise dull, unsophisticated, sometimes even loutish virtue had nothing to recommend it, except that it made the *Germanen* ready to receive the more advanced Christian virtues into the substance of their lives.

Was it a matter of luck that there was no trouble transplanting the incipient moral psychology of Christianity linked to Roman universalism into the habits of the *Germanen?* For Hegel, in fact, their own rather lackluster culture even helped to pave the way, since their attachment to their own religions was so weak (because their intellectual life was so undeveloped) that they quickly abandoned their native religions for the new one of Christianity without much protest or struggle at all. Because they were also imbued with a strong sense of fidelity to each other and to the leaders to whom they swore allegiance, they were therefore on Hegel's view the ideal clay to be fired into modern Europeans.

What they supposedly lacked was any commitment at all in their ethnic identity to any sense of universality. They recognized only particular rights and privileges, and thus, the states which they formed for the first few hundred years of their rise to prominence was itself only an amalgam of contradictions. It claimed a universality that was completely at odds with what is required of a state to be a free state. Instead, they formed irrational, even fanatical, murderous states that persecuted each other and continually waged war. Born out of their stubbornness, feudalism as a system of oppression and inequality ruled for hundreds of years. Although feudalism itself developed and shifted its shape over that period, the distinctive metaphysics of subjectivity that manifests itself in feudalism (or so Hegel's claim goes) remained throughout much of that reshaping until it finally broke down under its own self-imposed pressures and became something else. Nonetheless, since universality as a matter of principle can be learned, the deeper commitments to freedom and fidelity meant that they had a good many of the building blocks required to shape (eventually) the modern order of thoughts based on rights, moral duties, and the socially established goods of the modern family, the regulated although market-driven civil society, and representative constitutional government (which Hegel also thought had to be monarchical).[59]

To his credit, Hegel bought into none of the more rabid nationalistic myths of his own time about the Germans.[60] Rejecting the view that "Germans" were once pure but then had either let their native virtues degenerate or lost them altogether, and that modern Germans thus needed to reclaim their native purity and virtue (a view held by many others in his time), Hegel thought that the very idea of a "German" golden age that had to be recovered was simply ludicrous. There was no value in trying to resuscitate the practices and beliefs of those early *Germanen*. As Hegel put it, his German contemporaries who thought so, who thought that this was a way of recapturing "German-dom" simply demonstrated that they were "German-dumb."[61] For modern Germans, the cultural traits of the early *Germanen* had, as he put it, been "simply a past history, swept clean away with a broom."[62] Contemporary Germans could find much more of importance about themselves in studying the Trojan War than in reading any ancient tale about, for example, *Nibelungen*.

Nonetheless, he did more or less accept the part of the myth that the peoples described by Tacitus were in fact the ancestors of the Northern Europeans and that it was their particular love of freedom that made them the carriers of the Christian principle of freedom and therefore the "ethnie" forbearers of modern Europe. Only that would explain the close link between the psychology of the northern Europeans and the principles of freedom which had come to play such a core role in European life after the French revolution. Did he thus think that those *Germanen* had a special psychology that enabled them to be the leading edge of spirit's progress? Since Hegel also holds that "psychology" rarely names some set of merely given impulses or dispositions, the passions at play in such historical transitions are intrinsically linked to principles, such that a change of principles also brings along a change in the status, if nothing else, of the passions. However, if spirit bids nature adieu with the Greeks and Romans, how then does nature reappear several centuries later with the *Germanen*?

Path-Dependency with Infinite Ends

Hegel's account of how it is that European modernity came about is clearly a path-dependent story. On this account, it could not have happened without the particular twists and turns it took from Greece to Rome to the Christian *Germanen* and finally to the French Revolution. Thus, although the path to modernity may have been necessary to modernity being what it is, it does not follow that the path to modernity was itself necessary. Moreover, it also does not follow that there is no other path that could have arrived at much the same point, so that it could turn out that many alternative paths to that same point are possible. It could well be that perhaps some of them are even actual. Even though Hegel's argument may have established the historicity of subjectivity, that is, the conception of our basic norms being indexed to very specific historical situations, it would not have established Hegel's more fundamental claim to progress. What is at stake is whether without an appeal to the Germanic "love of freedom," Hegel could establish his argument.

Development in history is different from development in nature because history is the manifestation of spirit, of human collective mindedness.[63] As the manifestation of spirit, history presents a succession of shapes of life, that is, ways in which people are bound together by virtue of their common commitments and shared understandings of what it means and what it takes to put those commitments into practice. Viewed at its most general level, it presents us with different metaphysical shapes of subjectivity.[64] These shapes are, as already said, a unity of passion and principle, each mutually reinforcing the other. This means that, in history, people are, to put it in more bloodless terms than is the case in historical reality, giving and asking for reasons, along with other activities, such among others, engendering children, plundering, negotiating, laboring, threatening, just making do, and so forth. However, as self-conscious subjects, in all these activities, they seek a type of authority for their actions, beliefs, and tastes, and this self-consciousness—not always, or even typically, reflective—manifests itself in history. Each person is making (or trying to make) sense of her world in light of the way in which her social world has taken root in her as a set of habits, expectations, virtues, and the like. As a manifestation of spirit, history is an arena in which people seek and have sought reconciliation—that is, a kind of justification of their lives—in their social worlds, and they have sought this both individually and collectively. Stated like that, there is nothing in that conception that implies that there is progress in history, much less necessary progress and certainly nothing that implies necessity.

Hegel's argument draws on his discussion in the *Logic* about how the "Idea" of the Good" and the "Idea" of the True" mesh together.[65] Roughly, that argument takes the following shape. At least for modern subjects, the good is that which a subject posits as preferable or desirable in the face of a world otherwise indifferent to the subject, and the subject actualizes that good by using certain worldly means to bring it about. However, once a subject has come to a comprehension of itself as a subject—that is, as not merely knowing what is the case by means of its cognitive receptivity to the world but also as knowing *that* it knows this and by becoming reflectively self-conscious—what had been merely the contingencies of the past come to possess a meaning that they otherwise did not have, namely, as the manifestation of an infinite end, which is fundamentally that of subjectivity as *Geist* coming to an adequate self-consciousness.[66] That is, it now understands itself not merely as history but as history that has a meaning for it, as "comprehended history" (*begriffne Geschichte,* as Hegel calls it).[67]

History's contingent path-dependent development is the development of a certain way in which subjectivity both understands itself and evaluates itself. As subjectivity conceives of itself, it also conceives of what it takes to be a successful subject, and that has both changed and progressed over time. In Hegel's version of Aristotelian naturalism, it is subjectivity conceiving of itself as an entity that flourishes in a certain way—namely, by using its reason—and its flourishing takes different shapes as it collectively conceives of itself differently. Although Hegel substitutes "satisfaction," *Befriedigung,* for the Aristotelian *Eudaimonia,* there is a similarity in the overall purport of the two terms. (Hegel does, however, firmly reject the substitution of "happiness" for *Befriedigung*.) A satisfying life is one lived in terms of what is worth doing, suffering, undergoing, and entertaining, where the element of reflective self-consciousness plays a crucial role, and for both Hegel and Aristotle, this is characterized as an activity, not an achieved state.[68] It is an infinite, not a finite, end. New orders of thoughts institute new ways in which those lives can be led and effectively rule out certain other lives. The satisfying life is that in which one has been able to accomplish matters of importance. Thus, there is one way in which speaking of the "ends" of life according to Hegel can be misleading. The infinite end of self-comprehension (and of justice) is not an end at which one aims and then chooses the most appropriate or efficient means to achieve. The final end is more like an activity characteristic of the life of a self-conscious human subject—an "activity of soul in accordance with virtue," as Aristotle described the life of *Eudaimonia*.

The argument is that there is a conception of *the* "good" as something like—to keep matters very general—making sense of things and one's life, that is, living a life that is worthwhile. This good is collectively and individually realized in a variety of ways, each of them intrinsically limited (and therefore "finite" in Hegel's terms). A shape of life enters the path to dissolution when it stops making sense. That is, when the people in it begin to give up hope that there is a way of making sense of those determinate goods (which are embedded in the shape of life) in these kinds of circumstances (in the material and social world surrounding them).

Now, there are two ways of seeing this progression in time. On the one hand, there is the obvious way of viewing it as it genuinely appears. History is a series of different ways of life, and the reasons for change are varied and fit into very little order.[69] On that view, history presents a version of what Hegel calls the "bad infinite": We can delimit one period, one way of life, one epoch only in distinguishing it from another, ad infinitum. Or it might turn out that the series of events in history has no order to it, and it is more like that of the series, "1–1 + 1–1 . . .", that is, it converges on nothing. In that case, it would be only a bad infinite and nothing more—something along the line of, "One dynasty succeeds another. . . ." There is no a priori assurance that the world is not such an unintelligible infinite series. (This is true even in the *Logic*. It takes an argument to show that in fact a principle for a certain infinite series can indeed be developed, and that is what the *Logic* claims to be able to do. It claims, that is, to have constructed an argument for something for which there was no assurance in advance it would discover or be able to construct.)

However, Hegel's claim is that there is indeed an infinite end at work in history—even if nobody is entertaining the end as such an end—and that is the end of making sense of things.[70] Such an end need not be manifested in all behavior. One can, for example, have health as an end without making every single action in one's life being carried out as a means to further one's health. Nor need one subordinate all other ends to an infinite end. If one wishes to be healthy, it does not follow that one ought to consider everything else one does in light of how it contributes to one's health. To understand the "affirmative infinite," as Hegel calls it, is to understand an infinite series in terms of the principle behind it.[71] There is a way of understanding history in terms of an infinite end, and because there is, there is also a way of asking whether there is progress in history. Hegel's metaphor for this is the "cunning of reason," the way in which despite the setbacks and horrors which appear in human history, there remains the need for self-comprehension which picks up its pieces and sets out anew.[72] New forms of moral and ethical authority precipitate out of the breakdown of old ones. Reason, as it were, asserts its own authority and also tears it down.

Moreover, this series in history has to be an unending series of plural goods. A good is what makes a claim on a subject as preferable, but given the finitude of all subjects and the circumstances under which they think and act and feel, there will be many such goods, or, as Hegel puts it, "in terms of its content the good is something limited, there are many kinds of good. Good in its concrete existence is not only subjected to destruction by external contingency and by evil, but by the collision and the conflict of the good itself."[73] Hegel's claim that there is "a" good in history therefore cannot be the more Pollyanna claim that things are always getting better, nor is it the sweet (and false) banality that there is a silver lining in every dark cloud. It is certainly not that the idea that the good will always triumph since, as Hegel puts it, the good is always subject to "destruction by evil." In fact, without such a conception of the good, there could be no recognition of its persistent destruction by evil. The infinite end of self-comprehension cannot be self-assured that it will always or even eventually win out in its best form.[74]

There is an additional difficulty for Hegel's view. If the good of freedom is indeed contingent on there being a prior affective engagement, then it itself can be an unconditional good (and not, as Kant would say, a heteronomous good) only if either: (1) this natural affective engagement is itself conceptually necessary; Hegel thought he had that conceptual necessity in the *Germanen*, but, as we have seen, this stands in contradiction to his own version of the link between principle and passion in a shape of life, and, besides, no such *Germanen* existed anyway. Or (2) if this originally heteronomous good could detach itself from its prior grounding in the psychological makeup of the *Germanen* and transform itself into an unconditional good. This would be the modern shape of spirit itself in which the function of being a subject is determined as good in fulfilling the rational purposes required of such subjectivity. Especially, if there were no such *Germanen*, then the second alternative is the only one open to Hegel, and, fortunately, it is perfectly consistent with the rest of his views. His actual arguments do, however, still rest on some unfortunate assumptions about the *Germanen*.

In this sense, there is a necessity to history only if there is a logic of justice that requires that an adequate conception of justice cannot be based on the view that only "one" is free or that only "some" are free. If that argument can be made, then there is a necessity to history, although not a metaphysically causal one.[75]

From Feudal Dependency to Justice as Freedom

When seen from the standpoint of Hegel's "philosophical" history, the origins of post-Roman Europe took their shape mainly around themes of power and domination. The ruling groups fell by and large into two: the Christian church, which at least potentially could stake a claim to universality, and the various other tribes and rulers with claims to have descended from the *Germanen* (the Visigoths, Vandals, Ostrogoths, Lombards, Franks, etc.), who established dominion and rewarded their clients. Part of the authority they claimed and through which they tried to legitimate their rule was to have themselves recognized by the Church, and the Church likewise tried to retain and extend its power by claiming the right to anoint or appoint them. Behind it all was a natural human inclination to seize power where it could be seized and to hold onto it, a passion that the institutional arrangements of the time did little to check.

Charlemagne (748–814), one of the greater rulers of the early period, managed both to extend the power of the Franks by conquest and get himself crowned as a Roman emperor by the Pope. Nonetheless, however much Charlemagne's nascent Holy Roman Empire looked like it might be or was the beginning of "Europe" out of a constellation of petty principalities, and despite its successes and achievements, it was, all in all, a false start for "Europe."[76] Although Charlemagne's empire did indeed think of itself as "Roman" and more importantly as "Christian," it did not yet have the idea of "Europe" at its heart. (That was a later meaning cast upon it when "Europe" began to think of itself more in those terms.[77]) The institutional securing of the idea of justice and its elaboration within the appropriate set of practices were missing. Justice as an end was present but unsecured, "for religion had not yet such an authority over men's minds as to be able to bridle the rapacity of the powerful."[78] The empire established by Charlemagne thus collapsed soon after his own death.

In the early formation of "Europe," the shape of life, the particular union of passion and principle, of subjectivity itself, was not yet so structured so that such a "European" system could have been established. Instead, what counted as a practical reason was localized to particular peoples and particular warlords and ecclesiasticals. On Hegel's account, Charlemagne's goals and specific proposals for raising revenues, establishing armies, founding schools, setting up systems of legal justice, however admirable they may in retrospect appear, lacked the appropriate institutional underpinning, and his reforms were powerless against the other interests who took themselves to be entitled to do what served them best. In the violence that followed his death, what emerged was not justice but the more concentrated and continued rule of the more powerful. Nor was Charlemagne's failed attempt the only one. Others, such as the later rule of the Hohenstaufens (roughly 1138–1254), were also false starts. One of the Hohenstaufen emperors, Friedrich Barbarossa, looked at first as if he would unite the German empire with large parts of Italy. However, the power of local loyalties proved too great for either emperors or popes to overcome. Moreover, the legality of the system of subordinations was always itself under pressure from its own members. While the gradations of dependence of vassals on lords higher than them looked firm on paper, in practice, vassals were always keeping one eye open for a way out from under the subordination to their betters, and when they saw their chance, they took it. No "Europe" therefore emerged out of Charlemagne's or Barbarossa's conquests (or of others of the period). But what does it mean to say that these were all false starts?

The violence that characterized such a shape of life impelled people to look for protection where they could find it. The ideal of justice in this shape of life could therefore only manifest itself as an ability to defend oneself against other wills (something Hegel claims is typical of "barbarians"), and thus, the only system of justice really possible was that imposed by the rule of the strong, by those who could promise protection.[79] The development of this state of affairs, of dependency in a world characterized by widespread violence, was feudalism, a social order based on inequality and personal dependencies, in which everybody was subordinate to somebody else, and only a combination of a sense of personal fidelity and the threat of force could hold the whole system together. It was, in Hegel's words, a system of "universal injustice" that firmly planted itself and held sway for hundreds of years.[80] In order to sustain and legitimate itself, such a system had to develop a comprehension of itself as divinely ordained, as somehow very basically adhering to the order of the cosmos. However, as it developed itself, that kind of system showed itself in the long run not only to be impossible to defend philosophically, but also to become more and more difficult to live with as it made less and less sense and as the resistance against it became more and more successful.

In such a shape of life, a certain form of political psychology quite naturally took root. Its focus was formed in the sense that doing what is required of oneself consists in acting according to the commitments that one has to others by virtue of where one stands in the order of dependencies. Something like "honor," and not freedom per se, has to be seen as the final end of life, yet "honor" itself is something that one freely takes on by committing oneself to a certain lord. From the side of the subordinate, the sense of subjectivity at work in the relation was that of swearing fidelity to one's lord, to putting one's passions at the service of another. This was in its root a different conception from the Roman principle of mere recognition as occupying a position in social space.[81] Nor was it stoic in that it did not authorize a rejection or withdrawal or indifference to the social space. It instead gave subjects a reason to cultivate a certain code of honor and to see their own commitments to their superiors not merely as obligations assumed in a social space but as subjective activities which only they as individuals could carry out.

The very senselessness of this feudal way of living, embedded as deeply in the life of the times as it was, thus also had to make its appearance off and on in those periods. This ongoing threat of senselessness, of even nihilism itself was, by Hegel's lights, not merely a phenomenon of modern times but a phenomenon that extended over long stretches of European history. Worries about it swept over vast areas, and these anxieties about skepticism and nihilism were basic to the development of European history. It is the background of Hegel's metaphor that with the dissolution of the Greek model, the world's heart was, as he put it, broken, and it sunk into mourning.[82] The way in which life's purposes were embedded within a social world such that a kind of beautiful harmony could be expected when those purposes were adequately actualized became a defining memory and object of mourning for European history, something that it had to work through. The present was measured by that now idealized past and found wanting. The threat was that the loss might be irreparable, and dealing with that threat seems to occupy much of European history afterward. Nonetheless, such nostalgia, so Hegel thought, is almost always completely out of place. Or, as he put it, "One finds in recent times great and deep men . . . who seek what is better by looking backwards. That is a mistake. We will indeed eternally feel drawn to Greece, but we will not find the highest satisfaction there, for what is lacking in that beauty is truth. The higher principle always appears for what is earlier and lower as ruination, as that through which the laws of the existing world are denied, are not given recognition. This denial is what robs the states and the individuals of their virtue."[83]

Hegel realized that nihilism, although it can be entertained in theory, is psychologically impossible for almost everyone. The idea that it might nonetheless be real can thus only provoke various ways of carrying on that help to disguise it and thus help one to disengage with it, which often enough takes the form of engaging in actions that border on the monomaniacal or even the insane. Thus, Hegel took up the period surrounding the Crusades as particularly illustrative of this, since the Crusades themselves, as monumentally senseless as they were, came about when "as it were, a universal feeling of the *nothingness* of their condition coursed through the world."[84] Whatever other examples of courage and adventure they provoked, the Crusades were nonetheless more or less insane bids for power. They began "with the slaughter and plundering of many thousands of Jews, and after this terrible prelude, the Christian peoples set out," and, after conquering Jerusalem, "still dripping with the blood of the slaughtered inhabitants, the Christians fell down on their faces at the tomb of the Redeemer, and directed their impassioned prayers to him."[85] They did this to seek something that even their own views told them was unobtainable. In Christian doctrine, Jesus had risen, and the most they could ever hope to find was only the "empty grave," which, again according to the doctrines of the Christianity they claimed to profess, would prove nothing and resolve nothing. In Hegel's eyes, a similar madness arose in the sixteenth century with the burning of witches when the dawning possible senselessness of the world again provoked an explanation of its shortcomings in terms of some vast, indeterminate evil that had to be at work in the world. To counter this, many thousands of women were judicially murdered.

Hegel took the medieval period not as many of his Romantic contemporaries understood it, namely, as a time of religious certainty in which worries about meaninglessness were held at bay by the deep roots that religion had struck in life. In fact, on Hegel's interpretation, it was a time in which the senseless of the world that followed the dissolution of the ancient world began to bubble up in the minds of people with a potency that was tamped down only by a combustible mixture of feudal ideology, the exercise of brute force, and episodes that bordered on insanity. The very liveliness of the medieval world and its color were expressions of these deep doubts about itself. These bouts of folly that rolled around the medieval world extended into the early modern European world.

The institutional and practical context for the gradual abandonment of the ethos of the medieval world was already giving itself shape as people tried to keep the whole in working order, and the path was thus already being laid for the downfall of the *ancien régime* across what was to become "Europe," although almost nobody was consciously entertaining that idea. Moreover, that nature itself might be the ultimate source of the values that make a life satisfying was increasingly being undermined by the new science.[86] Technology, especially gunpowder, changed the context of battle and furthered the dissolution of the myth that the aristocracy was necessary as a function of military ethos and defense of the realm.[87] The senselessness of the order of dependencies and their required inequality that was at its root produced the rot of the rest of the practical edifice holding the structure up.

Whereas those ends of life had until then resided in some other ways of making sense of things, in the new order gradually taking shape "the new, final banner was unfurled around which the peoples gathered, that of the flag of the free spirit which is at one with itself, which exists in the sphere of truth and indeed only exists in that sphere—the flag under which we serve and which we bear."[88] Justice, rather than requiring a cosmically underwritten system of subordination in which some were by the very essence of things authorized to rule over others, began to seem to require instead freedom for the individual—to express a world in which "all were free." The metaphysics of subjectivity was beginning to shift.

The secularization that grew in tandem with these changes gave a new sense to what would be a legitimate order of thoughts. Religion would not vanish in the face of secularization but rather would continue to exercise an altered type of authority by occupying a new place in the emerging normative scheme of things. Likewise, the new ethos emerging from the medieval period's deep anxiety about the point of its whole order made the study of the ancients more attractive. Thus, the virtues championed by the ancients began to appear in the Christianized world as it further secularized itself.[89]

In this way, a new shape of subjectivity asserted itself, not by virtue of being invented by some clever philosopher or merely as the causal result of a vortex of social forces but as something arising closer to the ground. The honor-bound ethos of feudalism fell apart under its own weight. In its own self-conception, as articulated in many of its arts, the feudal order rested on a free choice by an individual to subject himself to the will of another and to stay bound to that individual only by virtue of the strength of the committed vassal's making it a point of honor for himself.

The late medieval and early renaissance sense of defending one's honor—whether directly through the defense of honor itself, or in matters of love, or in demonstrating one's fidelity to one's lord—had to do with the holdovers of the idea of "personal self-sufficiency," the primary quality of a free man since Greek times. It at first looked like the older model of subordination, and it took its initial self-understanding out of that. However, such subordination, in the aesthetic telling of the story, is supposed to arise out of the vassal's own free assumption of his obligations to his lord or lady in the name of honor, love, or loyalty. The loyal vassal campaigns not for anything like "rightness" in general but for something more like "recognition and the absolute inviolability of the singular subject," that is, himself, by another singular subject, namely, his lord or lady.[90] The deep thread of subordinations of feudal life become reconceived as freely chosen and therefore honorable subordinations.

Yet in all that the tension between freely choosing individuals and deep, natural subordinations only became more heightened. The contradiction at work in late medieval and early modern Europe was intense: When they thought of themselves via the aesthetic conception of their shape of life, they thought of themselves as inherently monadic individuals, whose only dyadic obligations to specific others rested on their free choice—for example, to promise fealty to a lord or faithfulness to an idealized lady. Outside of that kind of oath or act of swearing fealty, there were no obligations except those of honor and Christian duty itself. Yet at the same time, the entire order was one of overlapping dependencies. Everybody was subordinate to somebody else, everybody had demarcated duties to specific others, and there was no place for such monadic duties.

Eventually, under those normative pressures, the chivalric individual character shifted its shape and became a Shakespearean individual, an individual who has not severed him or herself completely from the idea of a cosmic order of justice but who now placed first and foremost the idea of being their own person and accepting all the idiosyncrasies that involved. Hegel describes Shakespeare's characters as "consistent within themselves. They remain true to themselves and their passion, and in what they are and in what confronts them they beat about according only to their own fixed determinateness" of who they are.[91] They are not embodiments of any divine pathos, as were the Greek characters, whose individual pathos reflected a deeper conflict within the divine order itself (something to be expected from a polytheistic view). They are instead the modern and different conception of subjects as "keeping the faith" with themselves and their social world, knowing that the contingencies of the world in general may knock them off their path or destroy them. Shakespearian characters are the prototypical "amphibians" of modern life.

What was Hegel's account of this transition from the old society of orders to a modern world in which the principle is that "all are free"? The crumbling of feudalism and its transformation into the forms in which a modern politics of "justice as freedom" could emerge itself took shape around a variety of contingent factors and false starts. None of that could go smoothly until the correct institutional supports for the new shape of subjectivity were in place. In Germany, after the "wars of religion," the old princes of the feudal era, who had been vassals to a higher lord, themselves became for their own part independent princes. At first primarily in Italy and then later across wider swaths of Europe, the towns became independent centers of power, and the townspeople in them formed themselves into estates and guilds, with the result that the princes were forced to cede authority to these new centers of power certainly not out of principle but out of practical necessity. The process was not uninterrupted, not smooth, and not free of violence, but it worked its way out into the rudiments of the modern form of family, society and state orbiting around a conception of individual rights and the presumption of a universal moral order. The "Idea" (in Hegel's sense) of freedom began to take on more specific contours: the opposition of "barbarian / civilization" became transmuted into a country-side / town opposition, where freedom was to be attained in the towns. The older ancient conception of free subjectivity as not being a slave was transformed into being a townsperson and not a serf, but with the new twist of the kind of self-direction that came in the wake of taking up an artisanal trade in the town and in the kind of new family life that emerged in those conditions. (The medieval German proverb for this was "Town air makes one free."—"*Stadluft macht frei.*"[92]) As Hegel had argued for all the cases, how this transition was carried out depended on the "nationalities"—what we would nowadays more likely call "cultures" and "traditions"—in question, so that there was not one single process of building this new status of subjectivity.[93]

During this development, for large parts of the early modern world to the people living through it, the meaning of events had to look as if the powers in Europe were closer to finalizing the shape of the feudal society of orders and not to anything as momentous as shifting allegiances to the modern state. The rule of the Hapsburg Charles V as the Holy Roman Emperor and King of Spain (1515–1556) looked as if it might finally be the realization of what first Charlemagne and then later the Hohenstaufens had attempted: A European, even a global "universal monarchy" in which the feudal order would be brought into a unified empire and system. In fact, Charles's empire was even more universal than what Charlemagne could have only dreamed about: As Holy Roman Emperor, Charles possessed many of the German domains as his property, he ruled Spain, the Netherlands, large sections of Italy and, to add to that, much of the Americas. His rule had the genuine claim to be a global kingship.

Nonetheless, from the point of view of the philosophy of history, his rule was "without internal interest."[94] Despite the worldwide breadth of his hold- ings and the grandeur and interest he himself exhibited as a person, his far- reaching ambitions eventually amounted to no new shape of subjectivity. Checked by France, forced to squabble forever with his feudal vassals, he was also led into the fight against the rise of Protestantism, and during his reign, both the Jesuits and the counter-Reformation movement were founded. In the beginning of the "wars of religion," where he took the side of the Catholics against the badly organized Protestants, he was eventually, and very surprisingly, even forced into a peace settlement by a much lesser figure, Moritz of Saxony. Even more strikingly, Charles V's empire (under Philip II) was later defeated by the Protestant Dutch in their war of indepen- dence. His "universal monarchy" had grown up in the structure of feudal- ism and was at odds with the now clearly conflicted shape of subjectivity that had grown up within it. However grand and imposing his achieve- ments were, they "left no world-historical result behind and proved to be powerless within themselves."[95] In the end, Charles V's empire crumbled and left only beautiful ruins in its wake.

Protestantism, which Charles was fighting, had carved out an excep- tional authority for private conscience, and the Protestant movement itself was the expression of a deeper sense of secularization at work in that emerg- ing shape of life. However, during Charles V's time, "the state had not yet divided itself into the duality of a secular and an ecclesiastical polity set off from the rest."[96] That in turn meant that without the recognition of this duality as a "rightful" (ethical and legal) distinction, there was really no way out for the Protestants to secure the legitimacy of their interpretation of the right to conscience without war since "the question was not one of simple conscience but involved decisions respecting the owners of public and private property," including those of the established church.[97] In this context, there could only be a situation of not relative but "absolute mistrust." Such "absolute mistrust" eventuated into a distinct kind of civil war—wars which are "internal" to a shape of life, shaped by contradictions in it that have taken political shape and exercise power, and not the typical civil wars involving rebellion of one center of power against another.[98] As it were, during the "wars of religion," the "absolute" seemed to go to war with itself.

The tension between the chivalric, monadic conception of one's duties and rights took shape as a conception of "rights" themselves. The early modern theorists of rights are well known. (The names themselves— Hobbes, Locke, Bodin, et al.—are famous enough.) The conception of inalienable or at least ground-level basic "rights" emerges as an answer to the dissolution of the more on-the-ground "dyadic" world of feudalism, in which all obligations were owed to specific individuals. (Of course, feudalism is not properly speaking dyadic but would be "multiadic," if there were such a word.) If a dyadic "right" (a duty to a specific other) emerges out of a things like a contractual duty to another person—such that by freely contracting, I now have a duty to another who as a correlative has a right to my carrying out that to which I contracted—then likewise, a monadically construed right to, say, noninterference or to liberty of expression can function as a protection in the same way. The great conceptual breakthrough during this time came with the great theorists of early modernity understanding that perhaps all of the political duties that formerly seemed necessarily dyadic (such as all the requirement of justice and all the other political relations of loyalty, etc.) could be reconstrued as essentially monadic duties whose only apparently dyadic shape was the result of a contract. This functioned to underwrite a shape of life that was seeking to conceptualize itself as a society of "individuals" for whom the appropriate structure of morals, ethics, and epistemology was monadic in all instances.

However, the real world and its contingencies, as Hegel always stresses, does not shape itself neatly along the lines of conceptual distinction: "To be sure, historical transitions are not always so pure as they have been presented here, and often many of them happen at the same time; but one or the other always forms the preponderant part."[99] Thus, the structure of social life was not completely done over to conform to the monadic rights of the social contract. Moreover, the "wars of religion," as conflicts generated internally to the tensions in the basic commitments of early modern Europeans, were in many cases also not purely religious conflicts. They also involved the kinds of political tensions that were ingredients of that shape of subjectivity as it was giving itself its shape. For example, in the one of the more famous incidents of the period, in 1685 Louis XIV of France revoked the Edict of Nantes, which had granted toleration to the Protestants. In doing so, he thereby provoked a religious war in France. Hegel notes that at its outset it was not even yet a purely religious war since the Protestants had been continually suspected of being too easily tempted by the English to take positions contrary or even antagonistic to the Catholic French court's interests. Thus, at the beginning of the conflict, this still bore many of the marks of a "rebellion."[100] Likewise, in England, the dispute between Protestants and Catholics took on the character of a constitutional conflict. Puritanism, "the high point of inwardness" as a shape of subjectivity, took over power under Cromwell, even though English puritan practice itself was a mixture, in Hegel's words, of the "fanatical" and the "ridiculous."[101]

In the transition to a confessionally divided Europe, the Thirty Years War in Germany (1618–1648) stood out. It took part mostly in Germany and devastated the country. The economy was devastated, entire villages were destroyed and disappeared off maps, and the population fell drastically. (Württemberg, for example, where Hegel was born and grew up, declined from a population of 445,000 in 1622 to only 97,000 in 1639.)[102] The end of the Thirty Years War ushered in the period of a balance of power among separate states, but otherwise it was simply the result of exhaustion—"without anything having been won for thought, without an Idea, with the exhaustion of everyone, a total devastation in which all forces has smashed themselves into pieces, which ended by leaving the facts on the ground in place for all parties on the basis of external forces."[103] As he noted, "The exit from the war was of a political nature. There was neither a basic principle recognized nor a union of co-religionists produced."[104]

The result for Germany was that it was splintered into a variety of independent states, some relatively large but many others resembling postage stamps stuck randomly on a map of central Europe. This result in the settlement was, in Hegel's terms, a "constitutionally secured anarchy," brought about through the *raison d'état* on the part of the French minister, Cardinal Richelieu, who suppressed the Protestants in France at the same time as he was siding with them in the war in Germany.[105]

The "wars of religion" hastened the development of the modern European state. The loyalties of people began to be focused on more central-ized authorities and bodies, and a form of economic dynamism began to show up in ordinary life, which in turn assisted in the consolidation of the often contending authorities into a more unitary source of authority, the "state," which built itself up out of the more archaic "ethnies" (to use Smith's term again) of the European world. Because of a variety of different factors (including the experience of warfare and the growing need for "standing armies" on the part of monarchs, in order for sheer self-defense), a reconcep-tualization of the various key statuses in social life came about. In 1757, a British writer could say that "Of all honour that's truest . . . hath been won by the sword in a purple field of blood" and "the 'best gentleman' was the one who made his fortunes by 'hewing them out of his enemies' bowels'."[106] Only a few years later, that seemed to make little sense at all and even to seemed to run up to the very point of ludicrousness. As new forms of author-ity crystallized around new movements and demand for recognition, new virtues began to form and older ones lost their place. The former ethos of aristocratic glory in pursuit of war was replaced by the ethos of professional armies, and the so-called virtues of the aristocrat seeking glory were effaced in by the professional officer who selflessly took his orders from the higher command.[107] Thus, by 1700, Oxford's professor of geometry could make the argument that not equestrian skill but logic and philosophy were better training for the upcoming elite, including the military elite.[108] Likewise, the "great Barons" of France became mere "office-holders" instead of indepen-dent sources of political power, and the similar lords in the Ottoman Empire became something more like civil servants.[109] What might have looked like mere rationalizations of existing practice were in fact the appearances of a new shape of subjectivity forming its practical and institutional life around itself.

On Hegel's account, the modern state thus arose in no specifically ratio-nal or conscious manner but instead grew out of a variety of factors. In some cases, the Catholic religion was the binding glue that led to the formation of the state. In those cases, the authority of the church manifested itself as a "externality within an inward turn," the mode in which subjects, instead of making up their own minds about what they believed, followed instead the directives of the church, of something they would understand as possibly even beyond their own capacity to understand.[110] Such a shape of subjectivity comprehends itself to be following something like the rules of a practice where the authority for determining what exactly counts as following those rules is turned over to somebody else, and it can only keep its grip on people when the basic social institutions maintain a purely "positive," given authority to themselves—when the key institutions that both embody and dispense authority "rest on positive possession," as he puts it, rather than on "genuinely eternal right," that is, on an institutionally secured reflective distance from all given institutions.[111] So he thought, such "reflective distance" can only be secured by some kind of Protestant religion within which the kinds of institutions that can secure such a reflective, conscience-oriented stance for the citizenry can develop themselves. Likewise, that kind of Protestant religion can ultimately be comprehensible in the source of its authority by drawing on something nonreligious, namely, philosophy as the rational consideration of what makes sense—or what it is to ultimately make sense of things and to make sense of making sense.

The modern nation-state, for Hegel, thus arises out of the different "ethnies" of early modern Europe being forced by economic factors, war, and contradictions within the bases of their structures of authority into more consolidated arrangements of power. This in turn both results in and results from a different shape of subjectivity which takes its locus in a modern order of thoughts based on a global system of "states" vying with each other, and the actors within those states no longer understanding the old set of virtues as relating to one's fixed place in a social hierarchy as making sense. This new shape of subjectivity was at first turned inward—in an *"Insichgehen,"* in Hegel's German—and tended to adopt a position that took itself as detaching itself from all social standings, that is, as having a more "moral" and less an "ethical" view.

However, as Hegel notes, given their self-contradictory natures, the embryonic states of early modern Europe basically concocted a recipe for continual warfare.[112] Simply listing the numbers of wars in the early modern period after the devastation of the Thirty Years War would take up many megabytes of information. Moreover, during this period, the cost of warfare kept rising with the advances in technology and in modes of recruitment. Indeed, the seventeenth-century arms race and the increasing costs of warfare put great strains on loyalty and especially on finances, which in turn contributed to setting the stage for the emergence of the modern state.[113]

However, as long as the "state" was seen to be something that the monarch possessed as his property, the traditional view of the purpose of monarchical rule as the striving for "glory" determined much of the course of events, and striving for "glory" meant striving for conquest. Louis XIV, whose form of absolutism (for Hegel) represented the turning point between the old, quasi-feudal "state" and the new modern state, summed this up in his own 1679 treatise on kingship: "when one looks to the state, one is really working for oneself. The welfare of the former secures the glory of the latter. The ruler who makes the state content, prestigious and powerful also promotes his own glory."[114] The state was his property, and the link was so close that the glory of one was equivalent to the glory of the other. (Unfortunately, for those who prefer the received story, he most likely did not actually say "L'état, c'est moi," even if the sentiment was indeed truly his.[115])

As Hegel saw things, Louis XIV represented the last failed attempt after the earlier failed effort by Charles V to establish a "universal monarchy," or indeed, as he put it, a system of "world domination."[116] Like Philip II earlier, Louis XIV also came to grief at the hands of the Dutch (in his case, in 1678). Louis XIV's plan for establishing French domination upset the emerging balance of power in European life whereby small states (particularly those postage-stamp principalities precipitating out of the ruins of the Thirty Years War) might manage to defend themselves against larger, aggressive states. Hegel notes that this emphasis on the balance of power itself indicated a departure from the older order of thoughts of political units in Europe, since the system of a balance of power "took the place of the earlier universal end, that of Christendom whose focal point was that of the Papacy."[117] No such religious epicenter could provide for the unity of European powers any more. The loss of a religious focal point also meant that, somewhat metaphorically speaking, subjectivity had to rethink itself and what its absolute aims were.

Although Hegel does not go into any detail about Louis XIV's wars in the lectures, in one place, he did not need to do so. The Dutch defeat of the

French was well known to his audience, and, in addition, all educated Germans knew about what in English is often called the "devastation of the Palatinate." In an attempt to force the hand of the Hapsburg Emperor and thinking that the English were too preoccupied by their "glorious Revolution" of 1688 to be worth worrying about, Louis launched a war on German territory in 1688 that, along with some other policy goals, was intended to show France's capacity for shock and awe (and thereby intimidate the Hapsburgs). Louis XIV's troops pillaged, sacked, and burned to the ground several German towns (including Heidelberg). This war lasted until a treaty was signed in 1697, and it created in many generations afterward in Germany a view that France was somehow Germany's natural enemy.[118] To his credit, Hegel did not in any way share that view about France. In fact, Hegel notes that unlike Charles V, Louis did not base his aspirations to establish a French "universal monarchy" on the basis merely of raw power but on the superiority of French culture itself, which, as Hegel put it, gave him a "higher entitlement" to such an aspiration than Charles had possessed.[119] After all, "France," Hegel said, "is the land of culture *(Bildung)*."[120]

The absolutist state—brought to its most nearly complete form in France—was the final abstraction resting on the modern idea of all political duties as having a monadic structure. The sovereign had the rights and duties of a sovereign alone. He owed them to no other specific individual or group. The elimination of almost all of the vestiges of what the Germans had called the *Ständestaat*—the state of estates—had removed the remaining "dyadic" duties of sovereign and the basic political and social groupings of society, where each had, as it were, duties to each other and corresponding rights (even though that very terminology of "rights" and "duties" is not quite accurate to describe how they saw themselves). The shift from the state as a property of the ruler to the state as an independent constitutional order of thoughts came quickly, but it was the French who accomplished it at first in principle and then later in practice with their revolution. Louis XIV had managed to defang the nobility and, by making himself the very pinnacle of state authority, turn himself into something approaching an absolute monarch. His failure to establish a "universal monarchy" for himself provoked the move to comprehend the state as a source of authority independent of the monarch himself. By successfully shifting all authority to himself as the living embodiment of the state, he successfully undermined the kinds of recalcitrant authorities still at work in French society and thus set the stage for the overthrow of the monarchy and the establishment of a constitutional state. That, by the standards of historical time, this happened rather quickly is illustrated by a remark made by a French observer in the middle of the eighteenth century—before the French Revolution—that "today, hardly anyone dare say in Parisian society, I serve the king. . . . You'd be taken for one of the chief valets at Versailles. I serve the state is the expression most commonly used."[121]

Central to Hegel's view of the shape of the modern world—but not as much emphasized in the edited versions of the lectures on the philosophy of history—was the Dutch resistance and victories over, first, the Spanish— with the revolt beginning against the empire of Charles V as inherited by his son and successor, Philip II, and ending in 1648—and then later the successful Dutch resistance against Louis XIV, ending in 1678. The Dutch put the new shape of subjectivity front and center and made it the center of their revolt and their founding of a modern commercial republic. Hegel was himself enormously impressed with life in Holland when he visited there in 1822, and he saw it as the embodiment of what he took to be the exemplary elements of the dynamic of modern life.[122] Nor did he neglect this theme in his other lectures. For example, in his lectures on the philosophy of art, he placed a heavy emphasis on the Dutch experience of the modern world. The Dutch had fought a successful war of independence against Spain between roughly 1566 and 1648, and they had established a successful, rich, and tolerant nation based on trade. They reclaimed their land from the sea, they established peaceful and efficient political orders, and, most importantly, they established a successful and flourishing shape of life whose art captured the Dutch sense of a "joy in the world as such . . . domestic life in its decency, cheerfulness, and quiet seclusion." With them, the distinction between nobility and commoner simply vanished in importance.

The principle that "all are free" was worked out in practice by the Dutch even before it had been fully formulated in philosophy. Their fight for freedom and independence from Spain was carried out, in Hegel's words, "not by a superior nobility expelling its prince and tyrant or imposing laws on him, nor a people of farmers, oppressed peasants, who broke free, like the Swiss" but by "townspeople, burghers active in trade and well-off, who, comfortable in their business, had no high pretensions, but when it was a question of fighting for the freedom of their well-earned rights, of the special privileges of their provinces, cities, and corporations, they . . . courageously shed their blood and by this righteous boldness and endurance triumphantly won for themselves both civil and religious independence."[123] Their art—by which he meant seventeenth-century Dutch painting— thereby "developed the greatest truth of which art is capable," at least under modern conditions.[124]

Hegel's claims for the revolution in France as the turning point of the modern world (a view he had held since his youth) are well known, but Hegel had also entertained the idea that the Dutch example, although much less celebrated, formed one of the other major alternatives in modern life. To Hegel, the Dutch, more than anybody else, seemed to have put into practice the modern structure of rights, moral duties, and goods (specifically, those of family, civil society, and state) that Hegel had systematically explicated in his 1820 *Philosophy of Right*. Nonetheless, the Dutch example might look as if it might be just a quirk of a particular type of personality on the part of the Dutch themselves since they did not carry out their war of independence nor establish their new "bourgeois" way of life on the basis of any clearly articulated set of universal claims. It was not the Dutch wars of independence but the French Revolution that rested its legitimacy not on anything particularly "French" but on the universal "rights of man." Without the French Revolution supplying the ideas behind a possibly reconciled modernity, the Dutch example would seem therefore to be only a one-off event. Although the French were the avant-garde in raising the issue of human rights as a basis of legitimacy, the Dutch seemed to have provided the more useful blueprint for a tolerant, free, modern order. The modern world thus generated two somewhat competing models of how to be a modern state: the Dutch and the French.

If the French were the avant-garde of the rights of man, the Dutch were the avant-garde, as it were, of the Protestant German lands. In effect, the Dutch example showed, in Hegel's view, that the Protestant German lands had in principle worked out the lineaments for the resolution of one of the bigger problems to which the modern world had given shape: It had established the idea of governance according to legal rules and fashioned a social space in which individuals could carry out their own aims in large areas of social life without much reflection on how that all added up to the good of the whole. All the Protestant lands now needed was the underpinning of the Rights of Man, which the French had provided and which German philosophy from Kant forward had underwritten.

The nihilism that had been a bubbling undercurrent of so much European history was submerged in the commitment to a new and better founded ideal, that of freedom as the condition of justice being actualized, and the way in which the kind of psychology that took root in the Protestant lands meshed, so Hegel thought, without much friction with those new principles. In the Dutch-German lands, the idea had taken deep root—again so Hegel thought—that the arbitrary will of the prince could not be the source of law's authority but rather that the prince's "will is worthy of respect to the extent that he wisely wills what is lawful, what is just, and for the good of the whole."[125] The rule of reason had usurped the rule of domination by the powerful. In the older order, the princes and the emperors had stood as symbolic fonts and dispensers of justice. As Louis XV expressed this order in a quite non-symbolic way: "The magistrates are my officers charged with administering on my behalf my truly royal duty to dispense justice to my subjects. . . . Sovereignty resides in my person alone . . . and my courts derive their existence and their authority from me alone."[126] What the various Louis's did not quite see was that such a role was now shifting, also very nonsymbolically, to the constitutional state and away from them. The Dutch put them on notice. The French Revolution closed the deal.

Enlightenment, Germans, and the Revolution

For Hegel, the rule of reason arrived on the scene not just because of the collapse of absolutism in European political life. The French also played a major role in laying the groundwork for the way in which that collapse came to mean something more special to the people living through those events. This was their contribution to the movement of the "Enlightenment," which was conceptually joined to the collapse of the authority of the absolutist court. That collapse in turn helped to make the way in which the building blocks of modern life as a free life showed up in all their salience.

In this period, "Enlightenment" contrasted with the emotionalist religions opening up in Europe such as Jansenism in France, Wesleyanism in Britain, and Pietism in Germany. The world of "faith" (as distinct from "religion" per se) looked to the emotions as disclosing the divine presence in one's world, the way God was supposedly at work in one's innermost life and outward deeds. It found its expression in baroque art for both Catholics and Protestants. (The great Catholic Baroque cathedrals sat comfortably down the road from Bach's great Protestant music.) Yet just as much as they took themselves to be opposites and to regard each other with something like distrust bordering on contempt, both were equally expressions of the way in which the people taking on the shape of subjectivity fitting to that shape of life tried to find new orienting points for themselves. In becoming gradually unmoored from the old order of things, people sought the immediacy of emotion in the new religious movements, or they sought to put the stakes of the tent into the ground on Enlightenment principles.[127] Likewise, just as so many sought an intensity of emotion in their religion, they also sought an intensity of emotion in their art, and many of the paintings of the day (especially the French school) celebrated it. The shape of subjectivity that was forming itself was cleft between a devotion to reason and a cult of feeling and "sensibility" (as it was called at the time). How it would be possible for subjects to be at one with themselves under what looked like the contrary pulls of those two seeming absolutes which shaped much of the tumult surrounding the growth of the "Enlightenment" and the French Revolution. (Hegel credits Friedrich Schiller for identifying the problem and its need for a reconciliation between reason and sensibility.[128])

The mythical early *Germanen*, in their mythical early condition, were (supposedly) virtuous barbarians, capable of admirable feats of loyalty and bravery to their lords (to whom they freely bound themselves) but on whom the rule of law and bureaucracy had no affective grip. It was supposedly the harsh education of a thousand years of feudal rule and its concomitant violence that led them to reshape their disposition and motivational makeup so that they were able to accept both the rule of law and the bureaucratic apparatus necessary for a free life that was also a satisfying life. Hegel quite famously characterized this fusion as the union of morality—as a system of rules and principles formulated from the standpoint of universality, coupled with a felt necessity to act according to such principles—and "ethical life," *Sittlichkeit,* as the kind of social formations and practices necessary to produce the kinds of characters who exhibit the virtues (the union of passion and principle) necessary for a free and satisfying life. Quite pointedly, Hegel also argued (or at least claimed) that universalistic morality could have no real grip on people unless it was integrated into the more particularistic modes of ethical life. One of the genuine places where the moral life is carried out, where morality becomes real, is in a civil society structured into various mediating institutions that in principle are both different from each other and yet harmonize with each other.[129] On its own, universalizable moral constraints do not provide sufficient content to enable people to make concrete decisions. For that they need more basic first principles for their more explicit practical reasoning, and those ends must appear in those shapes of life as settled dispositions. (They are values that have also become psychological facts.) To that end, civil society had to be structured in terms of various estates *(Stände)* and "corporations" (institutions that were more like guilds than like the impersonal modern globalized behemoths of today) that embody a kind of practical know-how in orienting oneself in an increasingly complex modern world.

To Hegel's own question—Why did the Revolution occur in France and not in Germany?—Hegel's answer was in part that France came to possess only a very thinly constituted civil society.[130] In France, the dissolution of feudalism had left a social world of individuals contending with each other in a patently unjust regime within which the structures of official power still rested in feudal orders. Without the mediating effect of the guilds and the estates, whose social authority had been decimated by the absolutizing tendencies of Louis XIV, each individual was abandoned to his own resources. With the feudal structure rotting out from within, the only loyalty had to be either to the family or to the "nation" itself and could not be mediated by loyalty to something like one's estate. If the virtues are the dispositions and passions connected to the concept of what is right—are a matter of character and good judgment—then without the mediation of a vital civil society, the virtues become mere dispositions to be of service to the state or loyalty to family. This puts the state in a position where it ought not to be, and when the state is still seen as embodied in the monarch himself, it leads to a form of policing society that places terror at its disposal.

Moreover, in Hegel's rather negative view of the potentialities of the Catholic religion, as a Catholic country, France was subject to an authoritarian religion that prevented the formation of a deeply grounded civil society because of its refusal to recognize the principle that private conscience had to be protected. Hegel cites in particular (and in several places) the role that the Inquisition played in Spain. Although it billed itself badly enough as the "persecution of clandestine Jews, Moors, and heretics," it of course became an organ to "persecute enemies of the state," that is, of the king, such that it even "claimed supremacy over bishops and archbishops."[131] By making one's suspected dispositions themselves an object of punishment, it laid the ground for the Terror of the French Revolution. Without the restraining elements of civil society, the Inquisition became the model for a well-honed tool of state power, and although the French did not have an Inquisition, they had all the tools to make one happen.

In particular, the court life of the *ancien régime* in France had pushed the modern conception of subjectivity into one of its penultimate forms. The structure of recognition at work in the Bourbon French court had resulted in a form of monarchical absolutism. The aristocratic ideal that they and only they were capable of governing since they were not bound to the essential purposes of the "middling" classes, namely, the more egoistic demands of pursuing wealth and status. They, the nobility, supposedly already had the required status and thus do not need to seek it, and (in the ideology that underwrote this claim) they were also willing to risk their lives for the good of the state and thus deserved the political power they wielded. (The "middling" classes were supposedly too self-involved to do any of these things.) Since position in the order of thoughts required recognition from those possessing the authority to confer recognition, a pyramidal structure resulted with the monarch sitting at the top: He recognizes but needs no recognition from others, since his authority comes from divine origin. However, since it takes quite a bit of wealth to be able to participate in court life, and because court life is itself an avenue to wealth, historically the nobility ceased to be the group dedicated to the martial glory it claimed for itself. Moreover, the technological and social changes in warfare in the sixteenth and seventeenth centuries had increasingly made soldiering into a specialized profession and war into a pursuit of strategic political objectives. The place for the satisfaction of the older aristocratic thirst for "glory" was vanishing.

In light of those pressures, the nobility ceased to be warriors and became instead courtiers, intent on gaining glory by recognition at court rather than by risking one's life on the battlefield. Even the noble who pursued a military career was no longer the knight of legend out to seek his own honor. He was now subordinate to his superior officers and was expected to make good on that.[132] In such a world, real glory consisted in moving up in the court's hierarchy of status, not in martial glory. In such a world, as Hegel put it, the alleged heroism of the medieval world had given way to a bourgeois world pretending it was still part of a medieval military aristocracy. Heroism on the battlefield was replaced by the insider maneuvering of courtiers, and, as Hegel put it, in such a world, "the heroism of silent service becomes the *heroism of flattery*."[133]

That the distinction between the nobility and the middling, merchant sort—the pursuit of glory versus the pursuit of wealth—was thereby not really actual any more became ever more obvious to all concerned. This paradigm of developing one's personality to succeed at court life meant that since each noble seeks, as his chief purpose, to receive recognition from the monarch, this also means that he must renounce his legal personality (since the monarch is the source of all legality). What is left open to him is contingent on the whims of other, more powerful individuals. The life of the court is thus that of subjectivity that seems to consist in pure recognition, but it is not a repetition of the Roman order. The subject is now, in Hegel's terms, "reflected into himself," and self-consciousness is now inherently self-distanced: "Self-consciousness is essentially judgment,"[134] thoroughly reflective, keeping a tally on itself and others, jockeying for position, and increasingly aware of the nothingness of its own position and social life.[135]

The result was a conception of subjectivity as self-directing but fundamentally theatrical. Within that shape of life, each is an actor writing his own script so that he shows up in the social world as somebody to notice, all the while realizing that he and everybody else in the scene is fully aware of this element of theatricality. In such a world, the actor's own individuality eventually becomes hollowed out and the issue of whether the play is worth continuing becomes more and more up for grabs. Success for this form of subjectivity is making oneself be noticed by others, but being noticed by others becomes less and less a matter of any obvious objective value.

The life of the court's witty ironies about itself—that all was vanity, that it was all just a show—helped to fuel the movement that came to call itself the "Enlightenment," and which at first, at least in France, defined itself almost entirely negatively, as "not faith." It quickly grew out of its own negative definition and took on the identity of a movement based in reason alone, with its own faith in science, publicity, and inquiry driving it forward.[136] The appeal to reason and the movement that went along with the Enlightenment—that of casting aspersion on the court and the government—put even more pressure on the ruling powers. That court life had become an empty theatrical playground of both deadly seriousness and disinterested wit finally pushed it over the edge. The abstraction of the absolutist state as embodied in an unlimited monarch evaporated and with it the lingering sense of natural noble entitlement.

The Enlightenment highlighted the shape that subjectivity had taken in the social tumult leading up to the French Revolution. As that shape of subjectivity understood itself, it was a shape of subjectivity that took itself to be an exercise in humility—in contrast to the arrogance of court life and the ecclesiastical practice of the time—in that it abjured superstition and "faith" in favor of reason, yet it recognized the limits of reason and steadfastly and honestly refused to cross those lines. In Hegel's terms, such a shape recognizes its own finitude and refuses to puff itself up beyond that finitude. Kant's philosophy is the most developed expression in which that shape of subjectivity gives voice to itself. In its conception of a necessary structure of appearance—the world as we must find it—and its denial that this could be knowledge of the way things are in themselves (of things as they are apart from all possible experience), Kant gives voice to this dual self-asserting and self-humbling conception of subjectivity. (That Kant also held that we could with precision know what practical reason requires of us, while at the same time putting strict limits on how far theoretical reason can go, made it all the more expressive of this shape of subjectivity.) This shape of subjectivity takes the ultimate—the "absolute"—objects of thought to be beyond its comprehension, beyond its capacities for knowledge, limited as they are by the need for a sensible, intuitive component to them.

Kant takes there to be a limit to what is thinkable, and he stands, as it were, above the limit. That requires us, as Wittgenstein was later to remark, "to set a limit to thought," which in turn requires that "we should have to find both sides of the limit thinkable (i.e., we should have to be able to think what cannot be thought)" and that is, on its own terms, impossible.[137] When it is taken apart from its Kantian expression, the same figure of thought as the "view from above" becomes less humble. In the terms that court life set for itself, such "finitude," which takes the shape of humility in Kantian thought, instead becomes the arrogance of the courtiers. The shape of noble and royal subjectivity that takes everything to be vanity takes itself to be better than the vanity of others since it knows that it is vain. This view from above, as an impersonal point of view above the fray, has no real content to itself except to know that it at least has the honesty to know the limits of its knowledge.

As it begins to formulate itself, it seeks a rational standard for this "view from above" the limits, and it finds it, so it thinks, in the abstract principle of utility. The appeal to utility is not, after all, an appeal to the vanity of personal interest but to something like the best state of affairs. It is a genuine view from above since it is impartial. It is not "my" utility that counts so much as it is utility in general, the best possible state of affairs achievable in our circumstances.[138] What counts is happiness, but not necessarily "my" happiness.

In the theatrical world of the court, "the view from above" consists in the witty assurance that it is all for show. In the world of the French *philosophes,* the "view from above" is the appeal to utility. In Kant's hands, that "view from above the limit" turned into a powerful set of arguments to underwrite the reality of human freedom and a secularized, although abstract, ideal of human freedom and equality as membership in a "kingdom of ends." After the twin events of Kant's moral philosophy with its "kingdom of ends" and the French Revolution with its declaration of the rights of man, the idea that all are free—that nobody by nature has authority to command others—became what was at work, actual, *wirklich* in modern life. It was actual not in the sense that suddenly all the forms of irrational domination suddenly vanished (they obviously did not), but rather in the sense that it was now impossible to give a rational legitimation of the natural domination of some by others. Nor did it mean that people gave up trying to give those arguments (they obviously did not), but that there was no way after that turning point for actually making that case. It also meant that there were necessary consequences of this new view—for example, the irrationality of the natural authority men had traditionally claimed over women—that many people, even Hegel himself, did not want to draw.

Ultimately, all these are various and different, but nonetheless penultimate, expressions of a more reconciliatory view that reason's grasp is itself unbounded, *unendlich,* and that reason can work out its own limits from within itself. That is the task of something like Hegel's *Logic*. Hegel's *Logic* is the articulation of the "view from within" modern subjectivity itself, and the practical consequence is that reason has the wherewithal to shape a habitable world with its own tools. However, that more reconciliatory view could only appear on the scene once the alternations between humility, arrogance, and the kind of impartiality that discounted the view from within subjectivity itself had played themselves out. A reconciliatory view of rationality that incorporates within itself the partiality of the different viewpoints of subjects—as a way in which "the universal particularizes itself"— had to be developed historically out of the breakdown of the Enlightenment shape of subjectivity as the impartial view from above. That was what Hegel took his own philosophy to be: Not the "view from above" but the logic of the "view from within," where the difference of the "inner" and the "outer" was reconceived along the lines Hegel took his dialectical logic to have explicated, in which they are distinguishable but not separable moments of a single whole.

Even if the Enlightenment was one-sided in its view of reason as "the view from above," it was nonetheless the driving and constructive force of the French Revolution. Whatever its limits, its elevation of the natural sciences was nothing less than positive: The world bequeathed by the Enlightenment "sets the external world free" and "people turn to nature in order to know it and the result is that the experiential sciences flourish and prosper anew and even finer than they did in Greece."[139] The leading ideas of the Enlightenment coursed through Europe, and, as Hegel put it, in the American war of independence "the thought of freedom came out on top."[140] The Enlightenment had finally put "thought in the driver's seat."[141]

Hegel seemed nonetheless to think that, world-historical as it was, the French Revolution was a unique event, the result of a perfect storm resulting from a failed authoritarian regime identified with an authoritarian, anti-progressive church totally out of step with the growing demand for equal justice as calling for equal liberty, together with the economic failures of the royal regime. Into that storm was tossed Rousseauian calls for emancipation and self-direction, French utilitarianism, and behind the tumult was a mix of Romantic and Mediterranean sets of passions.[142] But that is not to underestimate it—as Hegel told his students, "It was a glorious dawn. All thinking beings joined in the celebration of this epoch."[143]

The result was a modern world that could not turn the clock back, however much some continued to long to do so. The French Revolution had legitimated itself around the idea of the universal rights of man, and with his repeated victories, Napoleon in effect made the Revolution into the problem for all European states. Although, to put it more mildly than it should be put, Napoleon did not exactly have the promulgation of the rights of man first and foremost in his mind as he staged his conquests and victories, nor when he put many of his relatives on the thrones of his newly created duchies, he did nonetheless embody the new idea of the individual gaining stature on the basis of his (and eventually her) own merit. Whereas the old order had understood itself as a rigid hierarchy that claimed (and to many even seemed) to be natural and which brought with it an official set of virtues— in particular, that of being content with one's lot and not displaying the vice of pride in seeking to rise higher than God had intended for you—the new order quickly undermined that as a virtue at all. (The theory of the virtue of being content with one's lot had always been at odds with the practice in many ways, but that was a feature of the contradictory shape of subjectivity of medieval and early modern concatenations of authority.) Napoleon as the ideal (as distinct from Napoleon the actual man) seemed to be the living embodiment of how the disposition to ambition could in fact be a virtue. That he could have risen so high through his own ambition and work was enough to make him the symbol of the new individual which was to take shape afterwards, when so many ambitious industrialists expressed their aspiration as wanting to be the "Napoleon" of some or another area of life.[144]

For a while after the downfall of Napoleon, following his ill thought-out and completely calamitous Russian campaign, Hegel was indeed worried about which way the hands of the clock were turning, but he was reassured by the fact that the Congress of Vienna, which more or less consciously set out to turn the clock back, in fact did not really reverse things, even though it did its best to stop things dead in their tracks.[145] The old order had collapsed under its own weight and its inner inconsistencies. However, rather than collapsing into an unintelligible world, it was being succeeded by the post-Enlightenment world that had grown up within it, in which the intelligibility of the whole was rapidly coming into focus. Or so Hegel thought.

In Hegel's view, there were other lines of development that showed that the upheaval of the French Revolution was not a fate for all modern regimes.

For example, Great Britain had avoided the fate of the Revolution because of the strength of its own civil society (and because England had already had gone through its own gory, fanatical civil war to secure Protestant rule there). The establishment of the United Kingdom in fact showed that a modern state could arise out of very different "ethnies" in such a way that was not the end-product of some kind of organic growth out of a pre-existing ethnic-religious unity: "Great Britain is divided within itself, into England, Scotland, and Ireland, and each of these lands represents a shape of religious life: the Episcopal, the Presbyterian, and the Catholic."[146] Moreover, to their credit, the English (one of the ethnies) express this in their economic life and are the "missionaries of all peoples with respect to industry and technology, and, through legal trade, they connect the whole world."[147] (In the lectures, he seems to have failed to note the large Scottish presence in all of that British trade.) However, despite these advantages, the English part of the regime was still infected by too many feudal privileges: "The government is in the hands of the aristocrats. In England, law is in the worst state, and it exists only for the rich, not for the poor."[148] England nonetheless functions because it has an aristocracy that was both trained for and experienced in politics, which Hegel thought helped hold together what seemed otherwise a creaky and corrupt system based on "rotten boroughs." (He also had misgivings about the English aristocracy, insinuating that he took them to be mostly a rather debased set of pudding-eating fox hunters who mistook their noble birth for brains.[149] But he had never visited England, so it is unclear where he got his less than unenthusiastic view of the English aristocracy.)

Germany, on Hegel's view, had avoided the revolutionary upheaval largely because of accidents about its past. The German Empire (The Holy Roman Empire of the German Nation) had been an elective empire, with the nobles choosing the emperor, and thus, so Hegel claimed, "because it was an elective realm, it never became a state."[150] Germany also suffered both the bad luck of being decimated by the Thirty Years War into a myriad of nominally independent political units, and, as he put it, from "not having, as France did, the focal point of a conquering family."[151] These so-called deficiencies, however, in fact turned out to be an advantage for Germany in the modern world. Because it had not been a "state," it could accept the principles of the French Revolution (for example, those of human rights and meritocracy) without having to overthrow the king or storm the Bastille, in large part because there was no German king to overthrow or German Bastille to storm. Because its union of passion and principle was, so Hegel also thought, already founded in its deeply felt acceptance of the Reformation and the fundamental right of the protection of conscience, Germany also could dispense with the Revolution and simply accept its principles. This was in part because of the initial French victories over the Germans in the wars immediately following the Revolution. This "French oppression" de facto imported the positive results of the Revolution into Germany and was then made into the basis of a widespread reform of the German legal system by the Germans themselves.[152]

This was more or less true, he thought, despite the fact that "Germany" remained divided between Catholic and Protestant populations, since, so he also thought, "the Catholic church was also on its own part reformed through the Reformation."[153] In fact, Hegel argued against the idea that Germany was an ethnic nation that naturally needed unification, and even that the whole idea of German unification was altogether a bad one: "On a small scale, interests can be the same. On the large scale, as in Germany, the interests of the Bavarians, the Austrians, the Pomeranians and the Mecklenburgers are highly distinct."[154] By virtue of the historical accidents of its past, Germans had, so Hegel claimed, been developing a lively civil society (and thus the new set of appropriate modern virtues) and a commitment to the rational rule of law (and thus something like Kantian morality). They were thus were in the position to stage the necessary reforms to their economic and social structure without the calamity of a violent revolution.

Germany, in fact, had been the home where the penultimate development of the modern "moral" point of view had been pushed into grasping itself as embedded in a different practice. "Morality," as the doctrine that people have to act on universalizable reasons and not just in terms of the ethos of the particular communities in which the relevant actors were members, reached this penultimate statement of itself in the immediate Kantian aftermath in the 1790s and early 1800s. In that short space of time, the "moral point of view" that had been one of the driving forces in early modern European life had come to be adequately conceptualized. The "moral point of view" was to be conceived in monadic terms. The relation of the moral actor to principle was conceived as only mediately a relation to specific others. A moral injunction was to "do right" and not "do wrong," and the other agent whom one might wrong in one's actions was not essential to the action's being right or wrong. One might indeed do wrong in harming another, but what makes such an act wrong is its violation of a principle and (and perhaps "or") the relation in which the wrongdoer stands to the principle. Doing wrong is more like violating a rule in a game. The monadic conception of the moral order has as its correlate a monadic moral order in the world. To the extent that by doing something wrong, an agent fails at being an agent—fails in its most basic function, to put it in the Aristotelian terms Hegel tends to favor—the importance of acting morally and getting into the correct relationship with the moral order becomes crucial to such agency. It becomes the warp and woof of emotional life itself.

In the Romantic appropriation of Kantian morality in Germany, so Hegel thought, this led not accidentally to a doctrine of "beautiful souls," that is, a conception of agents who took their primary concern to consist in avoiding doing wrong (and, if one had done wrong, to have thereby stained and soiled one's soul). The beautiful soul is obsessed in a self-involved way with his own standing in the system of moral rules and is thus blind to the more justice-oriented concerns with the others as others. As it were, the beautiful soul is obsessed with whether he is winning or losing the game according to the rules and not with, say, a concrete concern for the other person. Such a conception of moral action leads such beautiful souls to a practice of inaction. Because of the contingency of all action in the world, any action can result in a nonforeseen "staining," and the only way thereby to preserve one's purity is either not to act at all or effectively to shift the moral register into a conception of purity of intention or true conviction which stands in sharp contrast to the impurity of almost all worldly action. The rules of the moral game, that is, seem to point to a refusal to act, since any action might cloud the purity demanded by the rules. The end-result of such a moral stance, Hegel rather sarcastically notes, turns out to be merely that of two monadic subjects hearing their own echoes within an empty space, each expressing its own self-involved relation to the moral order and not directly speaking at all to each other.[155] To borrow a term from Marx, each has fetishized the moral order as if it were some self-standing all important game which it was up to each to win or lose.

In his own time, the impossibility of sustaining this as a living, practical project had, so Hegel thought, more or less become clear, and, analogous to the way the ancient relations of mastery and servitude had proved to be unintelligible and ultimately unlivable, the relations among such "beautiful souls" were also proving to be either in or at the edge of a similar break-down. In Germany, so he thought, the deeper roots the Reformation had struck meant that the social nature of agency as involving dyadic and not merely monadic judgments of the normative social space therefore did not require a revolutionary breakdown for its adequate expression. It was instead to be found in a secularized version of Christian doctrine. Beautiful souls had to understand themselves as metaphorical sons and daughter of God, not as separate individuals focused on their own single relation to the moral order. The "dyadic" nature of such a conception—after all, one can be a "brother" or "sister" only to an other, another "brother" or "sister"— becomes expressed in acts of mutual forgiveness for taking such a haughty, moralistic, and self-involved stance to each other. Beautiful souls have to hold tightly onto the idea that whatever messiness their lives might seem to have, their inner purity (which is therefore invisible to others) remains untouched by that world's disarray. Because of that, beautiful souls inevita-bly fail in their agency—their "hard hearts," as Hegel says, have to break— since they cannot help but be involved in the messiness of life.[156] The hard heart necessarily breaks because the conception of the monadically con-ceived moral order as having the resources within itself to sustain itself has to break and acknowledge that it makes sense only within the context of a dyadically structured ethical order.

The monadic moral stance thus had to give way to its truth, which involves the way universalistic morality is made livable and secure by its being embedded within more rational, dyadic modern institutions. The individualistic shape of agency that had been developed in early modern Europe was in the process of giving way to a more dyadic shape of life in which individualism could be cease to be self-defeating. The very existence of monadic rights and duties could be real (or "actual") only within a com-plexly structured set of dyadic rights and duties, and thus, the Greek ideal of self-sufficient subjectivity as sustainable only in a certain political and social order could be realized in a modern and thoroughly non-Greek way. The British, French, Dutch, and German examples were all fair expressions of this new shape of self-conscious life in which individuals freely associated with each other in terms of the principles embodied within a rational political order. Or, again, at least so Hegel thought.

The idea that Germany had pushed the emerging monadic moral order to its breaking point and then resolved it by returning to its anchor in something like Protestant secularized Christianity and its emphasis on the necessity of our involvement with each other in a shape of life marked the difference in the German and the French responses to the breakdown of the *ancien régime*. As Protestant countries, the Germans and the English had long since, as Hegel bluntly put it, "finished their revolution."[157] The principle of monadically conceived individuals had slowly been displaced for them since the ideal of the individual confessing to other, equal individuals rather than to a priest had taken root.[158] Where this had not been established institutionally, the principle remained that of individuals conceived as "atoms" sharing a common space where they interacted.[159] Where the "atomic" conception of social individuals dominated was where the Revolution played out. (As Hegel notes, in France, Spain, and in Italy—Naples and Piedmont—and, he says in passing, "Ireland is also to be counted" as having the conditions for such a revolution.[160])

Where Hegel speaks of the Protestant versus the Catholic religion in these contexts, he makes it clear that he thinks that history has moved to the point where a modern state must not have its final authority resting on a church or residing in church officials: "It is indeed a matter of the most profound wisdom to entirely separate the laws and constitution of the state from religion, since bigotry and hypocrisy are to be feared as the results of a state religion."[161] However, the basic practices and shape of self-conscious life cannot be separated from the kind of political order of which one is speaking, so religion still plays a key role. Thus, even though in the Revolution the French had put more or less entirely correct principles into place (with their "declaration of the rights of man and of citizens"), they remained merely principles without the necessary practical backing in the practices that make up a shape of life. For a modern constitutional state based on freedom, the shape of life must have the kind of social or "dyadic" shape that he thinks has arisen in those places informed by the more Protestant way of comprehending one's place in the whole.

What holds the modern constitutional state together are the dispositions—

the *Gesinnungen*, or what might be better called the "cast of mind"—present in the lives of the agents who live under that common order. Such a cast of mind exists not just where all individuals each assent to the same principles but where they for the most part genuinely share an order of thoughts within a combination of passion and principle. Where the cast of mind is "atomic," monadic, the virtues can only be seen as tendencies to follow the correct set of rules. From that and the idea that each is an "atom," the logic leading to the guillotine is, as Hegel reconstructs the story, not that long a story. Since the revolutionary society can hold together only if people have internalized the habit or disposition to adhere to the principles of the revolution—to exhibit revolutionary virtue—it is crucial to be on the look-out for those lacking such a disposition, those who do share the right cast of mind. Once the state and the government realizes it has to investigate not merely whether behavior is lawful but also whether the cast of mind is correct, tyranny follows, since one can always be under suspicion for having the wrong cast of mind. Thus, the "atoms" of Revolutionary France seeking freedom but lacking the dyadic structure that grows out of a Protestant way of life only had the principle of reason taken to be guided by something like "utility." On that principle, it can well turn out that some must suffer so that the whole can prosper, so that Robespierre could say consistently with that point of view, "Louis must die, that the republic can live." None of that would be necessary, so Hegel thought, where individuality was to be respected as a matter of social union, as in the Protestant countries. For them, he says, "the revolution is over . . . in terms of their external constitutions the protestant lands are very different, for example, Denmark, the Netherlands, England, Prussia; but the essential principle is present that everything in the state ought to be validly in force, must proceed from insight, and thereby be justified."[162]

The situation in Europe in Hegel's own day—in 1830–1831, in the lectures where he spoke of the matter—had to do with what he termed the "bankruptcy" of liberalism—"first, of the grand firm in France, then its branches in Spain and Italy."[163] By "liberalism," Hegel meant the post-1815 French liberalism which for some of its adherents drew on the principles of Jeremy Bentham's utilitarianism. (Bentham had even been made an honorary citizen of France in 1792.) Bentham's ideas were influential in certain opposition circles in French life after the final collapse of Napoleonic rule in 1815.

However, they were never the dominant trend—even before 1815, French liberals such as Benjamin Constant had in fact subjected Bentham's approach to fierce criticism. (Late in his life in the 1830s, in one of the less probable meetings in history, Bentham himself tried to convince Hegel's friend and ally, Eduard Gans, that Gans the Hegelian was really on the same page as Bentham's own liberalism. It is not clear that Bentham understood just how Gans as a Hegelian might have deeper views that were at odds with his own views.)[164]

"Liberalism" was in Hegel's day a new concept. It was hardly in use anywhere at all before the 1810s. (Thus, those who in our own day are brought under the rubric of "liberal" thinkers, such as Hobbes, Locke, Hume, or even Kant, were not for those of Hegel's day really thought of as "liberals" at all.) The rubric of "liberalism" had in particular come to characterize certain aspects of the post-1815 French regime, even though a great number of the people in that regime who characterized themselves as "liberals" (or were so characterized by others) actually thought of themselves as standing in opposition to the regime. Hegel sarcastically characterizes the French governmental system from between the Congress of Vienna to the July Monarchy—1815–1830—as a "fifteen year farce." The constitutional document under which the government of France supposedly operated from 1814–1830 was itself given by the king, Louis XVIII (brother of the guillotined Louis XVI). Its terms were fashioned so as to create the fiction that the revolution of 1789 had never really happened and that the royal succession was continuing as if it had always been there. The "Charter," as it was called, mimicked the English setup of two houses and a king with representative government, but it had no democracy. It was quasi-liberal in that it recognized careers open to talent, civil equality, a free press (after a fashion) and freedom of worship (with the Catholic church nonetheless officially entitled to be the established church), but it was also non-liberal in its insistence on the power and status of the monarchy.[165] It was thus based on the strained idea that the Revolution never happened and that the major results of the Revolution were to be incorporated into the new regime pretending to be the old regime.

The other fiction underlying its legitimacy was that all the parties—taken as the sum total of all the rational individuals living under the regime—had agreed to its terms. However, it became very clear very quickly that the regime of the "Charter" was more of a temporary cease-fire rather than a truce between the adherents of the *ancien régime* and the secular "liberals" who looked to 1789 as their year of birth. Such liberalism is based on, as Hegel put it, "the atomistic principle, the principle of singular wills, which maintains that everything that happens should emerge out of their express power and have their express consent."[166] Liberalism, on its own abstract terms, could not conciliate the two opposing groups. The die-hard adherents of the *ancien régime*—the "ultras" as they were called—wished to see the Church and the nobility restored to what they imagined to be its traditional and rightful authority. They found no middle ground with the "liberals"—who were known as the *Doctrinaires*—who firmly held that the modernity of civic equality which the Revolution had brought into existence was not to be sacrificed. To that end, they pushed for an interpretation of the "Charter" that made it seem to call for limited monarchy and civic equality with something like a kind of Benthamite utilitarianism undergirding its policies. The whole edifice came tumbling down in a matter of days in 1830, with the "Charter" being replaced by a new, much more emphatically "liberal" social order, and the Bourbon king (by this time, Charles X) being dispatched to exile in England in favor of an *Orleaniste* king (Louis Philippe), who quickly became known as the "bourgeois king." That was to last until 1848, at which point "liberalism" made an even more forceful entry on the scene, contra to Hegel's prediction of its bankruptcy. At that point, "liberals" in France had also distanced themselves from Bentham's utilitarianism, a distance that never really got closed again.

Hegel's prediction of "liberal" bankruptcy was thus far off its mark. His critique, however, retained some of its force. The new modern order where "all are free"—the shape of spirit which underlay the revolutionary order in which the rights of man was the new banner—required more than just setting up principles and assuming the parties would agree. It required a new set of practices and institutions that would produce the requisite union of passion and principle. If the new "bourgeois" order was to succeed, and people were, for example, supposed to be inclined on rational grounds to trade, bargain and compromise with each other, then people needed something to trade, and the bargains they struck had to fit with people's expectations as being morally preferable to the alternative of continuing to fight. The psychology of mutual respect had to be in play, and an appeal to abstract principles alone would not necessarily bring it into play. The form this problem took in Hegel's day did not seem to have been overcome in France, or, for that matter, even to be on the horizon of being overcome.[167]

The liberals grasped the impossibility of repressing pluralism, and they wished in principle to merge that with a respect for different casts of mind and to throw into the mix the ideal of individual self-improvement. However, the "ultras" saw no reason to submit to such a bargain with the opposition "modernists." They understood that the modern shape of life spelled the end of the *ancien régime,* and they, at least, were still ready for a fight. In that way, the conflict between "ultras" and "liberals" seemed for the time being to be beyond reconciliation in France. The "liberals" put their faith in reason and the rational administration of government by something along the lines of utilitarian thought, but so Hegel argued, that could not suffice to overcome the conflict. For there to be the genuine acceptance of the liberal principle of mutual respect, such a principle had to be a living part of a rational practice. Otherwise, the conciliation could not succeed, or, as he put it, "it is a false principle that the fetters which bind right and freedom can be broken without the emancipation of conscience—that there can be a revolution without a reformation."[168]

For the impasse, Hegel blamed Catholicism and its nonmodern insistence on authority that was beyond rational criticism. As it were, on Hegel's interpretation, the standoff was between the Catholics, who adhered to the principle "Thy will be done," and the liberals, who held to the principle "My will be done." That put them both absolutely at odds with each other, and it meant that the liberal appeal to administrative rationality was bound to fail in light of such intransigence. Such obduracy in the confrontation of religion and public practice was not at least in principle the case, he held, in Protestant countries.

Alas, Hegel was succumbing to something like wishful thinking in sticking to his views about how German protestant worldliness was now more or less clearly taking the Dutch path. Armed with the 20/20 hindsight of those living later, it is not hard for us to see that Hegel was being unfoundedly optimistic in his views on how deep and how widespread was the conviction in German life that reason now ruled and the princes were mere figureheads.[169] Not all Germans, and certainly not all the noble elite, and surely virtually none of the Prussian royal elite thought that the prince's "will is worthy of respect" only when it conforms to a kind of post-Enlightenment rationality, nor did the cast of mind run deeply that no German prince could even get away with ruling in contravention of the principles of reason itself. It was not the case that this commitment to a form of reason in everyday life had by then become so widely accepted that it had counted as a fact, and not merely an aspiration, in the German shape of life.[170] In reality, the "rights of man" still remained far more of a distant ideal than a living reality in German life. Even Hegel himself near the end of his life began to have worries about whether things were starting to fall apart in his own time. Nonetheless, his belief that the principles of "justice as social freedom" had so set themselves firmly at root in the modern world even led him to conclude that "in Europe nowadays each nation is bounded by another and may not of itself begin a war against another European nation."[171] He was right about the utter irrationality of such a war, but he was, alas, dead wrong in thinking it therefore would not happen.[172]

5

Infinite Ends at Work in History

෨෬

Substances and Subjects?

The nature of temporal human subjectivity itself did not imply on its own that the French Revolution had to happen. Nor did it imply that Rome had to collapse, nor that feudal monarchy had to fade out into constitutional monarchy.

Even if there were such a thing as a people who just happened to possess a standing desire to achieve freedom—of the kind that the mythical *Germanen* were supposed to have had but which needed to be disciplined into the rule of law—such a standing desire itself would not guarantee that those events had to take place. There is no argument—or at least no discernibly good argument—in Hegel that supports the conclusion that these events, or even ones similarly like them, had to occur by virtue of some kind of metaphysical / causal necessity. Thus, the only conclusion is that the French Revolution, indeed the whole path to modernity, was not necessary at least in the sense that it did not have to happen in any conceptual sense implied by the very nature of subjectivity, *Geist,* itself. The modern world was not willed by fate.

Where then is Hegel's case for any kind of necessity in history?

Hegel's broad claims for his philosophy of history have to do with the success or failure of some other big claims he makes. First and foremost is the claim made in the *Phenomenology* that everything hangs on apprehending and expressing the true not just as *substance* but equally as well as *subject*"—as Hegel stresses, it is not just "some things" but "everything" depends on that view.[1]

This has several sides to it. First, there is the extended argument of the *Science of Logic* that a comprehension of the objectivity of things requires an equal comprehension of the subjectivity of the subjects making the judgments about objectivity. This is not the claim that the existence of things depends on the existence of minds, nor even that the existence of "mere" things is somehow "perfected" by the addition of minded creatures to the furniture of the universe. According to the *Logic,* very roughly, to make sense of things, we necessarily judge in two general ways—in terms of "Being" or "Essence," that is, by pointing out, classifying, generalizing, or counting; and by explaining things in terms of some underlying condition that is not immediately apparent in the mere observation of them and which ultimately requires various modal concepts (possibility, necessity, etc.) to make sense of itself. These two metaphysical structures of making sense of things require us to make sense of making sense, to look at the conditions in which we can say that sense has genuinely been made. (That is the logic of "Concept," and is thus capstone to the three "books" of the *Logic*: Being, Essence, Concept.) This thereby requires us to understand the role of the "concept" in making sense, and that way of speaking of the necessity of the "concept" works out into speaking of the necessity of self-consciousness in judgment.[2] To put it more in the form of slogans: Without an account of self-conscious subjectivity, we cannot make sense of how we could make sense of objectivity (which is very different from claiming that without our conceptual activities, there could be no such things as rocks and sea salt).[3] The *Logic* has to do with the intelligibility of our judgments about the world and the intelligibility of those judgments themselves.[4]

Second, given the *Logic's* account, Hegel's case for some kind of conceptual necessity in history comes down in part to his case for how it is necessary to move from making sense of things to making sense of making sense and how the conditions for that kind of reflection depended the formation of new institutions and practices in history. Hegel first made that kind of argument in the 1807 *Phenomenology* as the introduction to the standpoint of the *Logic* (or, as he also put it there, as the "ladder" one climbed to arrive at such a standpoint).

Third, there is also Hegel's more general argument that there are not merely sets of finite ends in history, there are also infinite ends at work. The most basic is that of the infinite end of self-comprehension.[5] Such an end is not one for which the other ends are simply means to it, nor is the final infinite end inclusive of all those other ends—not everything is an instance of a striving for self-comprehension—nor are those other ends approximations to that end. Such an infinite end can be actualized and manifested at various times in better or worse ways.

Fourth, if the move from "substance" to "subject" requires an infinite end to make sense of itself, that leaves it open as to whether a further case can be made that there has actually been a form of progress in actualizing that end in history—that we comprehend more clearly what it would mean to be actualizing that end. Hegel's argument is that although world history is not a "Whig" story of steady and unrelenting progress, there is nonetheless progress that has been made. This has come to pass through the ways in which people, working out of their own path-dependent ways of comprehending things, have been compelled to understand themselves not merely as creatures simply caught and swept up in a temporal river but as each possessing a kind of capacity for self-reflection and limited subjectivity in practical life.[6]

As Hegel realizes, one of the more contentious aspects of the view he put forth in his *Philosophy of Right* is that this work systematically reconstructs the "elements" out of which the modern social and political order builds itself. The obvious questions are: Why those elements and not others, and why those elements in that particular shape and not other shapes? Hegel's short answer: History. That in turn raises the equally obvious set of questions about the putative rationality of those elements themselves and whether they even can be rationally brought together or whether the clashes among them make a habitable modern life impossible. For example, Marxists who followed in Hegel's wake accused him of reconstructing merely the elements of an order based on bourgeois private property, itself based on the exploitation of the laboring classes, which falsely declared itself to be a system of freedom. Even if one rejects the specifically Marxist accusation, the overall charge is still obvious.[7] Another obvious worry is whether the pressures to assemble the "elements" that are on the plate because of path-dependent history inevitably push Hegel's theory into collapsing into a kind of self-defeating relativist historicism.

Like any path-dependent view, Hegel's philosophy of history has to start from some point from which the path takes shape, and the worry is about the arbitrariness of such a starting point. As we have seen, although his account embraces all of world history—involving some particularly unsatis-factory chapters on Africa, China, India, Persia, and Egypt—his real starting point is ancient Greece, which lays down the starting point from which the path in which he is interested supposedly begins.[8] Even if one grants that there is a logic to what develops out of such a starting point, that it was that particular point which developed as the starting point cannot itself be a matter of logic.

There are two reasons for taking this arbitrary starting point. One is ret-rospective and comes out of Hegel's more systematic, theoretical approach. On that approach, found in the *Logic,* there is an argument to the effect that the logic of the concept (aptly called by Hegel the "subjective" logic) is that of correct inferences and mappings of various coherences. A subject is an entity that, to put most abstractly, moves in the space of such reasons and is more than merely an individuated entity (as in "Being") that manifests itself in various appearances and causes itself to act by virtue of its intentions (as in "Essence"). A subject is both of those things, but as living in a normative space, it is also not just those things, and its self-conception of itself as such a normative creature changes the way it thinks of its individuation and of the way it manifests itself.[9] A self-conscious subject is not just an individu-ated being causing itself to act with an element of self-consciousness and rationality added onto it. Our being is transformed by our self-consciousness. We are rational animals, not animals with rationality bolted down onto our organic lives.[10] Although we are what we are only in terms of a collective enterprise, we are also individuals who manifest our inwardness in certain ways and who are responsive to reasons (the logic of the concept), and ulti-mately to ideas of what it is to be a "true" subject (to which we shall return).

Ultimately, the logic of Hegel's *Logic* pushes it to an "Idea" of itself—roughly, the unity of metaphysical and more concrete concepts—as such an individuated normative creature that is embodied in a particular social space in a historical period. When it acquires such an "Idea" of itself, agency becomes explicitly "subjectivity." That is just what first shows up as a live option, so Hegel thought, in Greece. The shape it specifically took was indeed contingent and shaped by all kinds of arbitrary factors, but the "elements" of such a conception of subjectivity as self-consciousness were now elements on the agenda of world history.

That itself at least raises the suspicion that it might just amount to little more than a kind of self-celebration, something like the idea that the real contribution of such past shapes of life was just to be the Mini-Me's of us. It also does nothing to assuage any further worry that however we judge the Greeks to be, it is a matter of huge amounts of historical contingency that those same Greeks were subordinated by the Romans, and that "Europe" resulted out of the cataclysms resulting from the collapse of Roman imperialism and the failures of feudal monarchy thereafter.

True Subjectivity?

The second reason for the arbitrary starting point in Greece has to do with the philosophy of history itself. Greece is Hegel's real starting point because it is the arbitrary place where, on his account, what became the agenda of world history began. It is in Greece that the concept of freedom makes its first appearance on the historical stage. It does this at first negatively, namely, as the concept of what it is that the slave has lost or that of which he is deprived (as in Aristotle's earlier cited dictum that "it is the mark of a free man not to live at another's beck and call").[11] It receives its positive meaning as "self-sufficiency," independence, which again is captured by Aristotle's fundamental conception that political justice is only to be "found among men who share their life with a view to self-sufficiency, men who are free and either proportionately or arithmetically equal."[12] To be independent, one had to be able to be free from dirty work and thereby able to participate as an equal in the life of the polis. Greek freedom thus ultimately meant "being your own person." However, Greek freedom not only was continuous with slavery, it required it. Greek practice simply obscured the fact that when all is said and done, that slavery is the subjection of people by force into being the tools and instruments of others.[13] In terms of the "Idea" of freedom, freedom as individual independence runs directly into the fact that in the unity of concept and reality, some can be independent only if others are dependent on them.

The Greeks did not, of course, invent slavery. Many other societies used slaves (or at least some form of forced labor) to do the dirty work or perhaps even to give some people the pathological psychological pleasure of having the power to dispose of others. The Greeks, however, made it especially problematic to have slaves because they, the Greeks, also developed the ideas of freedom and political self-rule. For example, for Hegel, just as it was for many other commentators since, it was clear that Aristotle's defense of natural slavery (on the basis of some people lacking the capacity for full deliberation) ran headlong into conflict with Aristotle's own views that "since slaves are people and share in rational principle, it seems absurd to say they have no virtue."[14] Greek thought and Greek life ran into a nonavoidable conflict with each other, and it was not a conflict they could resolve within their own terms.

For that reason, although the Greeks came upon a novel concept, that of freedom, they did not have its true "Idea"—that "Idea" of freedom, Hegel says, "was not possessed by the Greeks and the Romans, Plato and Aristotle, also not by the Stoics. On the contrary, they knew that people were actually free only through birth (as citizens of Athenians or Sparta), or by way of strength of character, through higher education, or through philosophy (the wise are free also in chains and as slaves)."[15] They understood that being free was to be your own person, but they did not comprehend that one could genuinely be one's own person only in a world where all were entitled to be their own persons. In the Greek conception, one was free if one could participate as a citizen in the deliberations in the polis since only in such practice were one's actions the manifestations of one's own thoughts and not subject to the external authority of another person. No Greek citizen was required to say to another citizen, "Thy will be done." Such a status was possible for those citizens because of Greek slavery.

The Greek concept of subjectivity required freedom, and thus it also required slavery. The free person was free only in possessing authority over others who in turn had no claim to authority vis-à-vis him, but that freedom became fully real only when he was able with other such free men (women being excluded) to participate in the democratic participation in the polis. In that context, free of being commanded by any others in the polis, he was free to be his own person in terms of what he acquiesced in and what he struggled for by means of speech and rhetoric and not violence. This tension-laden system was held together by an archaic sense of justice that depended on their being a cosmic order to things that laid out offices for each such that it underwrote the hope that if each were do what was absolutely required of them in their office, the whole would spontaneously harmonize with itself. Why that was the case and not something else was itself beyond the grasp of reason. It was just the way things eternally were.

The concept of free but natural agency thus took on a determinate historical shape. A just order involved equality, even though the cosmic order held that the natural differences among individuals mandated that those of different orders receive their due in highly different ways. Subjectivity assumed a particular historical shape: The true shape of subjectivity was for that view that of a self-sufficient male individual who emerged out of private life and actualized his freedom in his public participation in a small, face-to-face democracy in which the only rule was that of spontaneity and persuasion. Only such men manifested true subjectivity.[16]

Hegel's conception of true subjectivity rests on his conception of how subjectivity is established in his *Logic* as consisting of an individual substance occupying a principled space of reasons and exercising its powers within it. As this is fleshed out—as it is made more concrete, as Hegel would prefer to put it—it becomes the conception of a historically bound subject who, moving within a determinate social space, is constrained by her past, absorbed in her present web of commitments, and oriented to her future. The "Idea" of subjectivity is thus the concept of what would be the true realization of such a concept of subjectivity, that is, what would be the best actualization of such a concept in certain determinate historical conditions.[17] (This is Hegel's post-Kantian transformation of the Aristotelian conception of what makes for the most flourishing, best-realized conception of a human.) The concept of subjectivity, as living in a normative social space, cannot do without such a conception of what constitutes better and worse realizations of that concept since being a rational subject and bringing oneself under the concept of rational subject are one and the same for the self-conscious primates we are. Thus, he says what might otherwise be rather puzzling: "This Idea itself is as such the actuality of people, not something that they thereby *have* but something that they *are*."[18]

What undoes the Greek conception of subjectivity is the way it is pushed into its own ultimate unintelligibility. The Greek conception was, in the somewhat idiosyncratic Hegelian sense, not fully actual, that is, was not fully *wirklich* in that it did not have the right kind of effectiveness. It is not that its general "concept" of itself was at odds with itself in any obvious way (so that would show up clearly in an analysis of itself). It is that its "Idea" of itself—its concept as actualized, as the "unity of the concept and objectivity"—could not intelligibly be conceived. For the Greeks, as for the Romans, and as for most of European civilization (along with its offshoots in North and South America and the Antipodes), freedom meant command of others without being oneself commanded by them, and that conception was the worm in the apple for all of them.

It was a matter of contingency that Rome appeared on the scene, and it was equally a contingent matter that Rome took up various Greek achievements in the way it did. However, that it did set in motion a kind of logic to the Greek conceptions of self-sufficiency, freedom, and slavery. That much of Roman civilization survived through its transformation into Christianity is equally contingent. However, that path that was taken from pagan Greece to imperial Rome to Christian "Europe" had a logic to it which involved the development of a different ideal of justice as having to do with something new, the "infinite worth" of each individual, whether master or slave. As Hegel phrases it,

> For in the Christian world, the subject is not to be grasped as a mere accident of the divinity but as an *infinite end* in himself, so that here the universal end, divine justice in pronouncing damnation or salvation, may appear at the same time as an immanent matter, as the eternal interest and being of the singular individual himself. . . . in relation to God and in the Kingdom of God he is in and for himself an end in himself.[19]

However, that it was also equally contingent that this became the core as what came to be "Europe" turned out to be even more contingent than Hegel himself thought. The freedom-loving, loutish *Germanen* supposedly took up the central idea of Christian freedom and laid the roots for the development of an infinite concern with justice into a concern with justice as realizing the freedom of all. They were, unfortunately, a myth.

Nonetheless, if Hegel's arguments about mastery and servitude work, they serve to show how the conception of freedom as complete independence (and thus as requiring command over others) itself breaks down under its own weight as it tries to make sense of itself especially in light of the resistance on the part of the oppressed or those who were left out of the story.[20] It also shows the very powerful motives that those who are "masters" would need to have to distract themselves and to obstruct any deep effort to make sense of themselves. Once the Greeks had put freedom on the map as a way of thinking about justice, there was a push toward justice as equality and as the mutual recognition of the freedom of all, an actualization of the ideal of each being "his or her own person"—or, in Hegel's own terms: "These rights, demanded in the name of what we have described as the absolute end of reason and as self-conscious freedom, are thereby classed as absolute ends like those of religion, ethics, and morality."[21] After that, it was a matter of contingency that "freedom" got taken up and worked into the web of commitments so that it became the watchword of modern life. There was no necessity in history that such events had to transpire the way they did, but there was a necessity to the argument that only such a conclusion would have made ultimate sense and would have represented progress in the comprehension of subjectivity.

The way things makes sense is a matter for the *Logic,* of what the conditions of intelligibility are in the first place. What the *Logic* cannot determine are all the particular ways and paths the items of world history had to follow for it to end up making sense in just that way. For the Hegelian system, it is a contingent fact about history that it does make such sense, but the way it makes sense is not itself a contingent factor.

In Hegel's radical historical view, the claim that "all are free" is retrospectively true even though in earlier periods, it could not be seen to be true, nor was it a practical possibility at those times. For those operating under the demands of an order of thoughts in which only "some are free," it seemed to be false that "all are free," and it was true in that specific practical order that not all were or could be in actuality free. So the thought would have gone: If the economy requires slaves, or if the feudal order requires natural subordination, then it simply could not be true that "all are free." What turned out to be false was that order itself, and it came to be false when it could no longer be in self-agreement, when it broke down on its own terms. The older order of "some are free" failed not because it failed to live up to its ideal—in many ways, it more than succeeded and left in its wake great monuments to itself—but because its ideal turned out itself to be false. Only when "spirit" has changed and the resulting concatenation of passion and principle has also thereby changed, can it be actually true that "all are free," true not merely as a concept (a possibility) but as an "Idea," as a reality.[22]

Rather than arguing for an unchanging core to ethics or morality that is timeless, Hegel opts for the idea that the only timeless core is that of subjectivity in the more abstract conception to be found in the *Logic,* which itself develops the claim that such universal concepts must particularize themselves to be intelligible. We bring the form of self-consciousness (that is, of "being-for-itself") to bear on our lives, and that formal distinction makes us into rational animals, not just animals with rationality tacked on.[23] This is a "form" from which determinate contents follow historically. The moral dimension emerges out of the ways in which various shapes of life provoked within themselves struggles for recognition, which themselves distilled into arbitrary constellations of power and command (into various relations of mastery and servitude).

One of the innovations of the Greek world was in effect to provoke the establishment of "morality" as reasons whose authority binds all rational subjects, not just those of a more limited, "ethical" community.[24] However, as the concept of morality came more and more into conflict with the realities of politics—involving the structure of rulership and therefore of the real authority of command—the result was another innovation, that of the political ideal of "all are free," that nobody by nature was required to live under the arbitrary compulsion of another. What counted as justice shifted its shape from justice in a "cosmic order of things" to "justice as an organization of freedom," and that itself was embedded within the larger purpose of spirit's making sense of what it is to be spirit. The eternal "Idea" of justice is that of an order where everybody is where they are meant to be. In the modern world, that is an order that emerges from the institutional life of freedom and does not reflect a kind of cosmic ordering of things. (In what would most likely be surprising to Hegel himself, "justice as freedom" has since his own time even widened out into a critique of racial and gender injustice.)

Unlike the sphere of nature, history is the arena where "spirit"—as human collective mindedness—can innovate with regard to its truths. The laws of motion in nature remain true whatever spirit does, but the status of subjectivity depends on spirit's own work. For spirit, although not for nature, Hegel subscribes to Goethe's idea (which Goethe puts in the mouth of Faust): *Im Anfang war die Tat*—for history, in the beginning was the deed (and not the "word," as the Gospel of John has it).[25]

Justice and Self-Knowledge in History?

To put to work a metaphor that if pressed would pop like a soap bubble: Hegel has a kind of "big bang" conception of the development of the ethical and the moral. There is an unchanging principled core to subjectivity that underlies the way history developed so as to make it retrospectively true that each subject possesses an inherent standing. That core has to do with the "form of self-consciousness" that we bring to experience and action. He underlines this very point in his lecture notes:

> The religiosity and ethicality of a restricted sphere of life (for example, that of a shepherd or peasant) in their concentrated inwardness and limitation to a few simple situations of life, have infinite worth; they are just as valuable as those which accompany a high degree of knowledge and a life with a wide range of relationships and actions. This inner focal point . . . remains untouched [and protected from] the noisy clamor of world history, and not only from external and temporary changes, but also from those produced by the absolute necessity of the concept of freedom itself.[26]

This "untouched inner center" emerges as of "infinite worth" only in history as the emergence of human mindedness takes its shape, working out its relations of independence and dependence in the context of the natural dependencies already there in human nature. The "untouched inner focal point" is what, so Hegel thinks, is the "unmoved mover" of the value that rational subjectivity possesses.[27] It is where the argument stops in the normal regress of reason-giving. It functions a bit like a first principle, except that what follows from it is what historically follows in the path-dependent course of events that make up human history.[28] The idea is that once moral beings have made their appearance on the planet, new areas of value show up that are not merely harms to interests or well-being narrowly conceived but show up as maltreatments of the things to which a rational being must be committed (that is, to those matters which they come to find in historical time are practically unavoidable). There is, however, no getting behind this principled core to derive it from some prenormative state. As Hegel scribbled in a note to himself, the formation of people into subjects "is historical, i.e., belongs in time, in the history before freedom."[29] There is no "basic action" that establishes at some identifiable point when human life becomes "spirit." As spirit, human life is always, already in historical time as a problem to itself.

For subjects to come to see themselves and each other as "infinite ends" required a struggle and a demand that others recognize them as such and that such a form of equal and reciprocal recognition required a proper institutional and practical context if it was ever to be real and not just a "mere" ideal. The Christian conception had us all as sons and daughters of God working to carry out the will of the father. In that context, we remained somewhat passive, receiving our due from a sovereign ruler. When we demanded recognition from others, we became agents, not merely passive recipients of justice. Subjects had to struggle to become equal, in which individuals become moral persons as well as being agents and demand that others treat them as such. Without that "inner focal point," that would not be possible. Without the development of the proper practices and institutions, it could never become actual. Without history, people could never become their "Idea."

The obscure origins of the history of reason-giving and reason-demanding primates are a metaphorical "big bang" of subjectivity.[30] That consists in bringing the "form of self-consciousness" to work within the context of rational animality. A metaphorical space of reasons has developed out of that origin into a mixture of logic and contingency, and new reasons appear as old ones go out of existence. Nor can just any ethical or moral set of considerations be developed. They emerge out of the human space of reasons, and they remain in it. The "universal" becomes more specific, and although the paths that particularization takes are contingent on a variety of

factors, the overall shape of the paths is subject to the demands of intelligibility. The concrete specifications of the more general normative demands
of the "true" and the "good" depend on the kinds of things that do not show
up, except at the most abstract level, in a *Logic*.[31] However, it is in the *Logic*
that the concept of such a principled entity, a "thinking subject," is to be
given its status as the "first principle"—the "infinite end" at work in history—and it is in the works that systematically follow the *Logic* that this
principled creature takes shape as perceiving a world around it and as
demanding recognition from other subjects.[32] (However, to finally pop the
soap bubble: the space of reasons is not "expanding" as the universe seemed
to do after the big bang. It has, however, been shape-shifting in terms of how
it retrospectively reshapes itself.)

Hegel's insistence on the details of history is thereby not ancillary to his
project. It is part of his theory that the relation between our most basic concepts and that of empirical reality is not in all cases that of a general rule and
its applications. (That is an appropriate matter for the more day-to-day operations of the intellect, not for the kinds of metaphysical clashes that emerge
out of the employment of our rational powers—it belongs to what he calls
"the understanding," as distinguished from "reason.") What counts as a
practical reason is the significance that things have for creatures, which
depends on the possibilities open to such creatures, and since self-conscious
subjects change their possibilities in history, what will be a reason for them
will also change.[33] Reasons are thus part of life, not for any particularly
metaphysically abstruse grounds, but because significance (and the possibility of failure) only arise against the background of the development of life
itself. On this view, the hare indeed has a reason to start running when it
sees the hawk descending, and the mantis has a reason to move when it
detects its prey. What neither the hare nor the mantis has is the ability to put
those reasons into anything like an inferential articulation, a narrative
account, or even a pictorial showing. That is a capacity that, as far as we
know, only self-conscious primates possess. Only self-conscious primates
can stich *"Gründe"* (reasons) into *"Vernunft"* (reason), not because "reason" is
something that such primates "have" in addition to their self-consciousness.
They are self-conscious reasoners, which is not an external property that
these primates "have" but a statement of what they as self-conscious primates "are." As Hegel himself states it, people "are" their "Idea."[34] Their

"Idea" is always full of tensions and potential breakdowns. Reason's meta-physical clashes become in history the clashes we have about who we, the genus that is aware of itself as a genus, are.[35]

What renders such self-conscious primates so very problematic is that they are also historical creatures, whose possibilities change for them by virtue of the institutions and practices they themselves develop, and who therefore make what counts as a reason into a moving target for reason itself. What counts as a reason for them depends on what possibilities they have, which depends on the kinds of bodies they have and on where they stand in a historical line. In each of those developments, subjectivity has a kind of Aristotelian "functionalist" standing: what it is to be a good subject is to be he or she who fulfills his or her function well, and that function of subjectivity itself concretely metamorphoses over historical time. "True" human subjectivity is that which fulfills its "function" best, and such a con-ception of "best" has developed in history. It reaches its high point of devel-opment when each person can be their own person, and that is possible only in certain types of social, moral, and political order.[36] In such social, moral, and political orders, there are the goods which constitute the elements of a satisfying life—a life, as we said, in which there are things of importance within the real powers of real subjects to achieve and thus are not merely possibilities available only in daydreams or ethereal longings for a better future.

It seems therefore that Hegel rejects a widespread and common concep-tion of what it means to be in possession of concepts. On the commonplace view nowadays, possession of a concept means that one can use a word in the appropriate way—that is, a concept is thought to be something like a rule, and if one has mastered the rule and its application, then one is in full possession of the concept. Thus, if one can use the word, "moral," or "red," or "action" in comprehensible English (or the equivalents in some other lan-guage) in a publically approvable way, one fully possesses the concept. On that view, there can be, of course, expert users of concepts—only the lawyer can tell if you have really signed something that is a contract—but even in those cases, if one knows how to apply a given concept-rule in the appropri-ate speech situations, one is said to possess the concept fully.

Hegel holds, on the other hand, that at least for some concepts—those involving what he calls speculative thought, that is, the basic concepts that make up the shadowy world of the "unconditioned"—there can be publically validated uses of the concept that are incomplete or not yet fully developed uses.[37] In those cases, one can use the word but not in the full sense, which itself only emerges at points in the future where it is more developed.[38] The concepts that fill out the speculative realm can be refined by being developed in ways that bring out implications and features that are not present in the original use, implications that only show up as the concepts are developed in practice.

Paradigmatic for this kind of development is the way in which the key concepts relating to the nature of subjectivity itself are developed in history. The original use of a concept for something having to do with the "unconditioned" is our conception of the object "in itself." As this conception of the object "in itself" develops in history, its internal tensions—even its contradictions—become more evident as the pressures such tensions put on self-conscious individuals and communities becomes less tolerable. As that happens, the concept itself comes up for grabs, and as it comes up for more contested use and development—as, in Hegel's language, it becomes "posited"—it comes to have features not originally present in its original usage but which build on and modify that usage. It is one thing to say that there have been basic conceptual changes in history—lots of people besides Hegel believe that—but, in many cases, these changes are conceived as responses to empirical difficulties with the concept, not the way in which use of concepts can be actualized in better or worse shapes. Rather, the speculative concepts themselves develop over time such that our possession of them discloses a different set of possibilities for us and thus a new concatenation of reasons.

The existent public criteria in any period for possessing a speculative concept and mastering it therefore do not exhaust its meaning. As these concepts develop historically, we sharpen and distill our grasp on the world they purport to disclose. The refinement of a concept "in itself" shows up as a refinement of our grasp of the authoritative nature of things, and, in Hegel's terms, therefore as a developmental grasp of the "absolute." Changes in the speculative concepts do not simply make explicit what was already there, nor are they the result of a more fine-grained analysis of the concept. Hegel puts this idea to use in his various metaphors hovering around the term, "organic": Failure, for example, to act on a reason has to be explained in one way similar to the way we explain disease—as something lying in the nature of things that prevents (or places barriers to) the organism's fitting the standards the lie within its shape of life. In the case of rational subjectivity, some of the problems with subjectivity do not lie in external factors (as in disease) thwarting the appropriate functioning of our powers of knowledge and action. Our powers can be thwarted in themselves when they impose impossible conditions on themselves or make the lives lived in terms of those reasons unlivable. This is where dialectic arises, not when we simply find ourselves holding incompatible empirical commitments. On the Hegelian view, that our speculative concepts in some cases can be not merely changed but rather more nearly brought to completion in terms of their own logic is itself generated out of the practical failures of a purely rule-following conception of concepts.

For Hegel in particular, this move to a view of the use of terms that commits us to the surprising thesis that mastery of a "speculative" term does not mean that oneself or anybody else in one's social realm fully understands the term. The more nearly complete comprehension is something that arises out the failure of the rule-bound civilizations of the past to make a place for any kind of deeper criticism of the rules. (For Hegel, that takes place in his mythical versions of Africa, China, and India.) That these civilizations were not the rule-bound, rigid shapes of life that Hegel took them to be does indeed invalidate that part of his history but not his more general point, which has to do with the way in which Greek slave society put freedom at center stage and thus brought to full light the tensions between Greek political life, self-sufficiency, compelled labor, and the goods of individuality. At that point in history, the speculative concepts showed up in a more nearly full view, and that made a difference in the way those worries about making sense of things became embedded in the comprehension of power and empire in Rome, and in the failures of "Europe," as self-consciously fashioning itself in light of "Rome," to make good on such ideas.

It is out of those failures that the language of true subjectivity acquires its dynamic such that it becomes more self-consciously an open question about what it is to be a true subject. That puzzle about true subjectivity itself comes to center stage in modern life, where the term becomes articulated as freedom manifested in, variously and in different contexts, self-development, authenticity, and noninterference, and as it comes to understand that freedom is part of being one's own person, being, as Hegel puts it, *"bei sich,"* at one with oneself, in one's actions.[39] That an infinite end can be specified in many different ways is at the heart of an infinite end. That it has been specified in these ways, such that there is a story of limited progress to be told cannot be read off of a mere analysis of that end. It requires turning to the facts of history to see if that kind of philosophical significance can be found in it, but one must have an account of what philosophical significance is in order to see if we find it.[40]

On Hegel's account, the movement of European history has led to the view that what turned out to be really at work in its background is a struggle over and a concern with justice, which in its development in history has turned into a conception of justice as requiring freedom.[41] The demand for justice eventually became a demand for emancipation.

This freedom within justice is not a finite goal for which, for example, current people must be sacrificed, since such a sacrifice in fact contradicts the concept of justice itself as it has developed. Nor is justice a goal like happiness, for which some will almost certainly have to be made unhappy so that others can be happy. Nor is it even something like Aristotle's infinite end of *Eudaimonia*. In fact, Aristotle, like all the ancients, thought that for this end to be actualized, some would have to be denied such flourishing, and even perhaps some have to be incapable of achieving it at all, namely, the natural slaves.[42] There is nothing in the logic of *Eudaimonia* that implies that all must have it. The defectiveness of that interpretation meant, or so Hegel argues, that the ancients really did not understand freedom very much at all in failing to see its connection to universality and therefore justice in a broader sense.[43] The ancients, so we could put it, had conceptions of freedom, but they did not comprehend it. For them, it was ultimately an awareness of what slaves lost and what it was that those who were not slaves possessed. They did not fully articulate that view, and thus, they lacked its proper "Idea." It follows from what Hegel says, since for him, "the only difference between African and Asiatic peoples and those of Greece, Rome and modern times is just this: That the latter know that they are free, that this exists for them. The former are also free, but they do not know it, and they do not exist as free,"[44] and since the "Idea" of freedom "was not possessed by the Greeks and the Romans, Plato and Aristotle, also not by the Stoics,"[45] it follows that once "the new, final banner was unfurled . . . that of the flag of the free spirit which is at one with itself . . . the flag under which we serve and which we bear,"[46] the major turning point in world history has to do with the advantages gained by modern Europeans who have come to comprehend the "eternal justice" of their world as consisting in a kind of commitment to the equal freedom of all. It is modern history—roughly that starting around 1687 or 1789, depending on whether one marks it at Newton's *Principia* or the French Revolution—that forms the most distinctive breaking point in history.

The Building Blocks of the Modern World?

Hegel was not, however, arguing that everything was therefore completely in order in the modern world. What he was after was the nonetheless audacious claim that in modern Europe as a whole, all the relevant parts, as it were, were in order and ready for assembly for a more nearly reconciled life. The particular "elements" for assembly consisted of the modern doctrines of rights to life, liberty, and property; the idea of a universalistic morality that relies heavily on finding one's place in a universal moral system; and the more determinate social formations of the modern family, civil society, and constitutional state that anchor the lives within those practices and give them a determinate purpose and shape. These "elements" make up the body of the considered moral and ethical judgments of modern people and the proprieties of the practices in which they are engaged.

In particular, he thought that although "rights" and "morality" were more or less the cornerstones of the building blocks of modern life, the shapes of ethical life (family, civil society, and state) were also the fundamental ways in which a modern shape of life could get a grip on human passions such that it would matter—and matter deeply—to people whether they lived in a modern world. Modern morality is fundamentally monadic in its structure. It represents the will "reflected into itself," defining its own rules of the right. Our relations to others within the modern "moral" system is thus mediated via these monadically understood obligations as resting on something like a system of rules. In its own self-understanding, the modern moral subject is thus fundamentally aimed at the status of rational independence and is thus ultimately driven to asserting claims about inviolable personal conscience as to how these monadically understood moral rules are to be interpreted and how they are to result in determinate obligations. On the other hand, in "ethical life," we have dyadic relations embodied in practices that enact the ways in which we are deeply dependent on others even for this very moral independence. Ethical relations are more like relations of justice—the "greatest" of the virtues," as Aristotle called it—as the ways in which we express and live our dependencies on others in nonetheless free ways. Ultimately, the motivations for the system of morality, taken as finding one's place in a universal system of rules, end up aiming at something abstract such as "the good," but that motivation itself withers when it is divorced from more determinate, "dyadically" conceived goods. Only such dyadic goods—those of ethical life, Sittlichkeit—can make the motivations to place oneself truly in the space of reasons within the system of universalistic morality and can thereby sustain such moral motivation. The form of self-consciousness, reflected into itself and striving to be moral from within its own resources, is driven out of itself to the goods presented to the will by others, and, as self-consciousness, both responds to those goods and is aware of itself as responding to those goods without there having to be any further reflective act. Hegel remarks that "from these reasons the moral must be taken into account prior to the ethical, although the moral puts itself forward in ethical life, as it were, only as an illness of the ethical."[47] To respond to moral reasons as reasons, one needs the practices of "ethical life" as embodying a kind of self-conscious practical know-how as involving the form of self-consciousness without there having to be a separate reflective act of consciousness.

Hegel's claim was not that the goods to be found in those ethical shapes represented something that people naturally wanted, nor that they seamlessly fit certain natural passions, but that they gave an appropriate purposiveness to an intelligible and concrete shape of life within the conditions of modernity. They took on the logical shape of self-conscious "life" for those people. Just as the natural species defines the goods for the individuals that fall under it, Geist, or self-conscious life, divides itself into various self-conscious "species"—the shapes of ethical life—within which certain matters function as the good of that "species." For Hegel, the modern bourgeois family, for example, and the ethos surrounding were not the natural expressions of some deep unchanging human nature. The bourgeois family did, however, give a determinate shape to sexual desire, to the demands of children and child raising, to issues of fidelity and trust, to the issues of faithfulness in generational continuities, and so forth. The shape it supposedly provides makes sense within (and only really within) the larger context of modern life and its other goods (the rule of law, constitutionalism, civil society, progress in the arts and sciences, etc.) along with its fitting into a scheme of rights and morality. Likewise, the characteristic virtues and vices of the modern subject where "careers are open to talent" and where the competitive nature of a market economy puts pressure on the development of one's character is not something that is natural to humans, such that barring some type of external obstacle, people will naturally develop into those kinds of characters. Such characters are integrally related to the bundle of goods that form the basic purposes which constitute such a society, and with issues about whether it is even good at all to be such a person, or whether such a life is ultimately genuinely inhabitable.

Hegel's view is thus neither the naïve nor the utopian view that, in the right social arrangements, duty and desire neatly fall into line with each other in such practices. His view is rather that the goods, rights, and duties embodied in the practices and institutions surrounding the modern family, the hurly-burly of market-driven civil society, and the contested politics of a constitutional state give people various ends that together structure a satisfying life that fully expresses both our independence from, and dependence on, each other. Parents may, for example, be frustrated with the recalcitrant child and may even feel aggrieved that because of that, they cannot do what they want to do; but on Hegel's terms, they can feel "satisfied" that in attending to the children's needs, they have acted in light of important ends to which they have committed themselves and that those ends can stand up to the acid test of reflection if they are so subjected. They are free in that they have made what really matters in the world into effective elements of their own lives, and for them to do that, a certain ensemble of passion and principle must be in place. That is, in carrying out those ends, they most likely have run up against the grain of certain desires of their own from time to time, but they have performed actions that mattered, that were up to them, for reasons of which they were conscious, and which, from the standpoint of a whole life, make sense (so that they have not committed themselves to a fool's errand). In acting on them as ends, sometimes in accordance with their other wants and sometimes not, they display and actualize their freedom.

They are at one with themselves in all the divisions and fissures that such a life brings with it.

It is a central part of Hegel's thesis that the concrete form in which justice is given a determinate shape and put into practice depends on the shape of life—the shape of "spirit"—in which it is enmeshed. The necessity that follows from the "Idea" of the proper and good ordering among people—of what counts as the proper order in a world containing subjects who are free—is different in a Greek conception of there being a cosmic order to things and the modern conception of subjects living in a disenchanted world. In one respect, it amounts to Hegel's own historicizing of Aristotle's claim that the virtue of citizens is relative to the constitution in question.[48]

The conclusion that one can draw from Hegel's conception of the modern concept is that just as the "master" and "servant" at the initial stages of the *Phenomenology* may be coming at each other from different systems, by virtue of the struggle, their own subjectivity (and therefore the final ends guiding their lives) become implicated with each in a shared enterprise. After the European imperialism of the nineteenth century had extended its grip all over the world, world history became even more definitively "world" history, even in a way that Hegel himself could not—and perhaps even did not want—to grasp. Just as the destinies of master and servant had become inseparable in his own system, the destinies of the world's people became more closely intertwined.

To many of Hegel's contemporaries, it was certainly not at all clear whether all the "elements" he singled out were themselves in order and, for many, it was not clear that these were indeed the right "elements" at all. Moreover, there were competing ways—both theoretical and practical—as to how these "elements" were to be combined and what, if any, the relations of subordination should be among them. The elements are what is given to us by history, and there are obviously different ways of arranging them into a picture of what modern life should look like. Utilitarianism, for example, offers one way, a holistic-oriented balancing and weighing of competing goods offers yet another, and Kantian theories of the "right" offer yet another way, and so forth.

Hegel took it as the task of his own philosophy to aid in resolving that question of how the "elements" are to be understood and ordered. (That is why his book on the topic, the *Philosophy of Right*, claims to provide the "*Grundlinien*," the base, as it were, on which a solid figure stands, or to shift the metaphor, the baselines in which a game is played.) The various "elements" are given a systematic treatment in terms of what significance they have for people operating within those practices with their associated values such that their attempts to make sense of what they are doing, as that takes concrete shape in practical activity and of what it means to be engaged in such a practice, can be put into a systematic shape. Hegel's own theory is, of course, one account of how these building blocks—these basic collective ends—are to be combined, how are they are to be explicated, and so forth, but it may not be the only account, and his own account is at least relatively independent of his account of how history led to this.[49]

Hegel's systematic account of how the "elements" were to be combined with each other was intended to show that certain combinations should be seen as rationally ruled out (and that failure to do so theoretically would eventuate in some kind of practical failure in the world of institutions and practices). Shapes of life that think of themselves as operating in a social space bounded only by exercising and respecting the basic rights of life, liberty, and property will find themselves in practical situations that are always threatening to descend into futility unless they move on to understanding themselves as not merely exercising and respecting rights but also as acting and judging from a moral point of view. Once they have taken on that extended understanding of what they are doing, they also change their understanding of what they were doing in the first place. The initial self-understanding is thereby "sublated"—it is put aside in its original form and preserved in a new form.

Hegel's own more daring claim was that a group that only understood itself as a community of moral subjects respecting each other's rights would itself generate its own contradictions unless it were associated with a more comprehensive view of how moral practice works in a social order of families, markets, civil associations, and representative constitutional government. In other words, only the whole consisting of rights, duties, and social goods would turn out to be intelligible, even though that particular whole had the elements it had because of the particular shape history had taken. Moreover, those elements and their arrangement were not just a fortuitous outcome.

That arrangement had an intelligibility to itself as resulting from the fortuitous circumstances of history. Such an order would be just and would be the proper "habitat" for the kinds of rational subject-primates we are.

Hegel was not making the argument that the world in which he lived was therefore already in order. Much of it was obviously not. As Hegel himself noted about the accusation against his own philosophy that it assumed everything was in a nice and tidy arrangement: "And who is not clever enough to see a great deal in his own surroundings which is in fact not what it ought to be?"[50]

To take one of the more salient ways in which the "Idea" can be at odds with itself: For centuries, people in the West (and beyond) took slavery to be problematic yet nonetheless legitimate.[51] The conventional wisdom, including that of some of the most prominent philosophers, was that the economy, the social world itself, simply could not work without such forced labor. In Hegel's own day, North America proclaimed itself to be the land of freedom, but its freedom rested on its use of its slaves. So Hegel's account went, the contradiction at work in such modern slave societies—between slavery as an economic necessity and a moral evil—had now, historically, been shown to be "sublated." The roots of the breakdown of the modern slave society were therefore now firmly planted. The "Idea" with its norm that "all are free" was at odds with the purported reality of the economic and social world—the so-called fact that some must forced to labor for others, and they do this best when they are owned as tools for the satisfaction of other's purposes. As the "Idea" had developed, that so-called fact came to be seen as what it was, namely, as merely a so-called fact, that is, not a fact at all. There was no possibility of reconciling the reality of slavery with the "Idea" of freedom.[52]

This of course did not mean, nor did Hegel take it to mean, that the slave societies of the new world were going to immediately vanish. The powerful economic interests of slave owners and of those who, although they did not own slaves, still benefitted from the goods that a slave society could offer them, meant that slavery would have to be abolished by force, not merely by argument. The institutions of American southern slavery also meshed well with the modern financial tools of free-market societies, so there was no "modernist-economic" impulse per se coming in from the outside to undo slavery.[53]

Nonetheless, however powerful the interests of the slave owners were and however much it suited others not to think about it, the practice no longer made any moral sense except for those for whom freedom still meant that others had to be radically dependent on them. Nor did Hegel take it to mean that markets on their own did all the work needed and could be relied upon to bring to an end that kind of human and moral horror. He certainly thought that for a market to be part of a "civil" society—a society based on decency in interaction—there had to be regulations on the working of the market that protected water supplies, food supplies, attended to public health and, among other things, continually restructured itself away from the practices of misleading and exploitative exchanges. Hegel took himself to have shown that the enduring ancient argument—that slavery's economic necessity simply had to be acknowledged alongside any squeamishness about its moral disagreeableness in some kind of "it is necessary, so make the best of it" way—had already fallen apart.[54] The economic necessity of slavery could no longer be a real issue, and its moral horror was clear to those thinking rationally.[55] In effect, existing slave societies could at that point only appeal to the primitive self-interest of slaveholders and to spurious theories of "natural slavery," which had now become clearly indefensible in terms of any rational conception of human subjectivity.[56]

Necessity in History?

Did Hegel make his case for necessity in history? If he has made his case for these theses about self-consciousness, the necessity for its always taking a determinate shape (Hegel's claim about the unity of the universal and the particular), about its determinate shape arising in a path-dependent way; and if his investigation of the facts supports the view that we have moved from a world in which there was no real "Idea" of freedom to a world in which the "Idea" is that "all are free," then his philosophical interpretation of history as developing different metaphysics of subjectivity can stake a claim for itself. It is more than simply an interpretative claim that from the standpoint we now occupy in the temporal river, we can make a plausible case that this is what it has all been about. It is the more audacious claim that a certain kind of "absolute" has come into view, and that is the view of the infinite end at work in all human life and in history itself. In saying that the

state is the "absolute purpose of reason," Hegel is not engaging in state worship (although in light of later developments, he certainly could have used
less inflammatory language).[57] He is rather saying that the modern concatenation of rights, moral duties, and social goods that are held together by
something like the modern constitutionalist state is itself a rational end,
something that can inform a whole variety of individual actions without all
particular persons actually having its as her intention to promote just that
end. The purpose of modern life is, in part, to effect the transition from individuals as those who are subjected to a royal or aristocratic order into "citizens" of a modern state, and there can be no citizens without such states.
The state, as the "final purpose" of such life, sets the boundaries of what
enterprises are rational. If one of the conditions of practical reason is that he
who wills the end must will the appropriate means, the other enterprises of
modern life that would make it impossible to sustain the aim of equal citizenship—such as lack of appropriate means of life or the denial of basic
rights—must be acknowledged to be irrational. For Hegel, patriarchal families were one such irrational enterprise.[58]

Hegel himself recognized that the abstraction, "the state," was itself perhaps too thin to secure allegiance to itself, and thus he thought that the additional motivation for giving allegiance to such an abstraction had to come
from the appropriate religion as the realm of "feeling" or "passion" so that a
workable conception of a wider, shared good could get a grip within the
fragile psychologies of individual people. The possibility that such passions
might become murderous had, he thought, been securely circumscribed by
the exhaustion brought on by the carnage of the "wars of religion" in
Europe. As a result, confessional pluralism was now an accepted fact of life,
or at least so he thought, and the more violent motivations brought on by
religious difference had thus been effectively silenced. The hindsight
afforded to later generations lets us see that Hegel rather substantially under-
estimated the potential for murderous violence that the nation-state under
the cover of "nationalism" could provoke. However, that the state, taken on
the model of the European nation-state, might have outlived its time in the
sun is also compatible with its once having been the appropriate particularization of such an "infinite end." A different particularized concatenation of
rights, morals, and goods might be the true "infinite end" at work in modern
history since Hegel's time.[59]

If the philosophical case can be made that the post-Kantian conception of self-consciousness and its importance cannot be found fully explicitly in the premodern world, and if that conception of self-consciousness makes a difference to self-conscious beings about how they lead their lives or think about their own institutions (and if that is buttressed by the conception of subjectivity as embedded in a fundamental historicity about itself), then the case for such an infinite end at work in history can also be made.

However, Hegel did not make his case for Africa, Asia, and the other "Orientals" he groups with those he thought lived in merely "impulse-driven" or "rule-following" civilizations. Since he got that part wrong, a substantial portion of his philosophy of history is deficient in terms of the measures Hegel himself set up to evaluate those claims. Indeed, if there are different structures of subjectivity at work in those shapes of life, then the philosophical comprehension of history would also have to change. Hegel would have to go back to the drawing board. This would greatly affect his claim to necessity in history: If the "Africans" and "Orientals" were not just failed rule-followers, then it remains entirely possible that a better examination of their own history would put different conceptions of subjectivity on the table for philosophical consideration. It would also mean that Hegel's view of the "elements" for the assembly of the modern world need a better case for themselves than Hegel has made. That they are what European history had handed down to itself by 1820, and that they were rational developments out of earlier European failures, would not be enough. That consideration would show that his system is still open, not merely in that it not the "end of history," but that it is not closed off even in the ways Hegel himself might have thought it was.

There are, of course, a good many of Hegel's other more specific theses that do not fare well in later light. Fortunately, Hegel himself already built a case for his other major philosophical conclusions about whether in our accounts of the world, we must move from substance to subjectivity—that we may not be content to make sense of things without having to make sense of making sense—and it is there that his core claims about history stand or fall. Our self-conscious lives began long ago with a comprehension of ourselves as "substance," as natural beings and as part of the larger cosmic order of things, and under the pressures we have put on ourselves, we have been compelled to understand our lives also as "subject," as agential, self-conscious, and bound to each other. History itself is about the particulars and details of that past and how it came to be practically unavoidable to see ourselves as "subject."

Hegel's account avoids falling into a careless historicism by virtue of its appeal to the infinite ends at work in subjectivity, but it maintains its strong historicist commitment by virtue of the way in which Hegel takes himself to have shown that the universal has to particularize itself—a thesis we could formulate rather abstractly as the notion that for speculative (philosophical) concepts, meaning is determined by use but not exhausted by use, such that within a certain historical development, such concepts can be developed into better actualizations. Hegel's type of philosophical history is not an a priori theory about how those historical particulars were necessitated to line up with each other, nor is it some happy-talk Whig account of progress, nor is it a self-congratulatory tale of progressive enlightenment and error-correction, nor is it the explication of any laws of history or any claims about how various regimes inevitably converge at some final point or inevitably lead to a certain result.[60]

It is rather an examination of the metaphysical contours of subjectivity and how the self-interpreting, self-developing collective human enterprise has moved from one such shape to another in terms of deeper logic of sense-making and how that meant that subjectivity itself had reshaped itself over the course of history. It is not a thesis about what constitutes true causality in history, nor is it even a thesis that unintelligibility causes such breakdowns. Hegel's philosophy of history is concerned with what various things mean to subjects, individually and collectively, in the historical configurations into which they are thrown. Subjects may indeed be caught in the wake of forces that they cannot control or only vaguely understand, and they may be operating in terms whose implications they do not fully grasp or comprehend at all. However, the Hegelian concern is with what it means for those subjects to be caught in that vortex yet still be acting self-consciously, and not with determining the causal conditions of the vortex into which they might be thrown.

The Hegelian philosophy of history argues that there is progress in history in the area concerning the bases of human subordination and the sense in which agents acquire and sustain an understanding of recognition—the Hegelian shorthand of "from one is free to some are free to all are free."

That in turn requires a comprehension of what it is to be a subject in the first place, and, so Hegel's thesis goes, that is itself, surprising as at first it sounds, a social and historically indexed status. In philosophical history, different shapes of subjectivity itself show up for our view. In such a philosophical history, we come to comprehend the reason why some things are on the ethical and moral agenda and why some things fall off the agenda altogether and what difference falling off and on makes to the rationality of what is left on the agenda, since we should, by the end, have a more comprehensive understanding of what concatenations of subjectivity go best with what kinds of institutions and practices.

The necessity that is to be found in history as philosophically comprehended is only that of the necessity of making sense of things and making sense of making sense and whatever necessity those two activities bring in their wake. These views about subjectivity depend on Hegel's more speculative claim that the "universal particularizes itself," that the sense of subjectivity we seek cannot be determined apart from the ways in which it has been concretely embodied. Philosophy as done only by the philosopher and history as done only by the historian turn out, in the Hegelian story, each to be one-sided. In those matters, the "abstract" and the "decidedly concrete" are the two sides that require the full coin for each to be intelligible. Each answers the question, "What does it mean to be human?" from different angles, and only the two together add up to a real figure.

History at first looks like what Hegel calls the "bad infinite": "A vast spectacle of events and actions, of infinitely varied constellations of nations, states, and individuals, in restless succession."[61] But, so Hegel's claim goes, as we understand the principle of the series—the infinite end of collective self-comprehension and different ways of being a human subject—the series becomes intelligible, not in all its details and certainly not in terms of predicting the future. We simply comprehend its point as it has emerged in the series itself: Self-comprehension of what it is to be a temporal, self-conscious being and a struggle over the right terms of our lives with each other. This takes shape in the various "shapes of spirit," the concrete concatenations of human biological and cultural life as these shapes themselves shift their shape over the centuries. As the people living though these developments and unfoldings try to make sense of this, they give shape to an "Idea" that itself ultimately has come to take the shape of justice as based on the principle that "all are free." This is a freedom in which a modern form of independence has taken root within a modern web of dependencies which is the very condition for that kind of independence and which is only real, effective—"actual," as Hegel would say—within those webs of dependencies. In its paradigmatic modern form, such a relation to self is mediated everywhere by our relations to others and within which ultimately the reality of being one's own person in civil, decent concert with others as mediated by the right set of institutions and practices is the object of the satisfactions of social and individual existence. To comprehend that requires looking at the details of the paths on which we are dependent for having brought us to where we are, whenever we undertake to determine what we might become. Even though justice and freedom have very rarely been front and center in the "restless succession" of human history, nonetheless, as components of a conflicted striving for collective self-comprehension and thus for recognition, they have emerged as what the struggles have all been about.[62]

Notes

Bibliography

Acknowledgments

Index

NOTES

Book epigraphs: (Hegel and Hoffmeister 1994), pp. 26–27; (Hegel 1975), p. 26. Jean-Jacques Rousseau, (Rousseau and Kendall 1985)

Introduction

Note: In many places, I have taken the liberty of altering the cited English translations of Hegel's works.

1. The origin of the general charge, although not against Hegel, is found in (Butterfield 1951).

2. On the uses and abuses of the "tree analogy" in Hegel, see (Alznauer 2015), pp. 29–36.

3. This view has some affinities to views developed in (Jaeggi 2014). She argues for a view of history as presenting the material for a critique of forms of life, where she understands a form of life as a "cluster of practices" that presents both ways of resolving problems that it both faces and which it also poses. To this end, she develops a view that draws its elements of Hegel's conception of history as not having a goal but a principle behind it and links it to more contemporary thinkers such as MacIntyre and Dewey. As she puts it, for Hegel, "freedom is not the goal but rather the principle of history as that of a spiritual process . . . the principle of freedom must first unfold itself on the path of overcoming the ever new problems and crises that are displaying themselves." p. 425

4. The concept of domination, as being ruled by or being vulnerable to the arbitrary powers of others, should here be taken in the sense of normative

domination in which domination has to do with what turns out to be illegiti-
mate authority over the what counts as the normative requirements given to
others. On this idea, see (Richardson 2002), p. 34: ". . . these are all situations in
which the dominators acted under a claim to authority. . . . The purported
exercise of normative power—the power to modify the rights and duties of
others—is, I suggest, essential to the idea of domination."

5. Hegel described it in the following way in his dictations for his middle and high
school classes on philosophy of religion in his time in Nuremberg: "§5 Substance
is power and necessity. As reflection, it is the distinguishing of itself from itself
and the durable existence of various things,—absolute goodness. However, the
particular things are only transitory, every thing is differentiated, separated
from the whole; but its durable existence is the whole, and therein it has as the
same time its necessity; within its dissolution, it comes back—absolute justice."
(Hegel 1969c), pp. 280–281. This abstract idea of how the totality of things properly hangs together as a good is, he says, the root of a religious conception of the
world: "According to these relationships, the state rests on an ethical cast of
mind, and this ethical cast of mind rests on a religious cast of mind. With religion being the consciousness of *absolute* truth, that which is supposed to be able
to have valid force as right and justice, as duty and law, i.e., as *true* in the world
of the free will—that can only have valid force insofar as it shares in that justice, under which it is *subsumed* and *from which it follows*." (Hegel 1969a), §552,
p. 353, (Hegel et al. 1971), p. 283. It is noteworthy that Hegel says that "justice"
has to do with a "necessity" that obtains not in the natural world per se but in
the "world of free willing."

6. Michael Rosen has argued, however, that "history for Hegel is neither the proj-
ect of happiness nor the project of justice." (Rosen 2011) p. 546. But if it is not
about that, what is it? Rosen's answer: "history is the coming-to-itself of *Geist*."
(Rosen 2011) p. 546. Kant's religious views are, Rosen argues, at the heart of
Kant's project, however much the contemporary secular humanist advocates of
Kant's philosophy want to claim otherwise. Troubling to the secular humanist
Kantians is Kant's own assertion, as Rosen claims with numerous citations
from Kant's texts, that the real problem in history is not that bad things befall
good people (since we are not entitled to be happy, that is actually not a problem) but that the wicked might go unpunished. Punishment is thus, at least for
Kant, a good. However, that adds a new dimension to history: We can envisage
a history in which injustice will be corrected, and this is attainable in this life.
On Rosen's account, Hegel picks up this theme from Kant but transfers it to an
insupportable idea of "spirit" which realizes itself though the actions of individuals, not "*against* the rational agency of individuals or behind their backs but
through that agency itself." (Rosen 2011) p. 548. This implies the rather unbelievable

(for Rosen) claim that "when we act under the influence of some value or ideal, we are, thereby, registering in some immediate but not yet reflective way the ultimate, rational structure of Geist." (Rosen 2011), p. 549. My own position as laid out in this manuscript is that Hegel does indeed take justice to be a central concern of his philosophy of history and that the way in which spirit can be said to realize itself in history need not be given the monistic-metaphysical interpretation of which some commentators are so fond (and which the Heideggerians calls an ontotheological approach).

7. Although it is not explicitly concerned with the thesis about the historical shapes of the metaphysics of subjectivity, Robert Pippin's earlier work on "modernism" argued that the issues raised by those in the debate about modernity are at their root philosophical issues. He has since gone on to embrace more fully the "historicity" claims of Hegel's views on subjectivity. (Pippin 1991)

8. Michael Thompson has recently distinguished between agents and persons. On Thompson's account, agents act on reasons, and agents can be singular humans or collectivities. (You are an agent, but so is the World Bank.) A person, on the other hand, is a creature that can be wronged. (Some collectivities may be wronged, but it is possible to construct an agent—a collective—that can act but cannot be wronged. The informal Proust Appreciation Society might be an example.) (Thompson 2004) Likewise, "persons" can also be collectives (as in the definition of a limited liability corporation as a legal person in certain circumstances). For reasons such as those Thompson has laid out, I stay with Hegel's terminology of "subjects," which straddles both senses of agents and persons. For example, if put in Thompson's terms, it is indeed the "subject" as both person and agent which is the focus, for example, in the *Philosophy of Right* (which is not about agency per se, but agents who embody "right" and are therefore persons). This is also helpful in distinguishing those parts of Hegel's account where "agency" is at issue and those where being a "person" is at issue. (It is also the case that Hegel has a special use of the term, *"Person,"* in German that does not track English usage very well.) This approach is to be distinguished from those who wish to extract a conception of agency *per se* out of Hegel's discussion of "subjects" in the *Philosophy of Right*. For the latter, see (Quante 2004) Hegel himself marks the distinction differently: "The person is essentially different from the subject, for the subject is only the possibility of personality, since any living thing whatever is a subject. A person is therefore a subject which is aware of this subjectivity, for as a person, I am completely for myself: the person is the individuality of freedom in pure being-for-itself." (Hegel 1969b), p. 95; (Hegel 1991), §35 *Zusatz*, p. 68. A subject is that to which what it is does or typically does can be ascribed to the shape of life to which it belongs. The "subjects" in which Hegel is interested, however, are the subjects

who are both agents and persons, and it is this sense of "subject" that I am using here, a sense which Hegel for the most part also shares.

9. For an exemplary account, see (Hodgson 2012). See also the excellent overview by Hodgson and Robert F. Brown in (Hegel et al. 2011). Their account of the various sources Hegel uses for some of his historical claims is also invaluable. See also the very helpful account by Myriam Bienenstock in her introduction to (Hegel, Bienenstock, and Waszek 2007).

10. See (Dale 2014) and (Bouton 2004).

11. (Moore 2012) Pippin's and Moore's idea of making sense of making sense do differ. Moore stresses formal logic as the paradigmatic mode of making sense of making sense, whereas Pippin stresses the way in which logic itself has to be reconceived if making sense of making sense is to be thought to its conclusion. (Pippin 2014b); (Pippin 2014a); (Pippin forthcoming)

1. Preliminaries

1. (Hegel 1969a), p. 23; (Hegel 2010), ¶17.

2. Since the 1840s, the dominant reading of Hegel's philosophy amounted to reading Hegel as a version of Schelling's exuberant metaphysics of spirit with some sort of logic attached to it. This was the version propounded in H. M. Chalybäus' influential book, *Historische Entwicklung der spekulativen Philosophie von Kant bis Hegel* of 1839—translated into English into 1853, with a laudatory preface by no less an authority than Sir William Hamilton—and it has stuck. (Chalybäus and Edersheim 1854)

3. (Hegel 1969c), §246, p. 9; (Hegel and Miller 2004), p. 10: "There is a metaphysics which is all the rage in our time, which holds that we cannot know things because they are completely closed off to us. One could put it this way: Not even the animals are as stupid as these metaphysicians, for they go directly to the things, seize them, grasp them and consume them." Another version: "The free will is consequently the idealism which does not consider things as they are to be existing in and for themselves, whereas realism declares those things to be absolute, even if they are found only in the form of finitude. Even the animal does not subscribe to this realist philosophy, for it consumes things and thereby proves that they are not absolutely self-sufficient." (Hegel 1969e), §44, p. 107; (Hegel 1991), p. 76. Yet another: (Hegel 1969a), p. 91; G. W. F. Hegel, 'Phenomenology of Spirit translated by Terry Pinkard', (2010), (¶109): "Nor are the animals excluded from this wisdom. To an even greater degree, they prove themselves to be the most deeply initiated in such wisdom, for they do not stand still in the face of sensuous things, as if those things existed in themselves. Despairing of the reality of those things and in the total certainty of the

nullity of those things, they, without any further ado, simply help themselves to them and devour them. Just like the animals, all of nature celebrates these revealed mysteries which teach the truth about sensuous things."

4. This language of "showing up" in experience was suggested to me by Mark Lance and Rebecca Kukla. See also (Kukla and Lance 2009) (It seems that the original use of the term in this way comes from John Haugeland.)

5. This is one way of taking Robert Pippin's gloss on Hegel's claim that "self-consciousness is desire itself," namely, as a way of having certain things show up in experience. (Pippin 2010) It could be that Hegel draws this idea from Fichte: "But I also grasp those things through need, desire and enjoyment. Something comes to be food and drink for me not through concepts but through hunger, thirst, and satisfaction." (Fichte and Preuss 1987), p. 77. (Fichte and Fichte 1965), Vol. II, p. 260

6. To put it more cautiously, one should say: Although the point of view defended here requires an interpretation of Hegel that does not make him into such an exuberant spiritualized-Spinozistic monistic metaphysician, the jury is still out on that claim. For the most recent, robust and deep defense of the alternative monistic interpretation, see (Bowman 2013). For another metaphysical interpretation of Hegel that takes the core of Hegel's metaphysics as a matter of the implications of the kinds of reflexivity involved in self-conscious thought, see (Tinland 2013)

7. On the overall view of Hegel's philosophy of nature, see (Rand 2016). The topic is also discussed in (Pinkard 2012).

8. See (Kreines 2008); (Kreines 2006) This is given a fuller statement in (Kreines 2015). Similar to Kreines, Susan Songsuk Susan Hahn argues that there are contradictions in nature, specifically in life itself. However, in Hahn's view, Hegel's dialectic should be seen as naturalizing contradiction, such that the dialectic traces out the kind of contradictions at work in organisms and anything else having an organic structure (such as agency and thought). See (Hahn 2007). I have tried to give a fuller account of where Hegel takes these ideas in (Pinkard 2012). The point of difference has to do with assessing the importance of the dialectical two-in-one of self-consciousness in Hegel's *Logic* and his system as a whole. For Hahn, it mirrors and develops the tensions of life itself, and thus, she is driven to hold that Hegel is seeking something like an "intuitive" grasp of the unity of opposed elements. This makes her view very different from that represented by Kreines or by myself, and I find it difficult to square with Hegel's statements in the *Logic*. It seems more Schellingian in its aspirations than it does Hegelian.

9. Hegel notes, "The basic determination of the living being grasped by *Aristotle,* that it must conceived as setting itself to work purposively, has in modern times

been almost forgotten until *Kant,* in his own way, revived this concept in his doctrine of *inner* teleology, in which living being is to be treated as its end *(Selbstzweck).* The difficulty here comes mainly from representing the teleological relationship as external, and from the prevalent opinion that an end exists only in consciousness *(nur auf bewußte Weise existiere)."* (Hegel and Miller 2004), p. 389; (Hegel 1969c), §360, p. 473

10. (Hegel 1969c), §371, p. 521; (Hegel and Miller 2004), p. 429: "The stone cannot become diseased, because it comes to an end in the negative of itself, is chemically dissolved, does not endure in its form, and is not the negative of itself which expands over its opposite (as in illness and self-feeling). Desire, the feeling of lack, is also, to itself, the negative. Desire relates itself to itself as the negative—it is itself and is, to itself, that which is lacking."

11. I take Hegel to speaking of self-conscious life here (Hegel 1969c), §359, p. 472; (Hegel and Miller 2004), p. 387.

12. The characterization of nature's impotence occurs in various places. Here is one such occurrence: "The infinite wealth and variety of forms and, what is most irrational, the contingency which enters into the external arrangement of natural things, have been extolled as the sublime freedom of Nature, even as the divinity *of* Nature, or at least the divinity present *in* it. This confusion of contingency, caprice, and disorder, with freedom and rationality is characteristic of sensuous and unphilosophical thinking. This impotence of Nature sets limits to philosophy and it is quite improper to expect the Notion to comprehend—or as it is said, construe or deduce—these contingent products of Nature. It is even imagined that the more trivial and isolated the object, the easier is the task of deducing it." (Hegel 1969c), §25, pp. 34–35; (Hegel and Miller 2004), §250, pp. 23–24.

13. See the helpful discussion of how Hegel moves from the idea of drawing conclusions from premises to the structure of "life" itself in (Redding 2014).

14. (Hegel 1969e) §35, Zusatz: ". . . since any living thing whatever is a subject." (Hegel 1991), p. 68.

15. "Since the impulse can only be fulfilled through wholly determinate actions, this appears as instinct, since it seems to be a choice in accordance with a determination of an end. However, because the impulse is not a known purpose, the animal does not yet know its purpose as a purpose. Aristotle calls this unconscious acting in terms of purposes φύσις"; (Hegel 1969c), §360; (Hegel and Miller 2004), p. 389.

16. This way of explicating Hegel's conception of subjectivity draws on some views expressed by (Rödl 2007). See pp. 106–109; and (Thompson 2004). In what I now think to be a very confused way, I discussed this several years ago as the self-subsuming and self-explaining aspect of conceptual thought in (Pinkard

1988). Nonetheless, however clumsy and ultimately unsatisfactory my original treatment of the idea was, the basic idea behind it had more or less something approaching the right target in view (even if, while in flight, the arrow fell far away from the goal): A subject is a subject by being the kind of substance that does not sense itself as a substance and then apply a category to itself, but is rather a thinking substance that knows it is a thinking substance by being the substance that brings itself under that concept of thinking substance. Subsequent reading of several authors helped me to see the inadequacy of my earlier way of putting things. One of the other major failings of *Hegel's Dialectic* is its Adorno-ian infused suspicion of the absolute. This led me—in what I now think was a rather unfortunate way—to think that the question Hegel was posing in the philosophy of history was a kind of Kantian "what are the conditions of the possibility of history at all." This is not Hegel's primary question (or, if to the extent that it is a question at all for him, it is only one of the lesser worries he raises along the way for the purpose of explicating his real concerns).

17. (Hegel 1969f), p. 112; (Hegel 1988) p. 88: "Man is an animal, but even in his animal functions he does not remain within the in-itself as the animal does, but becomes conscious of the in-itself, recognizes it, and raises it (for example, like the process of digestion) into self-conscious science. It is through these means that man dissolves the boundary of his immediate consciousness existing-in-itself, and thus precisely because he knows that he is an animal, he ceases to be an animal and gives himself the knowledge of himself as *Geist* [spirit, mind]."

18. Here are a couple of relevant citations: "it is the concept alone . . . that has actuality, and in such a way that it gives actuality to itself." (Hegel 1969e), §1, p. 29; (Hegel 1991), p. 25: "On the contrary, it is by nature active, and activity is its essence; it is its own product, and is therefore its own beginning and its own end. . . . The business of spirit is to produce itself, to make itself its own object, and to gain knowledge of itself; in this way, it exists for itself." (Hegel and Hoffmeister 1994), p. 55; (Hegel 1975), p. 48.

19. (Hegel 1969f), pp. 80–81; (Hegel 1988), pp. 53–54.

20. I discuss the centrality of the metaphor of amphibians and how Hegel extends its use in (Pinkard 2012). See also the discussion about how this "amphibian" character relates to the status of modern art in Hegelian theory in (Pippin 2014).

21. See the discussion in (Boyle forthcoming): Boyle argues that the basic distinction between rational and nonrational animals should not be conceived as that of an "additive" property that is grafted onto an existing stock of animal powers, but rather that the distinction should be that between rational animals that realize animal powers in one way and nonrational animals that realize animal powers in another way. In particular, rational animals are self-conscious

animals, not merely animals that have a kind of self-consciousness sitting on top, as it were, of all their other animal properties. This is also the reason why Hegel uses the term *Geist* to indicate the species of humans about which he is talking: Not just animals who also "have" rationality as an extra power but who "are" rational animals. The concept of the "thinking animal" as *Geist* is at first in thought the concept "in itself." As the concept is publically developed— "posited" in Hegel's terms—it, as it were, divides itself into two in a recognitive struggle. This point is also taken up in a different key by Christopher Yeomans. For Yeomans, the "spiritual animals" to which Hegel makes reference in one of the chapters of the *Phenomenology* are "those creatures who are just starting to take reflective responsibility for their own individuation, and this is why the notion of the interest-guided development of talents, which is the primary mechanism for such individuation and has its most intense location in the human lifespan in later childhood and adolescence, is the focal point of the moral psychology of this self-understanding of agency in the *Phenomenology*." (Yeomans 2015), p. 27.

22. (Hegel 1969a), p. 145; (Hegel 2010)¶177: "What will later come to be for consciousness will be the experience of what spirit is, that is, this absolute substance which constitutes the unity of its oppositions in their complete freedom and self-sufficiency, namely, in the oppositions of the various self-consciousnesses existing for themselves: The *I* that is *we* and the *we* that is *I*." The way this sounds prima facie paradoxical has been noted by other philosophers than Hegel. Wilfrid Sellars remarks, ". . . I want to highlight from the very beginning what might be called the paradox of man's encounter with himself, the paradox consisting of the fact that man couldn't be man until he encountered himself." "Philosophy and the Scientific Image of Man," in (Sellars 1963). See also the very helpful piece: (Longuenesse 2012).

23. "The nonspiritual and inanimate, on the contrary, are the concrete concept only as *real possibility; cause* is the highest stage in which the concrete concept has, as the beginning in the sphere of necessity, an immediate existence; but it is not yet a subject that maintains itself as such in the course of its effective realization *(wirklichen Realisierung)*." (Hegel and Di Giovanni 2010), p. 740; (Hegel 1969j), p. 556.

24. (Hegel 1969b), §214, p. 370; (Hegel et al. 1991), p. 288: "The Idea may be grasped as *reason;* (and this is the genuine philosophical meaning of *reason*), further as *subject-object . . . as the possibility that has its actuality in itself* because the Idea contains all the relations of the intellect, but contains them in their *infinite* self-return and identity-within-themselves."

25. "Reason as the *Idea* appears here in the determination that the opposition of concept and reality itself, whose unity it is, here has the more precise form of the

concept existing for itself, of consciousness and the present object externally standing over and against it." (Hegel 1969d), §437, p. 227; (Hegel et al. 1971), p. 177.

26. The obvious terminological distinction is between Ideas as *Ideen* and ideas (or representations) as *Vorstellungen*. It would have been better had the original translations of Kant and Hegel used different terms, but the usage seems to have stuck.

27. In arguing that reason understands its own limits, Kant is implicitly committing himself to a view of reason which is, in relation to itself, unlimited. The "space of reasons," as today's terminology has it, is unbounded, or, rather, bounded only by itself. Hegel notes: "Even if the topic is that of finite thought, it only shows that such finite reason is infinite precisely in determining itself as finite; for the negation is finitude, a lack which only exists for that for which it is the sublatedness, the *infinite* relation to itself." (Hegel 1969c), p. 469; (Hegel and Miller 2004), p. 385. As Hegel puts it even more succinctly: "Where there is a *limit*, it is a negation only *for a third* [perspective], for an external comparison." (Hegel 1969c)"§359, p. 469; (Hegel and Miller 2004), p. 385. See also (Wittgenstein 1963) p. 3, where Wittgenstein noted that "to set a limit to thought, we should have to find both sides of the limit thinkable (i.e., we should have to be able to think what cannot be thought). It will therefore only be in language that the limit can be set, and what lies on the other side of the limit will simply be nonsense."

28. "But since the result now is that the idea is the unity of the concept and objectivity, the true, we must not regard it as just a *goal* which is to be approximated but itself remains always a kind of *beyond;* we must rather regard everything *as being* actual only to the extent that it has the idea in it and expresses it. It is not just that the subject matter, the objective and the subjective world, *ought* to be in principle *congruent* with the idea; the two are themselves rather the congruence of concept and reality; a reality that does not correspond to the concept is mere *appearance,* something subjective, accidental, arbitrary, something which is not the truth." (Hegel 1969j), p. 464; (Hegel and Di Giovanni 2010), p. 671.

29. A sharp critique of this way of interpreting Hegel's system with a specific focus on the concept of infinity is to be found in (Horstmann 2006). I hope that I have managed to respond to Horstmann's fine-grained criticism that in the last analysis, the interpretation at work here is a neo-pragmatist interpretation that, whatever its other virtues may be, is not true to the genuine novelty and therefore strangeness of Hegel's philosophy.

30. There is more, obviously, to the noumenal-phenomenal distinction, and even the use of "noumenal" (which Hegel himself avoids) can suggest that one is speaking of something "merely" posited, or of something that "cannot appear." Hegel's own proposal is to locate the philosophical worries about matters such

as "merely posited" and "cannot appear" in his *Logic* on "Essence" (where the basic issue is the relation between appearance and its substructure). In "Concept," this becomes a duality that is not really a duality in the "Idea" of a phenomenal subject who, by bringing itself under the concept of apperceptive life, is the noumenal subject.

31. See §247, where Hegel discusses his claim that "externality constitutes the determination in which nature exists as nature." (Hegel 1969c), p. 24; (Hegel and Miller 2004), p. 15.

32. "For the *cognition* already contained in the simple *logical* Idea is only that of the concept of cognition thought by us, not the cognition present at hand for itself, not actual spirit, but only its possibility." (Hegel 1969d), §381, p. 18; (Hegel et al. 1971), p. 8. He also notes: "absolute spirit, however, is the absolute unity of actuality and the concept, or, of the possibility of spirit." (Hegel 1969d), §383, p. 29; (Hegel et al. 1971), p. 18.

33. (Hegel and Hoffmeister 1994), p. 85; (Hegel 1975), p. 72.

34. This image of the "absolute" articulating itself appears in characteristic passages such as: "The task is indeed to demonstrate *(dargestellt)* what the absolute is. But this demonstration cannot be either a determining or an external reflection by virtue of which determinations of the absolute would result, but is rather the *exposition (Auslegung) of the absolute,* more precisely the absolute's *own exposition,* and only a *displaying (Zeigen) of what it is.*" (Hegel and Di Giovanni 2010), p. 466; (Hegel 1969j), p. 187.

35. (Hegel 1969d), §383, p. 27; (Hegel et al. 1971), p. 16: "As existing for itself the universal is self-particularizing and therein it is identity with itself. The determinateness of spirit is thus that of *manifestation.* It is not any old determinateness or content, whose expression, or, externality would be only that of form differentiated from it. It is not that that does not reveal something but that rather its determinateness is itself this act of revealing. Its possibility is thus immediate, infinite *actuality.*"

36. This has, I think, several points of contact with the views laid out in (Thompson 2008): Provisionally, Thompson has taken his view to imply the following: "I admit I don't know how the enquiry would proceed if this possibility is granted. But why not just grant that it's possible as far as anyone knows and say that you know it doesn't stand so in your own case, and thus in the case of the kind of thing you are, viz. a human being. *You don't know this empirically, but rather as a Faktum of reason in self-conscious exercise of concepts, in realizing them—that is, in action. It is not a cognition you gain 'from outside.'"* (Thompson 2013), p. 732. This differs from Hegel's version in at least one crucial way: The knowledge of the "Idea" for Hegel is not supposed to be a "Faktum of reason." This is why he goes to such lengths in the *Science of Logic* to worry about the issue, as he calls

it, of "with what must the science begin?," and the answer is that one must go to the ground-level zero of intelligibility to get the argument started in a way that does not beg a lot of other questions. That ground-level zero is the thought of "being," which is, without further inference, identical with the thought that if nothing else, "being" is not the same as "nothing" and that this is the most abstract and indeterminate of all shapes of intelligibility. To the extent that he can show that it breaks down in intelligibility and requires a very distinct form of supplementation so that he can logically march from there to the absolute "Idea," then he has carried out his program for rejecting the idea that our knowledge of ourselves as human rational animals is a *"Faktum"* of reason. To demonstrate that with the detail that dyed-in-the-wool Hegelians think is required would require departing from the "looser" version of the *Logic* which I have adopted here for the purposes of the exposition of Hegel's thoughts on history, but it is behind what Hegel says when he remarks in the *Logic:* "To bring to consciousness this *logical* nature that animates the spirit, that moves and works within it, this is the task." (Hegel and Di Giovanni 2010), p. 17; (Hegel 1969i), p. 27. It is also the case that Thompson's project aims to show that we get all the ethical considerations we need from an appropriate concept of "first nature," that is, ourselves as rational animals. I am not clear about how much or even whether this differs from Hegel's concept—which would be that our first nature is exactly to develop a second nature—or whether this is merely a trivially semantic distinction between Thompsonians and the Hegelians. So, it seems, the big difference between the Aristotelian-Thompsonians and the Aristotelian-Hegelians lies in the deep level of historicity that Hegel thinks is characteristic of the genus "self-conscious rational animals."

37. See the discussion of how the impulse to develop our "talents" necessitates the development of ourselves as "spiritual animals" in (Yeomans 2015).

38. As Hegel puts it, the first two books of his *Logic,* which he calls the "objective logic" are "therefore the true critique of such determinations—a critique that considers them, not according to the abstract form of the *a priori* as contrasted with the *a posteriori,* but in themselves according to their particular content" (Hegel and Di Giovanni 2010), p. 42; (Hegel 1969i), p. 62.

39. "Just as the simple determinations of the life of the soul have their severed counterpart in the universal life of nature, so that which in the individual man has the form of what is subjective, which has a particular impulse, unfold itself. it is within him as a being, without awareness, and it unfolds itself within the state into a system of differentiated spheres of freedom—into a world fashioned by self-conscious human reason." (Hegel 1969d), §391, p. 52; (Hegel et al. 1971), p. 36. This is also expressed in characteristic passages such as "If the doctrine of virtues is not merely a theory of duties and thus includes the particular aspects

of character which are grounded in natural determinations, it will therefore be a *natural history of spirit.*" (Hegel 1991), p. 194; (Hegel 1969e) §150, p. 299.

40. On this point, see the helpful introduction and essays in (Khurana 2013).

41. "The determinateness of spirit is consequently that of manifestation . . . its possibility is consequently immediately infinite, absolute actuality." (Hegel 1969d), §383, p. 27; (Hegel et al. 1971), p. 16.

42. I have tried to make a separate case for that in (Pinkard 2012). See also (Testa 2013). Another related version of reading Hegel in nondialectical but nonetheless loosely naturalistic terms is the classic work (Wood 1990).

43. Hegel notes: "It is on these grounds that the child is still in the grip of natural life. The child has only natural impulses and is not yet the actuality of being a spiritual person *(geistiger Mensch)* but only the possibility of being such a person in terms of its concept. . . . The concept progresses necessarily towards the development of its reality, for the form of immediacy, of the indeterminateness which its reality at first possesses, is something contradictory to it; what seems to be immediately present in spirit is not what is genuinely immediate but rather what is, in itself, something posited, something mediated. . . . To be sure, spirit *exists* already in its beginnings, but spirit does not know it as yet, does not as yet know that it is this spirit. It is not it itself which at the beginning has grasped its concept but only we who observe it. Only we know its concept. That spirit comes to know what it is is what constitutes its realization." (Hegel 1969d), §385, p. 33; (Hegel et al. 1971), p. 21.

44. This is slightly complicated by the various and numerous passages in which Hegel speaks of the "human spirit." That might seem redundant, but the contrast is always with the "divine spirit" as a way of conceiving of a human-like spirit that was nonetheless not a member of our species yet sharing in our species' interests.

45. Hegel speaks of a "shape of life" in his earlier, unpublished works, and the phrase reappears in the famous sentence in the *Philosophy of Right* about the owl of Minerva: "When philosophy paints its grey on grey, a shape of life has grown old, and it cannot be rejuvenated, but only recognized, by the grey in grey of philosophy; the owl of Minerva begins flight only with the onset of dusk." (Hegel 1969e), p. 28; (Hegel 1991), p. 23. The metaphor of the owl is perhaps unfortunate since the owl of which Hegel spoke most likely only flew in the daytime. See (Knowles and Carpenter 2010/2011).

46. Thus Hegel notes that "in short, life must be grasped as an end in itself *(Selbstzweck),* as an end which possesses its means within itself, as a totality in which each distinct moment is alike end and means. It is, therefore, in the consciousness of this *dialectical,* this *living* unity of distinct moments that self-consciousness is ignited, the consciousness of the simple, ideal existence that is

its own object and therefore differentiated within itself, in other words, the knowledge of the truth of natural existence, of the 'I'." (Hegel 1969d), ¶423 Zusatz, p. 212; (Hegel et al. 1971), pp. 163–164.

47. "To study this science, to dwell and to labor in this realm of shadows, is the absolute cultural education and discipline of consciousness. It drives itself therein to what is remote from the intuitions and the goals of the senses, remote from feelings and from the world of merely fancied representation. Considered from its negative side, this task consists in holding off the contingency of merely clever thought *(räsonierenden Denkens)* and the arbitrariness in the choice to accept one ground as valid rather than its opposite. / But above all, thought thereby gains self-subsistence and independence." (Hegel and Di Giovanni 2010), p. 37; (Hegel 1969i), p. 55.

48. (Hegel 1969a), p. 139; (Hegel 2010),¶167.

49. (Rousseau 1968), p. 87.

50. Speaking of "manifestation" (which is Hegel's term of choice) could perhaps be a little misleading in light of recent literature on self-knowledge that prefers to distinguish manifestation as a noncognitive expression of a mental state with representation of some mental state or expression of a meaning. Matthew Boyle distinguishes, for example, between crying as manifesting pain and a linguistic representation that one is pain, which is part of his longer argument to the conclusion that "a person who can represent her own mental states must understand that the subject to whom she ascribes those states is one who has the power to make up her mind." Boyle's point turns on the idea that even in "passive" self-knowledge (knowledge of our sensations), we are still ascribing such states to a subject, and this capacity for self-ascription is thus fundamental to claims to knowledge about such passive states. We do not merely "have" these mental states (for example, of sensation or brute desire), we also represent them as ours. (Boyle 2009).

51. See the discussion of "self-ownership" and the instability of separating deed from action in (Deligiorgi 2010). Deligiorgi takes these considerations to be indicative that Hegel holds something like an "error" theory of agency. However, on the view advanced here, Hegel does not hold such an error theory, but he also does not think that agency is a mere "thing" (with which Deligiorgi agrees). It is a "subject," a peculiarly self-relating organism, but it is not nothing, and it is not just "substance." It is an apperceptive life and not merely an animal life that has rational powers grafted onto itself. The unity of action I ascribe to Hegel is more similar to what Michael Thompson calls his "naïve action theory" in (Thompson 2008), pp. 85–148.

52. How to draw out the elements of the distinction between action and deed in Hegel's theory is the focus of (Pippin 2008).

53. In addition to Pippin's discussion of the "action/deed" distinction in (Pippin 2008), see also the discussion of doing something "intentionally" and doing something "anscombely" in (Thompson 2013). Mark Alznauer takes up Pippin's account of the action only really being expressed in the deed, but takes it in a different direction. Alznauer claims that Pippin's account has the implication that we can only really be agents in modern institutions (in which basic rights, moral obligations and modern ethical life are recognized), whereas Alznauer argues that Hegel has a much weaker condition for agency, namely, that people have a "shared membership in a state." (Alznauer 2015), p. 63. It is, however, not clear that there is much daylight between Alznauer's and Pippin's positions, except that Pippin might claim that we can only "fully" be agents in such modern institutions in a way that Alznauer would also affirm. The position I am defending here attributes to Hegel a much weaker condition for agency, which has to do with self-consciousness per se, and claims that agency is fully realized when it comes to a more complete understanding of what it is to be a *geistig*, "minded" being at all. The position being articulated here is of a piece with Pippin's and Alznauer's positions in that all three express versions of a metaphysical thesis about the "sociality" of agency.

54. See also (Boyle 2009). See also the discussion about how this is essentially Kant's point in speaking of representing something in consciousness "as combined" in (Yeomans 2015, Rödl 2007).

55. See the discussion in (Boyle 2009).

56. For example, in (Hegel 1969a), p. 181; (Hegel 2010), ¶235, "Now, this category, that is, the *simple* unity of self-consciousness and being, has the *distinction* in itself, for its essence is precisely this, that it is immediately selfsame in *otherness*, that is, immediately selfsame in the absolute distinction. Thus, the distinction *exists*, but it *exists* as a completely transparent distinction which is at the same time therefore no distinction at all."

57. (Hegel 2010), ¶494.

58. (Kukla and Lance 2009) argue that such pointing out is also part of a social practice of hailing somebody, of pulling them into one's social space. Hegel would no doubt agree with that, but it is not the focus of his discussion of sense-certainty. It is to show the presence of an apperceptive life in such activities, and then later, to argue that an apperceptive life can only be intelligibly conceived as participating in a social space.

59. (Hegel 1969a), p. 145; (Hegel 2010), ¶177. In explicating Hegel's discussion, I have especially drawn on the points raised in (Rödl 2007) and in (Lavin 2004). There is nothing, however, in Rödl's rather Kantian discussion that would lead to anything like a dialectic of mastery and servitude.

60. (Hegel 1969e), §7, p. 57; (Hegel 1991), p. 42. This responds to a criticism voiced in (Sparby 2014).

61. Hegel speaks of this other who succumbs as a *"Knecht,"* which could mean a "vassal," a "servant," and even a "slave." The general point is about "servitude." Hegel also thought that something like this idealized struggle occurred deeply in the prehistoric human past.

62. The phrase itself is well known as coming from Wilfrid Sellars. (Sellars 1963), p. 212.

63. (Thompson 2004).

64. (Thompson 2004), p. 353.

65. (Thompson 2004), p. 344.

66. There is a controversy about how to interpret the sections on mastery and ser-vitude concerning whether there really are two people in a dyadic relation to each other or whether the passages present a kind of allegorical treatment of the relation between the conceptual and the empirical within one subject. John McDowell has made the case for the allegorical reading, and part of his case has to do with what he thinks makes better sense of the shift from consciousness to self-consciousness in the *Phenomenology*. He accuses, for example, Robert Brandom of interpreting the shift as simply a change of topic, and he argues (rightly, I think) that this is at cross purposes with Hegel's stated aims about the shift. (McDowell 2009), chapter 8. Robert Pippin has agreed with McDowell on the point that it is not simply a change of topic, but he also claims that McDowell's interpretation does violence to the text and to the ideas at work there. (Pippin 2010) (The key troublesome passage in Hegel for McDowell's interpretation is: "The doubling, which was previously distributed between two individuals, the master and the servant, is thereby turned back into one individual." (Hegel 1969a), p. 163; (Hegel 2010) ¶206. McDowell says that is merely allegorical.) Pippin's retort to McDowell was to argue that the authority in question cannot be individualized since all authority exists only as recognized authority, and that agency itself exists only in the networks of mutual recogni-tion of such matters as authority, that agency itself is a social status. McDowell has in turn responded with the idea that, to be sure, nobody becomes an agent without being socialized into such a status, but once one has become an agent, one possesses an authority that is independent of such sociality. His example is that of speaking English: What counts as "English" is obviously dependent on social authority, but once one has acquired the capacity, one has it independent of being recognized by others. McDowell notes: "Suppose everyone around me dies just as light is dawning for me, so there is no one to recognize me as a self-moving speaker of English. It would be wildly implausible to think it follows

that I do not have that status. Suppose years later English-speakers from the Antipodes arrive on the scene of the disaster that I alone, of my local community, survived, and they recognize me to be expressing thoughts in English. It would be wildly implausible to think I had to wait for their recognition of me to acquire that capacity." (McDowell 2009), chapter 9, p. 169. McDowell is right on that point, and it seems to undermine the sweeping claim that we are the kinds of human subjects we are only in networks of recognition (or at least it demands that the claim be heavily qualified), and it thus seems to undermine, or to weaken, Hegel's own assertion: "Self-consciousness exists *in* and *for itself* by way of its existing in and for itself for an other; i.e., it exists only as a recognized being." (Hegel 1969a), p. 145; (Hegel 2010) ¶178. The view presented here departs from both views (or, perhaps, picks the happy middle). The subject is a subject only by being the life that brings itself under the concept of subject, and that concept of itself cannot be monadic at ground level. However, once it has acquired the relevant capacities (such as speaking a language, moving about in a normative social space), it is to that extent free-standing (as McDowell claims). But such a free-standing agency would in Hegel's sense only be "abstract," barely an agent at all. It would require further recognitive relationships. A concrete agent is part of a web of recognition. Once the step is taken to demand the kind of recognition that goes on in the dialectic of mastery and servitude, however, it pushes itself into a new practical enterprise that implicates itself with others in a non-escapable way.

67. (Kant 1929), p. 153 (B133): "As *my* representations (even if I am not conscious of them as such) they must conform to the condition under which alone they *can* stand together in one universal self-consciousness, because otherwise they would not all without exception belong to me. From this original combination many consequences follow."

68. (Hegel and Hoffmeister 1994) p. 82; (Hegel 1975), p. 70.

69. In systematic terms, this means that the concept of subjectivity in the *Logic* has to be filled out with the concepts of nature and concrete subjectivity in the other two books of the *Encyclopedia*. The *Logic* only gives us the "concept" of the thinking, acting subject. The rest of the system fills out the "Idea" of the thinking, acting, feeling subject—what it is for such a thinking, feeling, and acting subject to be real. (Or, if one wants to be picky, the *Logic* gives us only the abstract "Idea," whereas the rest of the system fleshes out the concrete "Idea.")

70. See the discussion in (Yeomans 2015). Yeomans makes the claim that that talents, as individual features of ourselves, are, relatively speaking, objective features of ourselves and our interests, as taking up those talents, are, relatively speaking, subjective features and are the way we make ourselves at home in the world by learning to exercise and actualize our talents.

71. (Hegel and Hoffmeister 1994), p. 81; (Hegel 1975), p. 70. Hegel also notes there that we must include the general concept of what "interests" the agent in his world, what pulls him as the person he specifically is into that particular con-catenation of passions and principles: "If I put something into practice and give it a real existence, I must have some personal interest in doing so; I must be per-sonally involved in it, and hope to obtain satisfaction through its accomplish-ment—in other words, my own interest must be at stake. To have an interest in something means to be implicated and involved in it, and an end which I am actively to pursue must in some way or other be my own end."

72. I tried making the case for this in (Pinkard 1992), although that attempt was flawed. The case for seeing Hegel as a version of "internalism" in moral psy-chology is made at greater length in (Moyar 2010). Robert Pippin had earlier made this point, (Pippin 1997) and (Pippin 2008). See also (Padgett-Walsh 2010); (Padgett-Walsh forthcoming). See also the excellent overview of the internal-ism debate in (Wallace 2005).

73. (Hegel and Hoffmeister 1994), p. 81; (Hegel 1975), p. 70.

74. See the discussion in (Moyar 2010), chapter 4, "Motivating and Justifying Reasons," pp. 43–80.

75. (Kant 1960), p. 19: ". . . the observation, of great importance to morality, that freedom of the will is of a wholly unique nature in that an incentive can deter-mine the will to an action only so far as the individual has incorporated it into his maxim (has made it the general rule in accordance with which he will con-duct himself); only thus can an incentive, whatever it may be, co-exist with the absolute spontaneity of the will (i.e., freedom)." For the "incorporation thesis" itself, see (Allison 1990).

76. Hegel's pre-*Phenomenology* arguments against Kant on these points have been explored by Robert Pippin in "Avoiding German "Idealism: Kant, Hegel, and the Reflective Judgment Problem," in (Pippin 1997), pp. 129–156. Sally Sedgwick has devoted a large part of a book to a careful explication and defense of Hegel's case against Kant mostly based on those early writings: (Sedgwick 2012).

77. On this conception of "distinguishable but not separable" in Kant and Hegel, see (Pippin 2005). For a discussion of how Kant's incorporation thesis translates into romantic and Wittgensteinian themes that also connect with Hegel's dis-cussion, see (Eldridge 1997).

78. This is not to deny the possibility that the desire may eventually overwhelm the subject and lead to something looking like an action, but in those cases, that is a matter of losing one's agency. One's agency is simply swept away by some-thing outside of itself, as if one is caught in a windstorm or wave of water and carried along by a superior force.

79. In the *Phenomenology*, Hegel had argued that point when he contrasted the knight of virtue to the way of the world. The knight of virtue thinks he is struggling to realize "the good" as opposed to the subject who embodies the wicked way of the world (the world of passions and egoism). The knight of virtue takes himself to have made reason his motive, whereas he takes the subject of "the way of the world" to be moved by only natural self-interested desire. This amounts only to shadowboxing (*Spiegelfechterei*—"fencing with a mirror") since what is at stake is what counts as a good or overriding reason for each of them. In Hegel's telling of the story, the way of the world wins out not because animal passion triumphs over virtue, but because the constellation of reasons at work in the emerging early modern world win out over the antiquated conceptions of virtue. After authors such as Mandeville in his *Fable of the Bees* had already made the claim that in the newly emerging modern world, private vice could actually be public virtue, Hegel broadened considerations like that into the view that the structure of reasons that we have can itself only be comprehended in terms of its sociality and historical embeddedness, and in the modern world that comes with market-oriented practices that provide a basis for thinking that self-interested reasons can be actually be legitimate, ethically based reasons. I discussed this in (Pinkard 1994). See the discussion of how this plays out in terms of self-individuation in Hegel's thought in (Yeomans 2015).

80. (Aristotle 1998), book III.

81. Dean Moyar conceives of this as in terms of a nesting of purposes within other purposes that provides the basic girders to Hegel's version of internalism. See the summary given by (Moyar 2010), p. 75. It is not clear that Hegel quite has such nesting in mind, since that draws on a largely Humean picture of action as always that of choosing means to an end, such that any action is, if not immediately directed instrumentally to a specific end, always at least part of a wider set of purposes to which it is directed. The subject may act in terms of a specific purpose that is manifested in the action without its being linked as a matter of conscious activity to any wider set of purposes, something Moyar acknowledges. Moyar's claim is not that we always have these wider purposes in mind (although we can) but that the wider purposes can and often do serve to justify the motivating reasons that are nested in the wider purposes without our having to have them in mind while acting. In making that claim, Moyar distinguishes the subjective way in which motivating and justifying reasons coincide and the objective way in which they do (which involves the nesting of purposes within wider sets of purposes), and he notes, "On Hegel's view complete justification depends on the systematic whole of the institutions of Ethical Life." (Moyar 2010), p. 74. It is unclear on Moyar's nesting proposal whether it still supposes that the means-end model of practical reason holds, even if it has to be

reconfigured into more complicated nesting relationships. Hegel, on the other hand, thinks that there can be manifestations of an overall end without the actions being able to be lined up so that they fit into an instrumental model of reasons. Spirit's purpose, to become self-conscious about what it truly is, is not an end to which ultimately everything else is a means. All our other purposes are not a means to spirit's self-comprehension (although they are ingredients of it), nor is spirit's self-comprehension inclusive of all those purposes, nor are other purposes merely approximations to spirit's self-comprehension. Spirit's overall purpose need not be modeled on that of conscious action—for example, Hegel's statement that "the difficulty here comes mainly from representing the teleological relationship as external, and from the prevalent opinion that an end exists only in consciousness." (Hegel and Miller 2004), p. 389; (Hegel 1969c), §360, p. 473.

82. (Hegel 1969b), §66, p. 156; (Hegel et al. 1991), p. 115. See the discussion of the puzzles associated with making the "ethical," which seems to require reflectivity, line up with the "habitual." (Novakovic 2015)

83. (Hegel 1969g), p. 40; (Hegel 1963), p. 21: "The person *(Mensch)* who in itself *(an sich)* is rational has come no further when he is rational for himself. The in itself is preserved, and, nonetheless, the distinction is huge. No new content is produced, but yet this form is a huge difference. All of world history concerns this distinction."

84. (Hegel 1969e), §7, p. 57; (Hegel 1991), p. 42.

85. He says that "Freedom lies neither in indeterminacy nor determinacy but is both at once." This is a component of Hegel's well-known rejection of orthodox Kantianism: On its own, the will is merely reflective, indeterminate and incapable of generating content for itself. That content as Hegel says in the same passage can come from nature or spirit. If it comes from spirit, it is content generated by others, and that can take the form either of convention (in effect, doing what others do) or of what is necessary to achieve success in attaining spirit's goals (the concepts with which Hegel is concerned). The agent's will as capable of reflective distance thus remains "indeterminate," and it becomes determinate when it is taken up with the (rational) wills of others (that is, the wills of others, and in the best case, insofar as they embody a shared rational will). In any event, the shared wills of others is, in concrete terms, social, and to the extent that the shared will is not rational, it is defective and subject to dissolution because of its own senselessness. Self-consciousness itself is at once both: It is awareness of itself and as such indeterminate; and it is aware of a content that comes from outside of itself (and is thus determinate), and as it is aware of itself as subject, it is aware of itself as aware of objects, without there having to be a separate and distinct act of reflection on this self-awareness. This

two-in-one structure of self-consciousness really is the core of the Hegelian dialectic. (Hegel 1969e), §7, p. 57; (Hegel 1991), p. 42.

86. (Hegel 1969g), pp. 41–42; (Hegel 1963), p. 23: "In coming around to itself, spirit attains its freedom. Genuine self-possession and genuine conviction on one's part come on the scene only in this. In nothing else but thinking does spirit attain this freedom. In intuition and in feeling, I find myself determined and am not free; but I am free when I have a consciousness of this my feeling."

87. (Hegel 1969g), p. 42; (Hegel 1963), p. 23: "In willing, one has determinate purposes, determinate interests; I am indeed free in this being 'my own' *(das Meinige)*; however, these purposes always include an other, or include the kind of things which is for me an other, such as impulses, inclinations, etc."

88. (Hegel 1969h), p. 493; (Hegel 1956), p. 413: "In this piety, there is superstition , a being bound to something sensuous, to a common thing—it occurs in the most various of shapes: that of the slavery to authority, for spirit, as external to itself within itself, is not free, is fettered to what is external to itself."

89. (Hegel 1969g), p. 42; (Hegel 1963), p. 23: "Only in thought is everything that is alien transparent, vanished; spirit is free here in an absolute manner. The Idea's interest, and at the same time the interest of philosophy, are given expression." See the discussion along similar lines in Yeomans' conception of the threefold activity of self-possession, specification of content, and effectiveness in (Yeomans 2015).

2. Building an Idealist Conception of History

1. The full quotation is: "The general perspective of philosophical world history is not abstractly general, but concrete and absolutely present; for it is the spirit which is eternally present to itself and for which there is no past. [Or it is the Idea.]" (Hegel and Hoffmeister 1994), p. 24; (Hegel 1987), p. 11. He also notes: ". . . the history of philosophy includes at the same time an inner conflict, because philosophy aims at knowing what is imperishable, eternal, and in and for itself. Its aim is *truth*. However, history relates the sort of thing which has existed at one time but at another has perished, displaced by its successor. If we start from the truth's being eternal, then the truth cannot fall into the sphere of the transient and it has no history. But if it has a history, and history is only a display of a series of past shapes of knowledge, then truth is not be found in it, since truth is not something past." Another formulation by him: "If the thought which is essentially thought, is in and for itself and is eternal. That which is genuinely true is contained in thought alone. It is true not just today and tomorrow but is outside of time. How does this world of thoughts come to have a history? In history what is given exposition is transient, is over with, is what has been

submerged within the night of the past and is no more. Genuinely true, necessary thought—and it is only with such thought that we deal with here—is capable of no change. The question raised here constitutes one of those matters which is first to be brought under our consideration." (Hegel 1969d), pp. 23–24; (Hegel 1963), p. 5.

2. Taken from (Lauer and Hegel 1983), pp. 68–69.

3. There is another possible answer to Hegel's own question that is usually ascribed to Hegel, but, so I shall argue, is not Hegel at all. It goes like this. Spirit is some kind of entity that begins undeveloped, develops itself according to its essence, and achieves its completion in history sometime around 1807 (or maybe as late as 1820). It is like a child that matures into an adult, and its history does not involve a change in its essence. This would in effect deny Hegel's historicism in favor of some kind of essentialism that Hegel rejects. The most sophisticated version of this interpretation comes from Heidegger's arraignment of Hegel to the effect that, like all Western metaphysicians, he took an "ontotheological" approach. By that, Heidegger meant that Hegel tacitly assumed that the "meaning of being *(Sein)*" consisted in determining that it lay in one entity *(Seiendes),* which usually involves claiming that such an entity is the most real, or perhaps the only real, entity of all beings. Once the problem is framed in that way—and, for Heidegger, all of Western metaphysics frames it in that way—one looks for some kind of semi-causal relation between the most real entity and everything else. That relation can be manifestly causal (as in Aristotle's causes) or disguisedly causal (as in Plato's idea of "participation" in the forms). All inquiry into origins (of truth, normativity, meaning, etc.) turn out to be thus ontotheological since they look for the "being" that "causes" the other beings to be what they are. (He called it "ontotheological" because of the way all such inquiries replicate the Judeo-Christian story of creation, and not because they are all explicitly theological.) On the Heideggerian reading, for Hegel, the meaning of being was supposedly "spirit" (subject) instead of substance. Heidegger bases his reading on a passage that is not from Hegel himself but was erroneously put into the text by Georg Lasson and which Heidegger cites. In that text, Hegel supposedly speaks of spirit's "falling into" time. Hegel said no such thing. See (Bouton 2004) However, this simply misunderstands Hegel's conception of spirit. Spirit is not an entity, although it is also not equivalent to the sum of all its members. It is something more like a joint commitment than it is like a separate entity. To be sure, Hegel speaks of what "the" spirit does in history, and he attributes various actions and motives to it, but this is a grammatical feature of the language Hegel speaks, not a feature of his metaphysics. In German (as in English), the use of "the" can refer to a genus without making any special metaphysical assumptions about it, as in the

sentences, "The Robin mates in Spring," and "The American Robin vocalizes differently in different regions." This assumption that Hegel is pursuing an ontotheological theory in Heidegger's sense drives the interpretation given by (Hodgson 2012). This "ontotheological" interpretation is also worked out in (Dale 2014). The idea that there is "a" spirit that functions as a final cause of the movement of history also animates Burleigh Wilkins' attempt to put Hegel's *Logic* to use in assessing Hegel's philosophy of history, which leads him, rightly, given the premise, to think that Hegel's view on how history develops in terms of its purpose has to be taken as a noble effort but fully indefensible: "I am no more inclined to campaign for the resurrection of Hegel's immanent teleology than Walter Kaufmann or J. H. N. Findlay is to labor for the resurrection of Hegel's dialectic." (Wilkins 1974), p. 120. This also leads Dennis O'Brien to think that Hegel must be taking the process of history as a kind of unitary "something" to which the categories of efficient, material, and final causes apply, so that states and constitutions are the material and formal causes and the passions and world historical individuals are the final causes. (O'Brien 1975) A thoroughgoing critique of the older "monistic" interpretation that sees what is nonetheless right about it is to be found in (Kreines 2008) Frederick Beiser seems to think it is just textually obvious that Hegel intends that type of immanent teleology and unitary structure and that a devout reading of Hegel's words simply has to go along with it. (Beiser 2005)

4. (Hegel 1969b), §383; (Hegel et al. 1971), p. 16.
5. The relation between the need for both a statement of principle and psychology draws on the discussion by Robert Pippin of how Western movies provide a partial account of such political psychology. (Pippin 2010)
6. On slavery and the ancient world, see (Finley 1964).
7. In essence, this was the basis of the dispute between Hegel and Leopold Ranke, which led to famous polemics in the 1820s and 1830s on the part of Ranke and his followers against the Hegelian school and vice versa. Superficially, it seems like a dispute between a fact-oriented empirical historian and a lofty and abstract philosophy of history, but the dispute went deeper. Both thought that particular shapes of life could be discerned and described. Ranke, however, seemed to think that each shape of life was sui generis and was, in his famous phrase, "immediate to God." On Ranke's view, as a historian, he was doing God's work by describing these shapes of life in the detail that he did and leaving the meaning of the whole to God himself. Yet, as scholars of Ranke's work have shown, he did actually think that there was a meaning to history, and he thought that the gifted historian (such as himself) could discern God's hand without having to have any systematic argument for it. Because the unity of a shape of life, as Ranke said, is a "spiritual unity, it can thus be apprehended in a

spiritual apperception." ("Idee der Universalhistorie 1831 bzw. 1831–32" in (Ranke, Fuchs, and Schieder 1964), p. 78). This divides the philosopher (i.e., Hegel) from himself: "There are two ways to learn to know human things. One is the knowledge of the singular and the other that of abstraction; one is the way of the philosopher, and the other is that of history." ("Idee der Universalhistorie 1831 bzw. 1831–32," (Ranke, Fuchs, and Schieder 1964), p. 87). Hegel, of course, rejected that alternative, namely, that one had to approach history either by adding up the singular events and fact or by abstracting from all of them to discover some larger pattern of meaning. Hegel's project in fact rejected the idea that the pattern of history could be discerned by a process of abstraction (as if one could look at say, Greece, Rome, and Germany and determine what was going on in history by way of the commonalities found in such abstraction). Hegel instead wished to see if there were any "infinite ends" in historical development. Hegel had two other main objections to Ranke and to his mentor, Barthold Georg Niebuhr. First, Ranke's claim to intuit the hand of God in history was empty, and when one starts from such an empty conception, one can conclude just about anything. Second, Hegel objected to what many took to be Ranke's strong point, his ability to construct a compelling narrative out of the facts. (Niebuhr did something similar.) For Hegel, such a narrative was just made up. In passages such as this—where Ranke says of Henry IV of France that he "was filled with great ideas. He fancied that he still saw his star hovering over him, destined to do something marvelous"—Hegel objected that this was the stuff of Walter Scott novels and best left to such novelists, who admitted that they were making it up, and not to historians. It is not clear that Hegel was simply denigrating one of Ranke's strengths, and the role of narrative-telling in a "scholarly" historical work remains a controversial flash point among historians. (The specific quote is taken from (Gay 1974). Gay discusses the tensions between Ranke the dramatist, Ranke the "scientist," and Ranke the theologian.) Frederick Beiser seems to think that there is not really much of an important difference between Hegel's and Ranke's approaches, except on technicalities.: "On the whole, Hegel's polemic against Ranke is limited to his misgivings about the narrative technique of the [Ranke's] *Geschichte* . . . [and] that Ranke himself . . . [later] admitted this shortcoming." Beiser thinks that Hegel's objection is that Ranke is too detail-oriented and has not adequately achieved a disclosure of the unity of the events (Beiser 2011). Beiser's view, however, underplays Hegel's objections to Ranke's idea of "spiritual apperception" in general, although Beiser does note that Ranke and F. H. Jacobi both share an appeal to intuition. On Niebuhr's use of Roman history to argue about contemporary Prussian politics—which Hegel also criticized—see (Ziolkowski 2004). On Ranke's ever-more-explicit commitment to the idea that there was a meaning in history that the Christian historian graced by God, and only by so being graced, could discern, see (Krieger 1977) and (Toews 2004). Toews' account is particularly insightful about the tension, if not outright contradiction, in the post-Hegelian historicism that arose in the 1830s and 1840s. Toews locates the tension in Ranke's thought as that between maintaining a stance that the final ends of life are completely transcendent—"Thy will be done"—and the conception of the final ends of life as being bound essentially to the development and constitution of a specific community ("Our will be done"). The project of the kind of historicism which shows up in Ranke's historical practice (and which, for example, shows up also in K. F. Schinkel's architecture and in some of Felix Mendelssohn's music), was supposed to be able to stabilize, as it were, that tension. Hegel would have thought such an approach had to fail, since it simply pitted one "finite" (a particular divine will) against another "finite" (a particular communal will).

8. On the idea that infinite ends have no internal limit, see (Rödl 2010).

9. In connection to the philosophy of religion and the establishment of religious cults at the earliest points in history, Hegel remarks, "As God's purpose, it has its being in the actual spirit; therefore it must have inward universality and be the genuinely divine end within itself; it must be the end that is substantive, that has substantive universality. A substantive end internal to spirit is one such that the existing spiritual individuals know themselves as one, behave as one, are united. It is essentially an inwardly universal, infinite end, an ethical end, for its soil is in self-consciousness, in freedom, in freedom realized. This is where the practical side first emerges, [God's] purpose in actual consciousness." (Hegel and Hodgson 1984), p. 435.

10. Hegel's mother-in-law reported that Hegel had promised her that the lectures on the philosophy of history would be intelligible "even for women." Leaving aside the sexism of the remark, the reference makes it clear that Hegel intended that series to be intelligible to a very general audience. As the history of the reception of the lectures shows, he by and large succeeded. (Hegel and Hoffmeister 1961), Letter #664.

11. (Hegel and Hoffmeister 1994), p. 108; (Hegel 1975), p. 91: "What makes men morally discontented (and they may even take a certain pride in this discontent) is that they find the present unsuited to their ideas, principles, and opinions concerning ends of a more universal content, which they consider to be right and good (among which we must nowadays include ideals of political constitutions in particular), or to their predilection for constructing their own ideals on which to lavish their enthusiasm. They contrast existence as it is with their own view of how things by rights ought to be. In this case, it is not particular interests or passions which demand satisfaction, but reason, justice, and

freedom; and, equipped with this title, such demands give themselves an air of authority and can easily take the form not just of dis-content with the condition and events of the world but of actual rebellion against them. To appreciate such feelings and attitudes correctly, we should have to make a thorough examination of the demands themselves and of the highly peremptory views and attitudes which accompany them."

12. "Now here, because we are discussing more precisely the state of the world of *spiritual* reality, we must take it up from the side of the *will*. For it is through the will that the spirit as such enters upon existence, and the immediate substantial bonds of reality are displayed in the specific manner in which the will's guides, i.e. the concepts of ethics and law, and, in short, what, in general terms, we may call justice, are activated." (Hegel 1969c), pp. 235–236; (Hegel 1988), p. 179.

13. (Hegel 1969a), p. 143; (Hegel 2010), ¶¶ 172, 173. "It is the *simple genus,* which in the movement of life itself does not *exist for itself as this 'simple.'* Rather, in this *result,* life points towards something other than itself, namely, towards consciousness, for which life exists as this unity, that is, as genus. . . . But this other life for which the *genus* as such exists and which is the genus for itself, namely, *self-consciousness,* initially exists in its own eyes merely as this simple essence and, in its own eyes, is an object as the *pure I.*"

14. (Hegel 1969e), p. 55; (Hegel and Di Giovanni 2010), p. 37.

15. "Freedom is that which is the in itself of spirit. Spirit must know what it is in itself. We know it, but at the outset spirit does not know it. World history begins with this self-knowledge, and it is a work of 3,000 years which spirit has made in order to know itself." (Hegel 2005), p. 37.

16. On the comparison of Kant's and Hegel's philosophies of history, see (Sedgwick 2015). See also the helpful discussion in (Dale 2014).

17. See the discussions in (Rorty and Schmidt 2009).

18. On the oddly teleological nature of Kant's short sketch of a philosophy of history, see (Deligiorgi 2012).

19. Polybius: "But the Romans have subjected to their rule not portions, but nearly the whole of the world and possess an empire which is not only immeasurably greater than any which preceded it, but need not fear rivalry in the future. In the course of this work it will become more clearly intelligible by what steps this power was acquired, and it will also be seen how many and how great advantages accrue to the student from the systematic treatment of history. . . . Previously the doings of the world had been, so to say, dispersed, as they were held together by no unity of initiative, results, or locality. . . . For what gives my work its peculiar quality, and what is most remarkable in the present age, is this. Fortune has guided almost all the affairs of the world in one direction and has forced them to incline towards one and the same end." (Polybius et al. 2010) Vol. I, pp. 7, 9, 11.

3. Hegel's False Start

1. See the very helpful exposition in Wang Hui's critical account of this Western view of Chinese history in (Wang 2014), especially pp. 41–53. Overall, Wang understands Hegel's philosophy of history in terms of its being the teleology of a single individual "thing" (spirit), which, so he also argues, skews Hegel's (and all his successors') views about China's possibilities, since China (or "Asia" in general) can only appear as the beginning stage of the development of this individual: "A major source of Hegel's philosophy of history is a psychological theory that developed out of an individualist and anthropocentric tradition. The goal of this psychological theory is to resolve philosophical difficulties produced by individualist discourse by using a construct of analogical relationships between world history and history of individual spirit." (Wang 2014), p. 47. That is indeed the traditional, but, so it is argued in this book, crucial misunderstanding of Hegel's view of spirit in history.

2. This interpretation of the *Phenomenology* is, of course, contested. There are interpreters who claim that the *Phenomenology* is not historical in any but the most superficial ways. Prominent among these interpreters is Stephen Houlgate, who interprets Hegel in a more or less Neo-Platonic form. Thus, Houlgate confidently asserts that "This development is to be understood not as historical, but as *logical*. The book does not examine how human consciousness has actually changed through time into modern self-understanding, but shows how certain general 'shapes' of consciousness necessarily transform themselves, because of their very structure, into further shapes. The development traced by Hegel overlaps in certain parts with European history (for example, in the analysis of 'Stoic' consciousness), but what gives Hegel's book its unity is the fact that it renders explicit what is logically entailed by being conscious." (Houlgate 2003), pp. 11–12. The interpretation offered here argues that it is indeed from what is involved in self-consciousness that we get the logic of history, but that rests on a different conception of the *Logic* than Houlgate allows. For him, the *Logic* is about structures of "Being" that we simply observe as they transform themselves into each other—much as in some interpretations of Plato, the philosopher observes how the forms mix with each other. See (Houlgate 2006). By sharply separating the kind of free, self-determining thought that he thinks Hegel espouses from empirical reality, Houlgate says that "Free, self-determining philosophy shows that human consciousness is impelled by its very nature to develop an awareness of its own freedom over time, and so to generate the process of history. . . . But, equally, it understands itself to be a product of a history which, given those particular natural and historical conditions, had to lead to the emergence of the consciousness of

freedom, because it was generated by the drive towards self-consciousness which is a necessary and intrinsic characteristic of human consciousness itself." (Houlgate 1991), p. 75. A similar but much more immanent view is also represented by (Winfield 2013). Like Houlgate, Winfield takes Hegel to be observing the course of free, self-determining thought: "Because the presupposed subject-matter develops itself through its own self-examination, what we observe is what our subject matter knows itself to be in function of how it distinguishes its object from its knowing." (p. 382) Like Houlgate, he also takes Hegel to have offered a timeless account that then finds external instantiation in history: "We observe empirically that the institutions of freedom are beginning to arise in modern times. On the basis of this nonphilosophical, empirical descriptive judgment, we can then look back over the given historical record and interpret it in light of the a priori normative history of what should occur. Thereby we represent what has happened as a history of freedom reaching its fulfillment in our time." p. 365.

3. On Hegel's rather careless and biased used of his resources on Africa, see (Bernasconi 1998).

4. Like probably most Europeans of his time (and for a good many European and American historians after that), Hegel did not have any idea of the dynamism and change going on across the African continent in the eighteenth and nineteenth centuries. For a corrective view on that (and also as a corrective for Hegel's views on the dynamism of Asian societies in that period), see (Bayly 2004). A concise and well-formulated version of the case against Hegel's view that Africa is somehow outside of history and what is at stake in the debate about Africa's "role" in history is to be found in (Appiah 1998). On the ongoing damage which Hegel's dismissal of African life has exercised, see (Taiwo 1998).

5. Hegel says of Africans, giving them some credit while at the same time deprecating them and brushing them aside: "They cannot be denied a capacity for education; not only have they, here and there, adopted Christianity with the greatest gratitude and spoken movingly of the freedom they have acquired through Christianity after a long spiritual servitude, but in Haiti they have even formed a State on Christian principles. But they do not show an inner striving for culture. In their native country the most shocking despotism prevails. There they do not attain to the feeling of human personality—their mentality is quite dormant, remaining sunk within itself and making no progress, and thus corresponding to the compact, undifferentiated mass of the African continent." (Hegel 1969a) §393, p. 60; (Hegel et al. 1971), pp. 42–43.

6. See Andrew Buchwalter, "Is Hegel's Philosophy of History Eurocentric?" in (Buchwalter 2012). Buchwalter's answer to his own question: "While not disputing

the presence of such a dimension, I have argued that it is less pernicious than is commonly assumed." p. 252. Each culture on Buchwalter's reading of Hegel is an end in itself and calls for its own transcendence (including Europe). That is true, but Hegel does nonetheless have a ranking of how things stand vis-à-vis what they contribute to European modernity, and therefore, or so I argue here, it is far more pernicious than Buchwalter gives it credit for, although Hegel's conception can within its own terms be corrected.

7. See the excellent account of Hegel's sources in (Hegel et al. 2011).

8. "The only distinction between the African and Asiatic peoples and those of the Greeks, Romans and modern times is just that the latter know that they are free. It exists for them. The former are also free, but they do not know it, they do not exist as free. This constitutes the enormous difference in the alteration of their conditions." (Hegel 1969b), p. 40; (Hegel 1963), p. 22. See the discussion of Hegel's conception of "savagery" in (Alznauer 2015), pp. 77–78. Alznauer thinks that this would mean that the individual is not responsible (in the expanded sense Alznauer attributes to Hegel) and therefore is not really an agent at all, since he or she does not engage in a self-subjection to a legal order but only follows a social norm out of fear of punishment of some sort. On the reading here, Hegel does think that savages are indeed agents but ones for whom the highest principles are simply social norms.

9. (Hegel 1996), p. 123; (Hegel et al. 2011), p. 214: "To that extent it has no history. So, in speaking about the most ancient history of this empire, we are not speaking of something past but instead of the shape that it has today."

10. Thus, Hegel claims: "Passing from the administration to the situation of law in China, we find the subjects regarded as in a state of tutelage in virtue of the principle of patriarchal government. No independent classes or orders, as in India, have interests of their own to defend. All is directed and superintended from above. All legal relations are definitely settled by legal norms; free sentiment, the moral standpoint in general, is thereby thoroughly obliterated."(Hegel 1969d), p. 161; (Hegel 1956), pp. 127–128.

11. (Hegel 1969d); (Hegel 1956), pp. 130–131.

12. "People only have respect for each other if they have a consciousness of something higher." (Hegel 2005), p. 68.

13. (Hegel 2005), p. 84. "The state's civil servants have no other religion than that of accomplishing the will of the emperor and carrying out his laws. Consequently, one calls this political atheism."

14. (Hegel 2005), p. 72.

15. In speaking of the Greeks in his *Encyclopedia,* Hegel notes that, "However, burdened with immediacy, the freedom of the subject is only custom without infinite reflection into itself, without subjective inwardness of conscience; with

that, the further development of devotion and the religious cult of beautiful art is also determined." (Hegel 1969a), §557, p. 368; (Hegel et al. 1971), pp. 293–294.

16. (Hegel 1969d), p. 201; (Hegel 1956), p. 151: "If China is entirely a state, then the Indian political existence is only a people and no state." In his illuminating work on Chinese philosophical and political thought, Wang Hui attributes to Hegel the view that China was not really a state but an empire and would have to become a nation-state in order to become modern. He thinks that is wrong and attributes this view to a Western binary of nation-state / empire which he argues is not appropriate for comprehending the different forms of political organization that China possessed and which thus puts China into a kind of historical teleology in which it looks as if he has to become thoroughly European to make any progress. Thus, "It is only in this implicit contrast between empire and state that Hegel is able to present Europe, which had been produced in Asia, as the center and terminus of the old world." (Wang 2014), p. 46. He also admits, however, that Hegel compares the state structures of China with those of Europe: "Hegel's concept of the Orient is a philosophical response to discourses on the Orient in European thought; at its core, it is a comparison of European state structures and Asian state structures." (Wang 2014), p. 49. Hegel's negative argument about China, however, is more about the suppression of difference within the state than of China's backwardness in failing to become a state and about the role of a form of "positivism" in understanding the status of law.

17. In criticizing what he takes to be the Chinese conflation of law and custom with morality, Hegel notes: "Legality may not intrude into matters of sentiment. If some moral point is commanded, the laws doing so can have an excellent resonance, can be in Solomonic language, although this in turn opens the door to a despotism that is all the greater in proportion to how excellent the law sounds." (Hegel 1996), p. 144; (Hegel et al. 2011), p. 233.

18. He even goes so far as to insinuate that some of the great achievements of classical Chinese civilization in fact had to be Greek imports, since they could not have come up with those things themselves: "For it was from the Syrian empire that extended out deeply into Asia . . . is that there was doubtless conveyed to the interior of India and China, by Greek colonies migrating to there, the meager scientific knowledge which has lingered there like a tradition, though it has never flourished. For the Chinese, for example, are not skillful enough to make a calendar of their own, and they are unsuited, so it seems, for everything conceptual. Yet they exhibited ancient instruments unsuited to any work done by them, and the immediate conjecture was that these had come from Bactria. The ideas about the sciences of the Chinese and the Indians are false." (Hegel 1963), Vol. II, p. 123–4; (Hegel 1969c), p. 138.

19. Hegel reports an anecdote from British emissaries in China: "When the last legation from England departed after vesting the supreme mandarin, the householder used a whip to clear a path for the imperial dignitaries. Corporal punishment can in one sense be considered something utterly insignificant, since the human being is only injured in his lesser aspect, merely outwardly, in mere mortal existence. But corporal punishment is the most humiliating for the very reason that human being so afflicted is supposed to be coerced with regard to his inner being." (Hegel 1996), pp. 147–148; (Hegel et al. 2011), pp. 235–236.

20. See the account in "How China Became the First Market Society," in (McNeill and McNeill 2003), pp. 121–127.

21. The classic but contested treatment of this point is to be found in (Fairbank and Goldman 2006). On the whole, the Fairbank school seeks to understand "why" China failed to become modern and "why" it therefore failed in the nineteenth- and twentieth-century competition with the West. Wang Hui goes after the entire "Fairbank school" for inserting Western categories into a context where, he thinks, they obfuscate more than they reveal (Wang 2014). On the idea of China's similarity to their contemporaries, the Romans, vis-à-vis their status and strategies for empire, see (Burbank and Cooper 2010). China's ancient development of its own civilization as resting on the way it successfully integrated its connections with other human developments is nicely told in (McNeill and McNeill 2003). The McNeills take the underlying story of world history to consist of what they call the "human web," which they define as "a set of connections that link people to one another . . . which may take many forms: chance encounters, kinship, friendship, common worship, rivalry, enmity, economic exchange, ecological exchange, political cooperation, even military competition . . . what drives human history is the human ambition to alter one's condition to match one's hopes. But just what people hoped for, both in the material and spiritual reams, and how they pursued their hopes, depended on the information, ideas, and examples available to them. Thus, webs channeled and coordinated everyday human ambition and action—and still do." pp. 3–4. Hegel's own concern is not with these quasi-causal conditions of what is "driving" history. It is not the place here, but it would be interesting to do a more detailed investigation of what the McNeills' view of the "human ambition to alter one's condition to match one's hopes" with Hegel's attempt at constructing a philosophical history of the world.

22. See the discussions in the accompanying notes in (Hegel et al. 2011).

23. See the discussion in (Wang 2014): "Chapter 3: Heavenly Principle / Universal Principle and History," pp. 61–100. Wang Hui attributes a kind of "internalist" Hegelian principle to some of the Neo-Confucian scholars of the Song period:

"... their criterion for evaluating change was not time, but rather an internal criterion—'the propensity of principle' *(lishi)*." (Wang 2014), p. 91. See also his characterization of the methodology of that particular school: Their "methodology is something that is inherently needed by the worldviews of Heavenly Principle and Universal Principle but is also the force that causes crises to occur within the worldviews of Heavenly Principle and Universal Principle and leads them to break down under their own weight." (Wang 2014), p. 95.

24. (Hegel and Hoffmeister 1994), p. 176; (Hegel 1975), p. 145.

25. Thus, Hegel's argument against the Africans is a part of his argument about the Chinese. Whereas he finds little to count in favor of the Africans, he views them as similar to the Chinese in that they are "stalled" ways of life. However, or so goes Hegel's account, African social lives do not change in anything other than arbitrary ways, and thus no civilization as such gets created. On Hegel's highly distorted view about the so-called stalled and therefore unhistorical nature of the Africans and where he thought he found evidence for this, see (Bernasconi 1998).

26. (Hegel 1969d), p. 174; (Hegel 1956), p. 139.

27. For a thorough look at what Hegel's sources were about India and how they could have misled him, see (Viyagappa 1980).

28. (Sen 2005).

29. See (Halbfass 1988), p. 87.

30. This criticism is reinforced by Hegel's review of Wilhelm von Humboldt's piece on the Bhagavad Gita in his 1826 review in the *Jahrbüchern für wissenschaftliche Kritik* in (Hegel and Hoffmeister 1956), pp. 131–204, where Hegel, confronted with scholarship that rejects his dismissal of Indian thought, dwells on what he takes to be the fundamental abstractness and therefore emptiness of Indian thought and religion and thus its way of carving out a space for tyranny in the kind of regime encouraged by that kind of emptiness.

31. The references to an "enchanted" world and to measuring it against human dignity seem to have occurred in the late 1831 lectures, as Hegel was hardening his already hard views against the calls for a return to a romanticized German past.

32. See the discussion in (Bernasconi 2002).

33. Hegel's 1827 review ("Über die unter den Namen Bhagavad-Ghita bekannte Episode des Mahabharata von Wilhelm von Humboldt") is to be found in (Hegel and Hoffmeister 1956). He says (p. 158): "This dissolution is impossible, because what is highest in the Indian consciousness, the abstract essence, Brahman, is within itself devoid of any determination, which consequently can only be external to the unity and thus can only be an external, natural determination. In this falling apart of the universal and the concrete, both are devoid of

spirit.—The former is the empty unity and the latter is the unfree multiplicity; the person, falling apart into this, is bound only to a natural law of life; elevating himself to the former extreme, he is fleeing from and in negation to all concrete, spiritual life." On the relation between Hegel's review and Humboldt's original piece, see (Viyagappa 1980).

34. See (Hegel 1999), p. 148: "Von Humboldt translate the word [Yoga] as absorption *(Vertiefung)*, in which the returning-into-itself remains the most striking feature of the person conceived in terms of yoga and what therein is also its own mystical disposition of mind; even though that rendering of an expression, which springs out of a wholly idiosyncratic viewpoint of a language, into the particular word of another language is insufficient." Hegel equates this *"Vertiefung"* with "absorption" in this way: "The higher impetus, or rather the most sublime depth which comes to light here leads us at once beyond the European opposition, with which we began this exposition, that **of the practical and the theoretical;** acting becomes absorbed in knowing, or rather in the **abstract absorption** of consciousness within itself." (Hegel 1999), p. 142.

35. Hegel was also at pains to argue against the rising tide of those who, like his good friend, Georg Friedrich Creuzer, were arguing that Indian religion showed itself to be both older and aiming in the same direction as the Christian religion. The Indians were said to be the recipients of an earlier divine revelation, such that Indian culture and religion led directly to the Greeks (and hence to the Europeans). This unnerved Hegel a bit, but he still insisted that the philosophy coming out of the Indian religions, as well as the religions themselves, were, when examined in detail, different in kind from Christianity. He also thoroughly rejected Friedrich Schlegel's speculation (in 1808, earlier than Creuzer's writing) about India being the source, since degraded, of the original Christian revelation. See the discussion in (Crawford 2014) (accessed 8/14/15 12:25 PM). An excellent and much more detailed account of the German "orientalist" project is to be found in (Marchand 2009).

36. Hegel says this of the Indians and Chinese in relation to the Europeans: "The English, or rather the East India Company, are the rulers of this land, for it is a necessary fate of the Asiatic empires that they are to be subjected to the Europeans, and China will also at some point be bound to this fate." (Hegel 1969d), p. 179; (Hegel 1956), pp. 142–143.

37. See the discussion in (Bayly 2004).

38. "The oriental world also has decay within itself; in the oriental principle there lies, however, the determination, the principle, which is opposed to itself, that it does not have itself within itself. It does not within itself release spirit into freedom so that it would turn itself against itself." (Hegel and Lasson 1923), p. 639. I sometimes refer to the Lasson edition of the philosophy of history in

those places where it includes materials not present in the Eduard Gans-Karl Hegel standard edition, but never in those places where it is at odds with the more limited Hoffmeister edition of the introduction to the lectures on the philosophy of world history. Although Lasson improved on E. Gans / K. Hegel edition—he wanted to weave the various lecture materials into a seamless book—that project does not accord well with contemporary philological standards. See the discussion in the editor's introduction in (Hegel et al. 2011).

39. (Hegel 1969d), p. 266; (Hegel 1956), p. 215. Hegel equates this with the idea that "the human individual has an infinite value in himself." (Hegel 1969d), p. 266; (Hegel 1956), p. 216.

40. Joseph McCarney makes the interesting suggestion that Hegel's discussion here is misled by his own metaphor of the sun rising in the East and setting in the West as the expression of what it might mean for Hegel to say that there is a great drama in history whose curtain is now starting to set (but not having already set). McCarney suggests that Hegel is putting too much weight on his own metaphor. (McCarney 2000): "Hegel is in the grip of, it might be suggested, of a crude kind of pictorial thinking which constrains his expression." p. 174. However, if the reading given here is correct, Hegel's misreading of the "Orientals," as a civilization whose glory is now a matter of the past is not driven by a failed metaphor but by his belief that rule-governed and essentially dream-driven societies are to be found in the East at the origins of civilization. See also the discussion about the so-called "end of history" in (Dale 2014). After analyzing various versions of the "end of history" thesis, Thom Brooks takes Hegel's view of the end of history as merely provisional: "We should view [Hegel's theses about history's end] in its systematic context and recognize that the court of world judgment must always revise its assessments over time. Thus, world history is a court of forever provisional and revisable judgments." (Brooks 2013), p. 157.

41. Hegel sometimes seems to explain ethnic backwardness in terms of geography (where he seems to be partially following Montesquieu), in which case he would have to say that were non-European peoples to migrate to a European climate, they too would become more "spiritual" and free. However, he never actually draws that conclusion. (Given that the premises are false, it is just as well that he doesn't.) In his meticulous study of Hegel's philosophy of history, Joseph McCarney claims that Hegel's conception of "peoples" *(Völker)* is most emphatically not an ethnic conception. He attributes instead to Hegel the claim "that world historical peoples are not be thought of an ethnic groups, a point on which Hegel is unequivocally firm." (McCarney 2000), p. 141. This seems too apologetic for Hegel since Hegel is simply not "unequivocally firm" about this. For example, in (Hegel 1969a), §394; (Hegel et al. 1971), p. 46, he says:

"The philosophy of history, on the other hand, has for its subject-matter the world-historical significance of races, that is to say, if we take world-history in the most comprehensive sense of the word, the highest development to which the original disposition of the national character attains, the most spiritual form to which the natural mind indwelling the nations raises itself." McCarney also takes Hegel's arguments against Schlegel's and Schelling's conceptions of there necessarily being a primitive "people" that preexists all other mankind (as a replacement for the idea of Adam and Eve in the Garden) to be Hegel's argument against "the idea of an Aryan race, an Urvolk, to which modern Germans belonged and from which 'all science and art has simply been handed down to us'" ((McCarney 2000), p. 140). Although such an idea of an Aryan *Urvolk* did appear in Friedrich Schlegel's work around 1819, the idea of an Aryan "race" did not really come on the scene until after Hegel's time, and in any event, Hegel's argument is mostly aimed against any conception at all of a primordial "state of nature," which would be humanity as its most pure form and therefore most authentic, a view, which, as Hegel notes, is simply writing history on the basis of pure fantasy.

4. Europe's Logic

1. See (Bayly 2004). Bayly convincingly shows that the origins of modernity have to be put into a global view, and that the story—economic, social and intellectual—is not confined to Europe or simply following Europe's lead. As he sums up his own findings: "Europe and its American colonies may already have had a competitive advantage in several areas as early as 1750. They may have been able to exploit their own and others' industrious revolutions in local production and consumption most effectively. But this does not mean that all significant change was initiated there. The origins of change in world history remained multi-centered throughout. We need not so much to reorient world history as to decentralize it." p. 470.

2. "To show that the spirit of the Egyptians presented itself to their consciousness in the form of a *problem*, we can call on the celebrated inscription in the inner sanctum of the Goddess Neith at Sais: *"I am that which is, that which was, and that which will be; no one has lifted my veil."* This inscription gives voice to the principle of the Egyptian spirit; although people have often had the opinion that it is supposed to be valid for all times. . . . In the Egyptian Neith, truth is still locked away. The Greek Apollo is its solution; his utterance is: *"Man, know thyself."* In this dictum, there is no intention to be a self-knowledge that regards the particularities of one's own weaknesses and defects: it is not the individual who is supposed to get to know his particularity, but humanity *as such* is supposed to

attain self-knowledge. This mandate was given for the Greeks, and in the Greek spirit the human exhibits itself in its clarity and its development." (Hegel 1969j), pp. 271–272; (Hegel 1956), p. 220.

3. See the account in (McNeill and McNeill 2003).

4. (Cline 2014).

5. See (McNeill and McNeill 2003). The MacNeills argue that the structure of Bronze Age ancient civilization in that area more or less resembled that of Egyptian rule: "Crete nonetheless resembled Egypt in the concentration of resources in the hands of a sacred ruler who probably controlled overseas shipping just Pharaoh controlled the boats on the Nile that undergirded his power." p. 68.

6. This is a point made by (McNeill and McNeill 2003), p. 72.

7. "In the case before us, the interest of the world's history hung trembling in the balance. Confronting each other were Oriental despotism—a world united under one lord and sovereign—and on the one side, separate states, insignificant in extent and resources, but animated by free individuality. Never in History has the superiority of spiritual power over the masses—and that of no contemptible amount—been made so gloriously manifest.—This war, and the subsequent development of the states which took the lead in it, is the most dazzling period of Greece. Everything which the Greek principle involved, then reached its perfect bloom and came into view." (Hegel 1969j), p. 315; (Hegel 1956), pp. 257–258.

8. In fact, Hegel uses the contrast between "China" and Greece to make a related but different point about negativity. If "China" fails to develop the differences and distinctions needed for its members to have a satisfactory life, Greece, which succeeds in developing the aspect of self-sufficiency of individuals *(Selbständigkeit)* could do so only be exaggerating the difference.

9. "But this immediate unity of the substantial with the individuality of inclination, impulses, and will is inherent in Greek virtue, so that individuality is a law to itself, without being subjected to an independently subsisting law, judgment, and tribunal." (Hegel 1969e), p. 244; (Hegel 1988), p. 185.

10. (Hegel and Lasson 1923), pp. 570–571.

11. (Hegel 1969f), p. 24; (Hegel 1988), p. 436; Hegel goes on to say on p. 437 (p. 25): "Nor, on the other hand, did the Greeks make the advance to that deepening of subjective life in which the individual subject separates himself from the whole and the universal in order to be independent in his own inner being; and only through a higher return into the inner totality of a purely spiritual world does he attain a reunification with the substantial and essential. On the contrary, in Greek ethical life the individual was independent and free in himself, though without cutting himself adrift from the universal interests present in the actual

state and from the affirmative immanence of spiritual freedom in the temporal present. The universal element in ethical life, and the abstract freedom of the person in his inner and outer life, remain, in conformity with the principle of Greek life, in undisturbed harmony with one another, and at the time when this principle asserted itself in the actual present in still undamaged purity there was no question of an independence of the political sphere contrasted with a subjective morality distinct from it; the substance of political life was merged in individuals just as much as they sought this their own freedom only in pursuing the universal aims of the whole."

12. (Hegel 2005), p. 125.

13. That this is an idealized picture is true. However, the animating idea behind the polis—as that of a place where male self-sufficient equals (many of them slaveholders) met without any natural authority to command each other—was indeed a reality of Greek life, even if it was not quite the fully democratic participatory milieu that Hegel portrays. See the discussions in (Finley 1983) ; and (Osborne 2004).

14. (Aristotle 1941b), 1367a 30–34, p. 1356. The passage can also be rendered as "under the compulsion of another." David Bronstein suggested to me that the model lying behind the idea expressed in the passage is that of the truly "noble" man who commands others as an architect might command the menial workers. Or, as we might put it, the noble (and therefore the free) man does not take orders from another—neither from his wife nor his slaves. As such a self-sufficient individual, he meets other such noble, free men in the democratic sphere of the polis where nobody is naturally entitled to give orders to the others. In the *Politics,* Aristotle extends this conception of having to exhibit theatricality to others, to let ourselves be guided by others, as inherently ignoble: "Thus then we reject the professional instruments and also the professional mode of education in music (and by professional we mean that which is adopted in contests), for in this the performer practices the art, not for the sake of his own improvement, but in order to give pleasure, and that of a vulgar sort, to his hearers. For this reason the execution of such music is not the part of a free-man but of a paid performer, and the result is that the performers are vulgarized, for the end at which they aim is bad. The vulgarity of the spectator tends to lower the character of the music and therefore of the performers; they look to him—he makes them what they are, and fashions even their bodies by the movements which he expects them to exhibit." (Aristotle 1941a), p. 1314 (1341b).

15. See (Pinkard 2008).

16. In his lectures on aesthetics, Hegel is fully explicit about how this idea of heroism is only mythical and has no place in a modern order of thoughts. For example: "Such a state of affairs is the one we are accustomed to ascribe to the *Heroic*

Age. Which of these situations, however,—the civilized and developed life of
the state, or an heroic age—is the better, this is not the place to explain; here
our only concern is with the Ideal of art, and for *art* the cleavage between universal and individual must not yet come on the scene in the way described
above, no matter how necessary this difference is for other ways in which spiritual existence is actualized. For art and its Ideal is precisely the universal in so
far as the universal is *configurated* for our vision and therefore is still *immediately*
one with particular individuals and their life. / (αα) This occurs in the so-
called Heroic Age which appears as a time in which virtue, in the Greek sense
of αρετη, is the basis of actions. . . . But this immediate unity of the substantial
with the individuality of inclination, impulses, and will is inherent in Greek
virtue, so that individuality is a law to itself, without being subjected to an
independently subsisting law, judgement, and tribunal. Thus, for example, the
Greek heroes appear in a pre-legal era, or become themselves the founders of
states, so that right and order, law and morals, proceed from them and are actualized as their own individual work which remains linked with them. In this
way Hercules was extolled by the ancient Greeks and stands for them as an
ideal of original heroic virtue." (Hegel 1969e), p. 244; (Hegel 1988), p. 185.

17. "Another circumstance that demands special attention here is that of slavery.
This was a necessary condition of an aesthetic (schönen) democracy, where it
was the right and duty of every citizen to deliver or to listen to orations respecting the management of the state in the place of public assembly, to take part in
the exercise of the Gymnasia, and to participate in the celebration of festivals.
It was a necessary condition of such occupations that the citizens should be
freed from handicraft occupations and therefore that what among us is performed by free citizens (the work of daily life) should be done by slaves." (Hegel
1969j), 311; (Hegel 1956), pp. 254–255.

18. Adorno only sees freedom as determinate negation, as the idea of what is lost in
some condition of unfreedom, as he puts it gnomically: freedom is the "determinate negation of any given concrete expression of unfreedom." This has to
do with Adorno's admission of only a "negative" dialectic. (Adorno and
Tiedemann 2006), p. 243.

19. See (Pinkard 2007) and (Pinkard 2008).

20. Raymond Geuss makes an allied, although not identical point, about the flaw
at the basis of the ancient conceptions of authority: "The ancient situation is
one that opens a space for a particular kind of tragedy, namely a misproportion
between a discretionary power that can, admittedly, be used appropriately or
inappropriately and the failure to specify any effective moral recourse to those
who, being subject to this power, might be disadvantaged by its inappropriate
use. The modern conception closes off this particular space by assuming a

certain moral equality among people and by vesting in each individual a prima facie right to self-protection, which means a right 'in principle' to resist." See the very helpful discussion in (Geuss), p. 118.

21. (Hegel 1969e), 513; (Hegel 1988), p. 400: "The *Dike* of the Greeks, for example, is not to be called an allegory; she is universal necessity, eternal justice, the universal powerful person, the absolutely substantial basis of the relations of nature and spiritual life, and therefore herself the absolutely independent being whom individuals, gods as well as men, have to follow."

22. See the discussion in (Osborne 2004). For a less-rosy picture than that of Hegel of the freedom of the polis, see M. I. Finley's discussion: "What gave it an uncommon twist in Greece was the city-state, with its intimacy, its stress on the community and on the freedom and dignity of the individual which went with membership. The citizen felt he had claims on the community, not merely obligations to it, and if the regime did not satisfy him he was not loath to do something about it—to get rid of it if he could. In consequence the dividing-line between politics and sedition (*stasis* the Greeks called it) was a thin one in classical Greece, and often enough *stasis* grew in into ruthless civil war." (Finley 1977), pp. 59–60.

23. An argument for its falsity is to be found in (Romm 1989). An argument for its plausibility can be found in (French 1994).

24. On the overestimation and mythologizing of Alexander by later historians, see (Beard 2013). On Beard's account, the epithet, "the great," is probably a Roman addition to Alexander's name—which would make sense for a new conquest state seeking to legitimate itself in its Mediterranean world. (Beard also notes that this idea is not original to herself—others have also suggested that "the great" was a Roman invention). See also (Green 2012) and (Osborne 2004).

25. "Greek ethical life had made Greece unfit to form one common state, for the dissociation of small states from each other, and the concentration in cities, where the interest and the spiritual education pervading the whole, could be identical, was the necessary condition of the freedom. It was only a momentary combination that occurred in the Trojan War, and even in the Median wars a union could not be accomplished." (Hegel 1969j), p. 324; (Hegel 1956), p. 265.

26. Mary Beard has noted how conflicted the origin stories were for the Roman themselves: "More often, though, ancient theorizing broaches a cluster of issues that underlie so much of Roman cultural debate more generally: What was Roman about this characteristically Roman institution? Do the roots of Roman cultural practice lie outside the city? How far is traditional Roman culture always by definition "foreign"? These themes are familiar from the conflicting stories told of the origins of the Roman state as a whole, where the idea of a native Italic identity (in the shape of the Romulus myth) is held in tension

with the competing version (in the shape of the Aeneas myth) that derives the Roman state from distant Troy. They are familiar too from the more self-consciously intellectualizing version of Dionysius of Halicarnassus, the aim of whose *Antiquitates Romanae* (Roman Antiquities) was to prove that Rome had been in origin a Greek city." (Beard 2007), p. 322. In more recent work, she has laid out how problematic the differing origin stories were for the Romans themselves, both in terms of how they conflicted with each other and in terms of the conflicts within each of the stories themselves. Roman "self-consciousness" about this was quite developed. See (Beard 2015).

27. Hegel thought that history was only possible for states. His reason for thinking so was that until a "people" had organized itself into a state, it could not be recognized as a genuine "people" by other states who by virtue of being such states have the authority to bestow recognition or to withhold it. Until it formed a political unity and fought for recognition, a "people" would have to be formless or ambiguous about who they were and hence could not collectively struggle for recognition. This seems contentious at best. For example, the Greeks could not form a single state, but they were recognized nonetheless as "Greeks." The Persians recognized them as a unitary force even though the Persians did not establish political relations with a unitary Greek state because they could not. Nonetheless, the idea that only as a "people" is a "nation" can it thus be recognized as a "state."

28. "The Roman people were not produced from a natural unit. They were something made, and thus made violently. By birth, they were not something originary. *(Ursprüngliches)*." (Hegel 2005), p. 143.

29. "Such an origin brought with itself the hardest discipline. The sacrifice must be the strongest in a band of robbers who in stand in hostile relations to everyone outside of themselves and which have no legitimacy, unlike other peoples whom they revered, since they knew that these others had occupied their land from time immemorial. The bond was not a liberal bond but that of a forced condition of subordination." (Hegel 2005), p. 144.

30. On the contingency of the formation of Rome's imperial ambitions, see (Woolf 2012); and (Beard 2015).

31. See the discussion about Rome's being a conquest state and tributary state in (Woolf 2012). See also (Finley 1983). See also the discussion in (Burbank and Cooper 2010).

32. See (Woolf 2012), p. 37.

33. See (Woolf 2012), p. 226.

34. "The influence of Greece also reaches into the Roman world, and hence, we have to speak of philosophy in the territory of the Roman world; but the Romans produced no proper philosophy any more than any proper poets. They

have only received from and imitated others, although they have often done this with *esprit;* even their religion comes from the Greek, and the special character of Roman religion makes no approach to philosophy and art, but is philosophical and inartistic." (Hegel 1969h), p. 123; (Hegel 1963), Vol. I, p. 101.

35. "Of the general character of the Romans we can say that, in contrast with that original wild poetry and inversion of everything finite to be found in the Orient and in contrast with the beautiful, harmonious poetry and the equally tempered freedom of Spirit of the Greeks, here, with the Romans the *prose* of life makes its appearance: The self-consciousness of finitude, the abstraction of the understanding and the hardness of legal personality, whose intractability even in the family is not expanded all the way to natural morality but rather remains the unfeeling non-spiritual, heartless "unit," which posits the unity of this "unit" only in abstract universality." (Hegel 1969j), pp. 350–351; (Hegel 1956), p. 288.

36. See the nice discussion in (Beard 2015).

37. "In considering the Roman World, we have not to do with a concretely spiritual life, rich within itself; but the world-historical moment in it is the *abstractum* of universality, and the purpose which is pursued with severity, devoid of spirit, is mere *dominination,* in order to that *abstractum* into valid force." (Hegel 1969j), p. 340; (Hegel 1956), p. 279.

38. (Hegel 1969j), p. 273; Sibree nicely renders : "Mit dem Lichte der Perser beginnt die geistige Anschauung, und in derselben nimmt der Geist Abschied von der Natur" as "With the 'Light' of the Persians begins a spiritual view of things, and here Spirit bids adieu to Nature." (Hegel 1956) pp. 221–222.

39. The overall conception of Roman subjectivity as contrasted with Greek subjectivity is summed up at (Hegel 1969j), pp. 239–240; (Hegel 1956), pp. 278–279: "Here in Rome then, we find from now on this free universality, this abstract freedom, which on the one hand posits an abstract state, politics and power, over concrete individuality and thoroughly subordinates individuality to politics and power, while on the other side it creates a legal personality *(Persönlichkeit)* in opposition to this universality—the freedom of the I turned within itself *(Ichs in sich),* which really must be distinguished from individuality. For legal personality constitutes the ground-level determination of right: It comes into existence chiefly [the institution of] property, but it is indifferent to the concrete determinations of the living spirit with which individuality is concerned. These two elements, which constitute Rome—political universality for itself and the abstract freedom of the individual within itself—at first have to do with the form of inwardness itself. This inwardness—this turn into the self which we saw to be the corruption of the Greek spirit—becomes here the basis on which a new side of world history arises."

40. (Hegel and Hoffmeister 1994), p. 19; (Hegel 1975), p. 21.

41. "That, therefore, which was abidingly present to the minds of men was not their country, or any kind of ethical unity; rather, they were directed only to yield themselves to fate, and to achieve a perfect indifference to life—an indifference which they sought either in freedom of thought or in immediate sensuous enjoyment. Thus man was either at odds with existence, or entirely given over to sensuous existence. He either found his destiny in the task of acquiring the means of enjoyment through the favor of the emperor, or through violence, testamentary frauds, and cunning; or he sought repose in philosophy, which alone was still able to supply something firm, something existing in and for itself, for the systems of that time—Stoicism, Epicureanism, and Skepticism—although opposed to each other, were oriented to the same thing, namely, rendering spirit absolutely indifferent to everything which the actual world had to offer. These philosophies were therefore widely extended among the cultivated: They produced in man an imperturbableness within himself through thinking, through the activity which brings forth the universal." (Hegel 1969j), pp. 384–385; (Hegel 1956), pp. 317–318.

42. ". . . The imperturbableness of skepticism made the will's purpose into the willing of purposelessness itself." (Hegel 1969j), p. 385; (Hegel 1956), p. 318.

43. "Through its being the state's purpose, that the individuals in their ethical life should be sacrificed to it, the world is sunk in melancholy: Its heart is broken, and it is *all over* with the natural side of spirit, which has sunk into a feeling of wretchedness." (Hegel 1969j), p. 339; (Hegel 1956), p. 278.

44. He takes this in a decidedly Johannine direction to the effect that the divine is reason itself as it manifests itself in life: "Already in John (εν αρχη η ο λογος, και ο λογος ην προς τον θεον, και θεος ην ο λογος [I, 1]) we see the beginning of a more profound comprehension." [In the beginning was the Logos, and the Logos was with God, and the Logos was God.] (Hegel 1969j), p. 401; (Hegel 1956), p. 331. In effect, Hegel makes the Christian God into Aristotle's god as that divinity is described at the end of the *Nicomachean Ethics*. (Or, conversely, he sees Christianity as the Aristotelian god "becoming flesh," the concrete, flesh and blood embodiment of "thought thinking thought.")

45. In discussing the Roman conquest of other "peoples," Hegel says: "The relation to other nations was purely that of force. The national individuality of peoples did not, as early as the time of the Romans, demand respect, as is the case nowadays. The various peoples were not yet recognized as legitimate, and the various states had not yet recognized each other as essentially existing. Equal right to existence leads to a union of states, such as exists in modern Europe, or a condition like that of Greece, in which the states had an equal right to existence under the protection of the Delphic god." (Hegel 1969j), p. 374; (Hegel 1956), p. 308.

46. To return to an earlier citation: "For the *cognition* already contained in the simple *logical* Idea is only that of the concept of cognition thought by us, not the cognition present at hand for itself, not actual spirit, but only its possibility." (Hegel 1969c), §381, p. 18; (Hegel et al. 1971), p. 8.

47. In the case of Rome, so Hegel thought, this meant that the abstract philosophies of stoicism, skepticism and Epicureanism were the only real possibilities for Roman philosophy: "And thus philosophy stepped over into the Roman world. And even though these philosophies belonged to Greece, and the Romans' great teachers were always Greeks (these philosophies arose in Greece), these systems in particular constituted under Roman rule *the philosophy of the Roman world.*" (Hegel 1969i), p. 252; (Hegel 1963), vol. II, p. 234.

48. "In other words, that which exists only in itself is a possibility or potentiality *(Vermögen)* which has not yet emerged from being an inner into existence. A second moment is necessary before it can attain actuality—that of actuation or actualization; and its principle is the will, the activity of mankind in the world at large. It is only by means of this activity that the original concepts or determinations existing in themselves *(an sich seiende)* are realized and actualized." (Hegel and Hoffmeister 1994), p. 81; (Hegel 1975), p. 69.

49. In his lectures on the philosophy of history, Hegel credits this to the development of monotheism in the Jewish religion. However, Hegel also held that the Jewish religion could only be a national and not truly universal religion and thus turned out not to be the point in history where the device of "all are free" came to expression. Although Hegel's rather narrow views on Judaism did indeed expand and change over his career in Berlin, he remained dead set against the idea that Judaism could really be a philosophy of universal humanity. It was, so he argued in the lectures, in fact the destruction of the temple by the Romans and the anguish it produced that pushed some of the Judaic monotheists away from Judaism as a national religion into a religion of humanity—that is to say, Roman power and its abuse created the conditions for Christianity. See the discussion in (Hodgson 2012). This idea of the impossibility of universality for the religion of Judaism was countered by the celebrated neo-Kantian, Hermann Cohen in his updating of Kant's idea of a religion of reason. (Cohen 1995)

50. (Hegel and Hoffmeister 1994), p. 59; (Hegel 1975), p. 51.

51. Hegel notes that: "The racial differences depicted in the *Zusatz* to §393 are the essential ones, the differences of the universal mind in nature as determined by the concept." (Hegel 1969c), §394, pp. 63–64; (Hegel et al. 1971), p. 46. A. D. Smith's conception of "ethnies" in his sense is that they are "are constituted, not by lines of physical descent, but by the sense of continuity, shared memory and collective destiny, i.e. by lines of cultural affinity embodied in myths,

memories, symbols and values retained by a given cultural unit of population"
(Smith 1991). Smith uses this concept to explain the phenomenon of nationalism: "A nation . . . is a *named human population sharing an historic territory,*
common myths and historical memories, a mass, public culture, a common economy
and common legal rights and duties for all members. By definition the nation is a
community of common myths and memories, as is an ethnie. It is also a territorial community. But whereas in the case of ethnies the link with a territory
may be only historical and symbolic, in the case of the nation it is physical and
actual: nations possess territories. In other words nations always require ethnic
'elements.' These may, of course, be reworked; they often are. But nations are
inconceivable without some common myths and memories of a territorial
home." (Smith 1991), p. 40. Smith notes elsewhere that an "ethnie" is fundamentally a matter of the "sense of cultural unity and intimacy that ethnicity provides. For the sense of cultural intimacy is what binds the various classes and
strata of an ethnie." (Smith 1998), p. 128.

52. On the idea that Hegel was a racist, see the discussion in (Bonetto 2006).
53. This is the idea lying behind his remarks about "national character," from
which the more general theory of the historical embeddedness of subjectivity
must be distinguished, at (Hegel 1969c), (Hegel 1969c), §394, p. 64; , (Hegel et al.
1971), p. 46.
54. (Hegel 1969c), §393, p. 57; (Hegel et al. 1971), p. 41: "But descent affords no ground
for granting or denying freedom and dominion to human beings. Man is in
himself *(an sich)* rational; herein lies the possibility of equal rights for all men—
and the nothingness of a rigid distinction between races which have rights and
those which have none." p. 41.
55. This the subject of Christopher Krebs's excellent and very important book:
(Krebs 2011).
56. See (Krebs 2011), p. 48. Mary Beard notes that Tacitus' style of argument—to
the effect that the "barbarians" may have more virtue than contemporary
Romans—had a long history even before Tacitus used it. (Beard 2015), p. 183.
57. Since Hegel held that nature is "impotent"—that it cannot determine sharp
boundaries among species, make itself better, etc.—it made little sense for him
to think that there even could be clearly demarcated ethnic units. There could
be sharp differences among concepts but not in natural unities, whose determinateness always depends on their relation to some "other." In his *Logic,* the
"something" and its "other" are said to pass over into each other, since there are
only provisional boundaries between them that can be drawn.
58. "The ancient Germans *(Deutschen)* are famed for their love of freedom, and the
Romans at the very outset correctly and wholly comprehended them in that
way. Freedom in Germany has been the watchword down unto the most recent

times." (Hegel 1969j), p. 425; (Hegel 1956), p. 353. However, he did note that the German tribes were many and racially mixed. For example, he notes: "Germany was originally a set of tribes, which were of partly Germanic *(germanisch)* origins and partly Slavic origins who had been Germanized. They never made a whole, as happened in France." (Hegel 2005), p. 200. In his 1822–1823 lectures, he also seems to equate these *Germanen* with *Deutschland*. See (Hegel 1996), p. 451; (Hegel et al. 2011), p. 470.

59. In a continuation of his reliance on part of the myth of the *Germanen*, Hegel mentions the importance of the forests—especially ancient, virgin forests—for them, a point Tacitus makes and which became one of the basic bricks of German mythic folklore. In alluding to the idea that it was Roman penetration into "Germania" that forced the *Germanen* to convert to Christianity and which thus began the modern story, Hegel claims: "A comparison of the free states of North America with European lands is therefore impossible; for in Europe, such a natural outlet for population, notwithstanding all the emigrations that take place, does not exist. Had the woods of Germany been in existence, the French Revolution would not have occurred. North America will be comparable with Europe only after the immeasurable space which that country presents to its inhabitants shall have been occupied, and civil society shall be pressed back on itself." (Hegel 1969j), p. 113; (Hegel 1956), p. 86. The mythology is even more fraught than Hegel could have known—there also were no longer any virgin forests in Germany by the time of Tacitus. See (Woolf 2012), p. 55.

60. This is a point nicely drawn out by Myriam Bienenstock in her introduction to (Hegel, Bienenstock, and Waszek 2007).

61. (Hegel and Hoffmeister 1961), II, #241. (Hegel, Butler, and Seiler 1984), p. 312. For Hegel, those who sought to recapture pure *"Deutschtum"* were really just showing that they were *"Deutschdumm."*

62. (Hegel 1969g), p. 347; (Hegel 1988), p. 1057: "The story of Christ, Jerusalem, Bethlehem, Roman law, even the Trojan war have far more present reality for us than the affairs of the Nibelungs which for our national consciousness are simply a past history, swept clean away with a broom. To propose to make things of that sort into something national for us or even into the Book of the German people has been the most trivial and shallow notion. At a time when youthful enthusiasm seemed to be kindled anew, it was a sign of the grey hairs of a second childhood at the approach of death when an age reinvigorated itself on something dead and gone and could expect others to share its feeling of having its present reality in that."

63. In his 1807 *Phenomenology*, Hegel makes his case for not allowing the term, "history," to be used with regard to nature: "In that way, *consciousness,* as the middle term between universal spirit and its individuality, that is, sensuous

consciousness, has for its own middle term the system of the shapes of con-sciousness as a life of spirit ordering itself into a whole—the system which is here under examination and which has its objective existence as world history. However, organic nature has no history; organic nature immediately descends from its universal, that is, life, into the individuality of existence. . . . This is so because the whole is not present within it, and the whole is not present in it because the whole does not exist here *for itself* as a whole." (Hegel 1969a), p. 226; (Hegel 2010), ¶295.

64. (Hegel 1969a), p. 327; (Hegel 2010), ¶440. "Spirit is the *ethical life* of a *people* inso-far as it *is* the *immediate truth;* it is the individual who is a world. It must advance to a consciousness about what it immediately is, it must sublate that beautiful ethical life, and, by passing through of a series of shapes, it must attain a knowl-edge of itself. However, these shapes distinguish themselves from the preced-ing in that they are real spirits, genuine actualities, and, instead of being shapes merely of consciousness, they are shapes of a world."

65. Interestingly, the argument made in the *Logic* rests, as Hegel notes in the text, on an argument made in the *Phenomenology* to the effect that the subject "is absolutely free in knowing its freedom, and it is this very knowledge of its free-dom which is its substance, its purpose, and its sole content." He cites the *Phenomenology* as the place where he makes that argument. ("[Es] ist absolut frei darin, daß es seine Freiheit weiß, und eben dies Wissen seiner Freiheit ist seine Substanz und Zweck und einziger Inhalt.") (Hegel 2010), ¶598. The claim in the *Logic* is found in (Hegel 1969l), p. 545; (Hegel and Di Giovanni 2010), p. 731. ("Consequently the idea enters here into the shape of self-consciousness, and in this one respect coincides with its exposition.")

66. See also the discussion in (Tinland 2013), pp. 218–230, where he argues that it is precisely in this kind of self-reflexivity that distinguishes Hegel from Schelling. Tinland, however, continues to see this as a kind of "transcendental" project of uncovering the conditions of possibility of subjectivity rather than a series of achievements on the part of historically structured mindedness (or *Geistigkeit*), although he does not deny the "achievement" part of Hegel's line of thought.

67. (Hegel 1969a), p. 591; (Hegel 2010), ¶808.

68. One of Hegel's extended discussions of action and satisfaction is found in (Hegel and Hoffmeister 1956), p. 152: "Action means nothing other than bring-ing about some end. There is action in that something is 'brought out' with it, in that success comes about. The actualization of an end is an achievement *(Gelingen);* that the action has success *(Erfolg)* is a *satisfaction (Befriedigung),* an inseparable fruit of the completed action. Between the acting and the achieve-ment of an end something can place itself in between them and separate them; and someone acting from duty will in many cases know in advance that he can

have no external success; but duty is something other than that merely negative indifference vis-à-vis success."

69. "We witness a vast spectacle of events and actions, of infinitely varied constellations of nations, states, and individuals, in restless succession. Everything that can occupy and interest the human mind, every sensation of the good, the beautiful and the great, comes into play; everywhere we see others pursuing aims which we ourselves affirm and whose fulfillment we desire, and we share their hopes and fears. In all these events and contingencies, our first concern is with the deeds and sufferings of men; we see elements of ourselves in everything, so that our sympathies constantly oscillate from one side to the other. Sometimes we are captivated by beauty, freedom, and riches, sometimes we are impressed by human energy, which can invest even vice with greatness. Sometimes we see the accumulated weight of a popular cause lose its impetus and finally disintegrate, to be sacrificed to an infinite complex of minor exigencies. Sometimes we see how a huge expenditure of effort can produce only a trifling result, or conversely, how an apparently insignificant thing can have momentous consequences. Everywhere we see a motley confusion which draws us into its interests, and when one thing disappears, another at once takes its place. / The negative aspect of the idea of change moves us to mourning." (Hegel and Hoffmeister 1994), p. 34; (Hegel 1975), p. 32.

70. "The concept of spirit involves a return upon itself, whereby it makes itself its own object; progress therefore is not an indeterminate advance ad infinitum, for there is an end present—namely that of returning upon itself. "(Hegel and Hoffmeister 1994), p. 18. (Hegel 1975), p. 149.

71. (Hegel 1969k) , p. 289; (Hegel and Di Giovanni 2010), pp. 210–211: "The fact is that the *infinite series* contains the bad infinite because what the series is supposed to express remains an *ought,* and what it does express is encumbered by a beyond which does not go away, and it is *diverse* from what it is supposed to express."

72. When Hegel speaks of the "cunning of reason," he often hedges it to make sure that he intends it as a bit of a metaphor and not a statement of a law of any sort. Thus, he says in the *Logic* in his discussion of teleology that "but that the purpose posits itself in a *mediate* connection with the object, and *between* itself and this object *inserts* another object, may be regarded as the *cunning* of reason." (Hegel 1969l), p. 252; (Hegel and Di Giovanni 2010), p. 663. Likewise, in the lectures on the philosophy of world history, he says, "It is what we may call the *cunning of reason* that it sets the passions to work in its service, so that those by which it gives itself existence must pay the penalty and suffer the loss." (Hegel and Hoffmeister 1994), p. 105; (Hegel 1975), p. 89. He is less cautious in the *Encyclopedia* (§209): "This, that the subjective purpose, as the power over these

processes within which the *objective* the processes abrade themselves against each other and sublate each other, and the subjective purpose holds itself *externally to them* and is what within them is *self-preserving*—this is the *cunning* of reason." In the *Zusatz,* he says, "Reason is as cunning as it is powerful. Its cunning generally consists in the mediating activity which, while it lets objects act upon one another according to their own nature, and work each other off, executes only *its* purpose without itself mingling in the process." (Hegel 1969b), §209, p. 365; (Hegel et al. 1991), p. 284.

73. (Hegel 1969l), p. 544; (Hegel and Di Giovanni 2010), p. 731: "Further, since this good is restricted by virtue of its content, there are several kinds of the good; the existing good is not only subject to destruction by external contingency and by being subordinated to evil, but also because of collision and conflict within the good itself."

74. It is probably worth pointing out that although Hegel is often saddled with a "great man" theory of history, he actually does not hold such a view. Although it was a view that was becoming common enough in his day, he notes that such "great men" were simply lucky. Their greatness was thrust on them by future events, not by any intrinsically superb quality they possessed. Their achievement of their particular ends contingently turned out to be of historical importance, but that was not necessarily their aim. This is part of Hegel's view of historical development. He does not hold that history consists solely of powerful forces such that there is no room for agency in history. But he also holds that role that agency plays, at least on the part of individuals, is by and large small. He says, "If we go on to examine the fate of these world-historical individuals, we see that they had the good fortune (to be] the executors of an end which marked a stage in the advance of the universal spirit. But as individual subjects, they also have an existence distinct from that of the universal substance, an existence in which they cannot be said to have enjoyed what is commonly called happiness. They did not wish to be happy in any case, but only to attain their end, and they succeeded in doing so only by dint of arduous labors. . . . Their actions are their entire being, and their whole nature and character are determined by their ruling passion. When their end is attained, they fall aside like empty husks." (Hegel and Hoffmeister 1994), pp. 99–100; (Hegel 1975), p. 85. The idea that Hegel thinks these "great men" are also thereby excused from moral responsibility by virtue of answering to the "higher call" of world-spirit is also effectively demolished in (Alznauer 2015). Alznauer also deals effectively with what had been the standard and best articulated defense of reading Hegel on the "great men" as endorsing a form of amoralism, namely, that given by (Wood 1990).

75. On Hegel's idea of history as not involving causal laws, see also (Stekeler-Weithofer 2001) ; and (Jaeggi 2014).

76. On this point, see also (Lopez 1967).

77. See (Le Goff 2005) pp. 4–6.

78. (Hegel 1969j), p. 438; (Hegel 1956), p. 364.

79. See (Hegel 1969j), p. 445; (Hegel 1956), p. 369.

80. "Universal injustice, universal lawlessness is brought into a system of private dependence and private obligation, so that it is the formality of requirements that solely constitute the aspect of right." (Hegel 1969j), p. 446; (Hegel 1956), p. 370.

81. On the more general conception of recognition and social space, see (Testa 2009). See also (Pinkard 1994).

82. (Hegel 1969j), p. 339; (Hegel 1956), p. 278.

83. (Hegel and Lasson 1923), p. 640.

84. "Es ist durch die Welt gleichsam ein allgemeines Gefühl der *Nichtigkeit* ihres Zustandes gegangen." (Hegel 1969j), p. 449; (Hegel 1956), p. 373.

85. (Hegel 1969j), p. 470; (Hegel 1956), pp. 391–392.

86. "The discovery of the laws of nature enabled men to contend against the monstrous superstition of the time, as also against all representations of mighty alien powers against which magic alone could win victory . . . [it turns out that] the Host is simply *dough,* the relics [of the Saints] mere *bones.* The rulership of subjectivity was posited against belief founded on authority, and the laws of nature were granted recognition as the only bond connecting the external with the external. Thus all miracles were disallowed: for nature is now a system of known and recognized laws, man is at home in it, and only that which has binding validity is where he finds himself at home; he is free through the knowledge he has gained of nature." (Hegel 1969j), p. 522; (Hegel 1956), p. 440.

87. "Another technical means was then found to deprive [the nobility] of their superior strength in weaponry—that of *gunpowder.* Humanity needed it, and it immediately appeared. It was one of the chief instruments in liberating the world from the dominion of physical force, and equalizing the various orders of society. As the distinction between the weapons [of the nobility and non-nobility] vanished, that between lords and serfs also vanished." (Hegel 1969j), p. 481; (Hegel 1956), p. 402. Hegel also casts doubt on whether the Chinese really invented gunpowder. That is yet another place where he simply gets the facts wrong about matters in Asia. See (Hegel 1969j), p. 481; (Hegel 1956), p. 137.

88. By calling it the "new, final banner," Hegel indicates that this was not at work until that point, that is, until freedom as this kind of unconditional commitment has emerged as a response to the irrationalities of what came before it. He says: "In the Lutheran Church subjectivity and the individual's own conviction is just as much necessary as the objectivity of truth. To the Lutherans, truth is not something made; the subject himself is supposed is to become truthful

(*wahrhaftes*), surrendering his particular content vis-à-vis the substantial truth, and making that truth his own. . . . Thus Christian freedom is actualized. . . . With that is unfurled the new, the final banner round which the peoples gather—the flag of *free spirit,* at one with itself, which is indeed existing in the truth and being at one with itself only in that truth. This is the flag under which we serve, and which we bear." (Hegel 1969j), p. 496; (Hegel 1956), p. 416.

89. ". . . the principle of holiness had falsely characterized the virtues of the ancients as attractive vices. This ceased." (Hegel 2005), p. 204.

90. "For honor's fight for personal self-sufficiency is not bravery defending the polity and the call of justice in the polity or of rectitude (Rechtschaffenheit) in the sphere of private life; on the contrary, honor's struggle is only for the recognition and the abstract inviolability of the individual person." (Hegel 1969f), p. 171; (Hegel 1988), p. 553.

91. "But Shakespeare's characters are self-consistent; they remain true to themselves and their passion, and in what they are and in what confronts them they beat about according only to their own fixed determinacy of character." (Hegel 1969f), p. 202; (Hegel 1988), p. 579.

92. See (Le Goff 2005), p. 100.

93. (Hegel 1969j), p. 479; (Hegel 1956), p. 400: "The chief point is that the basis and presupposition of such a formation of the state is in the *particular nations*. [In Europe] there are particular nations present, constituting a unity in their very nature, and which have the absolute tendency to form a state. All did not succeed in attaining this unity of a state." Some might find Hegel's invocation of "nations" problematic. One line of thought is that Hegel's mode of speech is anachronistic since at that time there was no any real conception of "nation" (at least in the later eighteenth- and nineteenth-century sense of the word). Instead, there were other functional terms, such as "race," "country," or "kingdom," that played similar roles. See the discussion in (Le Goff 2005), pp. 174–176. On the other hand, one can make a good case for Hegel's view that although modern nationalism (with which he was not particularly sympathetic) was not yet present, the embryonic idea of "nations" was taking shape already in the early Middle Ages. See the discussion in (Lopez 1967), pp. 96–98. Seen in light of the functional similarities between "country" and "kingdom" and the nascent ideas of "nations" in the middle ages, Hegel's usage does not seem quite so problematic.

94. (Hegel and Lasson 1968), vol. 4, p. 893. See also (Hegel 1996), p. 512; (Hegel et al. 2011), p. 510.

95. (Hegel and Lasson 1968), vol. 4, p. 893. See also (Hegel 1996), p. 512; (Hegel et al. 2011), p. 510.

96. (Hegel and Lasson 1968), vol. 4, p. 895.

97. "Without war the existence of Protestants could not be secured, for the question was not one of simple conscience but was about respecting public and private property which had been taken possession of in contravention of the rights of the church, for which the church demanded restitution. A condition of absolute mistrust supervened; absolute, because mistrust bound up with the religious conscience was its root." (Hegel 1969j), p. 515; (Hegel 1956), p. 434.

98. (Hegel and Lasson 1968), vol. 4, p. 895.

99. (Hegel 1969j), p. 479; (Hegel 1956), p. 400: "These historical transitions are assuredly not always so pure, as they have here been presented. Often we find more than one appearing contemporaneously ; but one or the other always predominates."

100. (Hegel and Lasson 1968), vol. 4, p. 896: "In the way civil wars arose, and one can call these internal wars, although they were not wars of rebellion."

101. (Hegel 1969j), p. 516; (Hegel 1956), p. 435.

102. That figure is taken from (Fulbrook 2004), p. 64.

103. (Hegel and Lasson 1968), vol. 4, p. 897.

104. (Hegel and Lasson 1968), vol. 4, p. 899. See also (Hegel 1996), p. 512; (Hegel et al. 2011), p. 512.

105. ("konstituierte Anarchie"). (Hegel and Lasson 1968), vol. 4, p. 899.

106. Quoted by (Thomas 2009), p. 60.

107. See (Thomas 2009), p. 64.

108. Cited in (Thomas 2009), p. 64.

109. (Hegel 1969j), p. 509; (Hegel 1956), p. 428: "The rights of the leaders of dynasties and the barons were suppressed, and they were obliged from that time onward to content themselves with official positions in the State. This transformation of the rights of vassals into official functions took place in the several kingdoms in various ways. In France, for example., the great Barons, who were governors of provinces, who could claim such offices as a matter of right, and who like the Turkish Pashas, maintained a body of troops with the revenues thence derived—troops which they might at any moment turn against the King— were reduced to the position of mere landed proprietors or court nobility, and those Pasha-positions became offices held under the government. Or the nobility were employed as officers, generals of the army, that of an army belonging to the state."

110. (Hegel and Lasson 1968), p. 903. (The phrase is: *Außersichsein im Insichsein*).

111. (Hegel and Lasson 1968), vol. 4, p. 904.

112. "Among these states there arose many-sided wars. . . . The purpose and the genuine interest of the wars is now and ever conquest." (Hegel and Lasson 1968), p. 908.

113. (Hegel 1969j), p. 509; (Hegel 1956), p. 429: "In this aspect the origination of *standing armies* is so important an event, for they supply the monarchy with an independent force and are as necessary for the security of the central authority *(Mittelpunkts)* against the rebellion of the subject individuals as for the defense of the state against foreign enemies." [In dieser Beziehung ist das Aufkommen der *stehenden Heere* so wichtig, denn sie geben der Monarchie eine unabhängige Macht und sind ebenso nötig zur Befestigung des Mittelpunkts gegen die Aufstände der unterworfenen Individuen, als sie nach außenhin den Staat verteidigen.]

114. Quoted in (Blanning 2007), p. 286.

115. See (Blanning 2007), p. 286.

116. (Hegel and Lasson 1968), p. 909.

117. (Hegel 1969j), p. 513; (Hegel 1956), p. 431.

118. See (Blanning 2007), p. 547.

119. "The pretensions of Louis XIV were founded not on the extent of his power (as was the case with Charles V) so much as on that culture *(Bildung)* which was everywhere, with the French language, taken up and was the object of universal admiration. Ludwigs pretentions could therefore plead a higher entitlement than those of the German Emperor." (Hegel 1969j), pp. 513–514; (Hegel 1956), p. 432.

120. This ascription of the cultural centrality to France is hedged a bit by Hegel when he notes that "What we call *Bildung* is the act of thinking of abstract universality. France is the land of culture." Hegel also thought he had made it clear in the *Phenomenology* that German philosophy after Kant was the successor to being the land of "thinking of abstract universality." (Hegel and Lasson 1968), p. 905.

121. Quoted in (Blanning 2007), p. 286.

122. See the discussion in (Pinkard 2000).

123. (Hegel 1969g), p. 129; (Hegel 1988), pp. 885–886: "And what we find here in political matters is neither a superior nobility expelling its prince and tyrant or imposing laws on him, nor a people of farmers, oppressed peasants, who broke free, like the Swiss; on the contrary by far the greater part, except the courageous warriors on land and the bold heroes on the sea, consisted of townspeople, burghers active in trade and well-off, who, comfortable in their business, had no high pretensions, but when it was a question of fighting for the freedom of their well-earned rights, of the special privileges of their provinces, cities, and corporations, they revolted with bold trust in God and in their courage and intelligence, without any fear of exposing themselves to all sorts of danger in face of the tremendous repute of the Spanish domination of half the world; courageously they shed their blood and by this righteous boldness and endurance

triumphantly won for themselves both civil and religious independence. If we can call any particular trend of mind *'deutsch'* [i.e., Dutch or German], it is this loyal, comfortable, homely bourgeois type: this remains in house and surroundings simple, attractive, and neat, in a self-respect without pride, in a piety without the mere enthusiasm of a devotee, but instead concretely pious in mundane affairs and unassuming and content in its wealth; and it can preserve unimpaired an ancestral soundness in thorough carefulness and contentedness in all its circumstances along with independence and advancing freedom, while still being true to its traditional mores *(Sitte)*."

124. (Hegel 1969g), p. 129. ; (Hegel 1988), p. 886: The question of how modern conditions limit the role that art can play is one to which Hegel devoted much thought. The depth and intricacy of his views on this topic have been explored very convincingly in (Rutter 2011) and in (Pippin 2014). See also (Rebentisch 2012).

125. (Hegel 1969j), p. 527; (Hegel 1956): "on the contrary their will is regarded as deserving of respect only so far as it wisely wills right, justice, and the well-being of the whole."

126. (Blanning 2007), p. 288.

127. Hegel does not discuss this two-in-one nature of Enlightenment and "Faith" so much in the lectures on the philosophy of history. His discussion of it does, however, form a major chapter of his 1807 *Phenomenology*. See the discussion in (Pinkard 1994).

128. "It is *Schiller* who must be given great credit for breaking through the Kantian subjectivity and abstraction of thinking and for venturing on an attempt to get beyond this by intellectually grasping the unity and reconciliation as the truth and by actualizing them in artistic production. For Schiller in his aesthetic writings has not merely taken good note of art and its interest, without any regard for its relation to genuine philosophy, but he has also compared his interest in the beauty of art with philosophical principles, and only by starting from them and with their aid did he penetrate into the deeper nature and concept of the beautiful." (Hegel 1969e), p. 89; (Hegel 1988), p. 61.

129. See (Hegel 1969d), §207, p. 359; (Hegel 1991), pp. 238–239: "The ethical disposition within this system is therefore that of *rectitude* and the *honor of one's estate,* so that each individual, by a process of self-determination, makes himself a member of one of the moments of civil society through his activity, diligence, and skill, and supports himself in this capacity; and only through this mediation with the universal does he simultaneously provide for himself and gain *recognition* in his own eyes and in the eyes of others.—*Morality* has its proper place in this sphere, where reflection on one's own actions and on the ends of welfare

and of particular needs are dominant, and where contingency in the satisfaction of the latter makes even contingent and individual help into a duty."

130. (Hegel 1969j), p. 525; (Hegel 1956), p. 443: "Two questions therefore suggest themselves: Why di the principle of freedom remain merely formal? And why did the French alone, and not the Germans, set about realizing it?"

131. (Hegel 1969j), p. 510; (Hegel 1956), p. 429: "This, which was established for the persecution of those who secretly adhered to Judaism, and of Moors and heretics, soon assumed a political character, being directed against the enemies of the State. Thus the Inquisition confirmed the despotic power of the King: it claimed supremacy even over bishops and archbishops, and could cite them before its tribunal."

132. As Hegel notes: "Likewise, today even a General or a Field Marshal has indeed great power; the most essential ends and interests are put into his hands, and his discretion, courage, determination, and spirit have to decide the most important matters; but still what is to be ascribed to his subjective character as his own personal share in this decision is only small in scope. For one thing, the ends are given to him and have their origin, not in his own individual self, but in matters outside the province of his power. For another thing, he does not by himself create the means for achieving these ends; on the contrary, they are provided for him; they are not subject to him or at his beck and call as a person; their position is quite different from that accruing to the personality of this military individual." (Hegel 1969e), p. 254; (Hegel 1988), p. 194.

133. (Hegel 1969a), p. 378; (Hegel 2010), ¶510.

134. (Hegel 1969a), p. 369; (Hegel 2010), ¶494

135. (Hegel 1969a), p. 389; (Hegel 2010), ¶¶524–525: "The self-conscious and self-expressing torn-apartness of consciousness is as much the derisive laughter about existence as much as it is about the disorientation of the whole and about itself. At the same time, it is the fading sound of this entire disorientation as it still takes note of itself. . . . From the aspect of the return into the self, the *vanity* of all *things* is its *own vanity,* that is, it *is* itself vain."

136. "These universal determinations, based on contemporary consciousness—the laws of nature and the content of what is right and good, is what one has called *reason.* The binding force *(Gelten)* of these laws was called Enlightenment. From France it passed over into Germany, and a new world of ideas *(Vorstellungen)* opened up. The absolute criterion—taking the place of all authority based on religious belief and positive laws of right (especially constitutional law)—was now that the content of spirit itself in a free present was be itself a matter of insight." (Hegel 1969j), p. 523; (Hegel 1956), p. 441.

137. (Wittgenstein 1963), p. 3.

138. (Hegel 1969a), p. 430; See (Hegel 2010), ¶581: "This culmination [of faith and pure insight] still lacks the *actuality* of self-consciousness, which is what belongs to the *vain* consciousness—the world from out of which thought raised itself up to itself. What was lacking is attained in utility insofar as pure insight achieves positive objectivity in utility." Hegel thought, as the very chapter titles of the *Phenomenology* show, that Kant's theory of the infinite worth of subjectivity, while still an expression of the "view from above," was the rational successor to the failed shapes of subjectivity to be found in "vanity" and "utility" and not merely one expression among the others. It is in Kant's philosophy that "thought raised itself up to itself" in its penultimate form.

139. (Hegel and Lasson 1968), p. 910.

140. (Hegel and Lasson 1968), pp. 919–920. "Catherine II of Russia also put the general principles into force, and in the American wars [of independence] thought came out on top." Hegel was more or less silent about the American war of independence for his adult life. He thought it to be rather unimportant for European history since it was an event that took place far away and in a not yet significant part of the world, at least as far as European affairs were concerned. Although he did rather vaguely anticipate Frederick Jackson Turner's thesis about the significance of the closing of the frontier in America, and he also famously described the United States as the "land of the future," for him, these were more or less just rhetorical asides to forestall any further discussion of what the American example might mean for Europe. (Some early critics of the 1820 *Philosophy of Right* complained about his ignoring of the American example.) However, in some of his lectures on the philosophy of history, he did praise the American spirit in the war of independence, comparing the heroism of the militias to those of the Dutch resisting the Spanish, although he also noted how, shortly after the glory years of the wars of independence at a time later when not so much was at stake, they completely folded against the British in 1814. (The militia of the North American republic proved themselves quite as brave in the war of independence as the Dutch did under Philip II [of Spain]; but generally, where such self-sufficiency is not at stake, less power is displayed, and in the year 1814, the militia posted bad grades against the English in 1814. against the English. (Hegel 1969j), p. 114; (Hegel 1956), p. 86). In his youth in Berne, he gave overt praise to the Americans and their war for freedom. (This was in his youthful commentary on a pamphlet denouncing the Bernese oligarchy. It was a pamphlet he translated from the French and published anonymously. Even his own family in Berlin did not know of his authorship.) See the discussion of Hegel's time in Berne in (Pinkard 2000).

141. (Hegel and Lasson 1968), p. 920. (". . . in that way the Enlightenment puts

thought in the driver's seat.) [. . . so ist der Gedanke doch durch sie [die Aufklärung] auf den Stuhl der Herrschaft gesetzt worden.]

142. Hegel does throw cold water on the idea that the real distinction between the German response to the breakdown of the feudal state and the French response had to do with Mediterranean passion: "As respects the second question—why the French immediately passed over from the theoretical to the *practical,* while the Germans remained stuck with theoretical abstraction, it might be said: The French are hot-headed [*ils ont la tête près du bonnet*]; but the ground lies deeper: The formal principle of philosophy in Germany stands over and against a concrete world in which Spirit finds inward satisfaction and in which conscience is at rest." (Hegel 1969j), p. 526; (Hegel 1956), p. 444.

143. (Hegel 1969j), p. 529; (Hegel 1956), p. 447.

144. This is nicely summed up in (Hobsbawm 1996), p. 75: "Napoleon was the 'little corporal' who rose to rule a continent by sheer personal talent. (This was not strictly true, but his rise was sufficiently meteoric and high to make the description reasonable.) Every young intellectual who devoured books, as the young Bonaparte had done, wrote bad poems and novels, and adored Rousseau could henceforth see the sky as his limit, laurels surrounding his monogram. Every businessman henceforth had a name for his ambition: to be—the clichés themselves say so—a 'Napoleon of finance' or industry. All common men were thrilled by the sight, then unique, of a common man who became greater than those born to wear crowns. Napoleon gave ambition a personal name at the moment when the double revolution had opened the world to men of ambition. Yet he was more. He was the civilized man of the eighteenth century, rationalist, inquisitive, enlightened, but with sufficient of the disciple of Rousseau about him to be also the romantic man of the nineteenth. He was the man of the Revolution, and the man who brought stability. In a word, he was the figure every man who broke with tradition could identify himself with in his dreams."

145. See the discussion of Hegel's reaction to the Congress of Vienna in (Pinkard 2000).

146. (Hegel and Lasson 1968), p. 906. See also (Hegel 1996), p. 505; (Hegel et al. 2011), p. 508.

147. (Hegel and Lasson 1968) "They are the missionaries for all peoples with respect to industry and technology; by legal trade, they bring the whole world into contact." Lasson notes that one of the student notes replaces "*Technik*" (technology) with "*Kunst*" ("art").

148. (Hegel and Lasson 1968).

149. This was discussed in his late pamphlet, "On the English Reform Bill." This is translated in (Hegel, Dickey, and Nisbet 1999). See the discussion in (Pinkard

2000). Hegel notes that in England, instead of relying on university training in rigorous science, the "crass ignorance of fox-hunters and *Landjunker*" is prized, and the state's interests are is in the hands of those whose "education [is] acquired simply through social gatherings or through newspapers," where political influence is reached after an evening of "pudding and dark beer." (Hegel and Hoffmeister 1956), pp. 103, 112; (Hegel, Dickey, and Nisbet 1999), p. 310.] As he puts it: "Nowhere more than in England is the prejudice so fixed and so naive that if birth and wealth give a man office they also give him brains."

150. (Hegel 1969j), p. 508; (Hegel 1956), p. 427.

151. (Hegel 1969j), p. 449; (Hegel 1956), p. 373.

152. Hegel remarks: "One of the leading features in Germany are the laws in the general legal code [*Gesetze des Rechts*], which was certainly occasioned by French oppression, since this was the especial means of bringing to light the deficiencies of the old system." (Hegel 1969j), pp. 538–539; (Hegel 1956), p. 456. This point about the necessity for the Revolution's results to be imported into Germany is also made in (Weiss 2012), p. 191.

153. (Hegel and Lasson 1968), p. 910.

154. (Hegel 2005), p. 128.

155. (Hegel 1969a), p. 483; (Hegel 2010), ¶658: "Thus, as consciousness, absolute self-certainty is immediately converted into a dying sound, into the objectivity of its being-for-itself, but this created world is its *speech,* which it has likewise immediately heard and whose echo is all that returns to it. That the echo returns to it does not therefore mean that consciousness therein exists *in* and *for itself,* for the essence is in its own eyes not simply any kind of *in-itself* but is rather its very own self. Nor does it have *existence,* for what is objective does not reach the point of being a negative of the actual self just as this self does not reach the point of being actual."

156. A beautiful soul eventually has to take on the character of what in biblical terms is called the "the hard heart." The confessing agent in Hegel's language confesses, "Ich bin's" ("I am he") who has done this—perhaps a reference to Isaiah 47:10 in Luther's rendering: "Denn du hast dich auf deine Bosheit verlassen, da du dachtest: Man sieht mich nicht! Deine Weisheit und Kunst hat dich verleitet, daß du sprachst in deinem Herzen: Ich bin's, und sonst keine!" In the 21st Century King James Version (KJ21): "For thou hast trusted in thy wickedness; thou hast said, 'None seeth me.' Thy wisdom and thy knowledge, it hath perverted thee; and thou hast said in thine heart, 'I am, and none else besides me.'" When Hegel also says that in this forgiveness and reconciliation between beautiful souls, "The wounds of the spirit heal and leave no scars behind; it is not the deed which is imperishable," he is not offering the rather Pollyannaish idea that

all evils just could or should be forgotten and forgiven, but the idea that a new shape of life has arisen that has picked up the pieces so that, wounded as it might be, modern life has reason to carry on in a very determinate way that involves opposition within itself: "The word of reconciliation is the *existing* spirit which immediately intuits in its opposite the pure knowledge of itself as the *universal* essence, intuits it in the pure knowledge of itself as *individuality* existing absolutely inwardly—a reciprocal recognition which is *absolute* spirit." (Hegel 2010), ¶670. From the standpoint of the *Logic,* the early modern "monadic" world gives way to a "dyadic" world in which the motivations for establishing such a "monadic" world are recognized and given their rightful place. It is a process of *Aufhebung* in which the shape of life picks up the pieces, keeps what works and reshapes itself. Thus, even though, to use his own metaphor, the collapse of the ancient Greek life broke the world's heart, it nonetheless regathered itself and fashioned a new life for itself, instead of being continually haunted by the distress of having lost a non-alienated political world. To have held onto it, after all, would have meant accepting the continued existence of slavery and the exclusion of women.

157. (Hegel and Lasson 1968), p. 925.

158. The great archetype of this for just about everybody in Hegel's generation was, of course, Rousseau's autobiographical *Confessions,* where, unlike Augustine in his book of the same title, Rousseau confesses not to God but to his public.

159. "Soon the whole attention of the inhabitants was given to labor, and the substance of the whole lay in the human needs, peace and quiet, civil rights and justice, security, freedom, and a community that takes as its starting point atomic individuals, so that the state was merely something external for the protection of property. From the Protestant religion sprang the principle of the mutual trust of individuals—trust in the dispositions of other people, for in the Protestant church its entire life, its activity, is that of its religious works themselves. Among Catholics, on the contrary, the basis of such a trust cannot exist, for in secular matters, what rules are only force and voluntary subservience, and the forms which are here called constitutions are in this case only a resort of necessity, and are no protection against mistrust." (Hegel 1969j), pp. 111–112; (Hegel 1956), p. 84.

160. "In the way, revolutions have taken place in France, Italy (Naples and the Piedmont) and finally in Spain. The revolution thus makes its entrance in the Romance countries (and Ireland is to counted as belonging to this group)." (Hegel and Lasson 1968), p. 925.

161. "It is, indeed, regarded as a maxim of the profoundest wisdom entirely to separate the laws and constitution of the state from religion, since bigotry and hypocrisy are to be feared as the results of a state religion. But although the

content of religion and the state are different, religion and the state are radically one; and the laws find their highest confirmation in Religion." (Hegel 1969j), p. 531; (Hegel 1956), p. 449.

162. "In terms of their external constitution the Protestant lands are very diverse, for example, Denmark, the Netherlands, England and Prussia. However, the essential principle is present: everything that is to have binding force in the state must have its starting point in insight and be justified by it." (Hegel and Lasson 1968), p. 933.

163. (Hegel 1969j), p. 535; (Hegel 1956), p. 452;

164. See the delightful account by Eduard Gans, Hegel's friend and follower, of his unexpected invitation to dinner at the elderly Bentham's house in 1831, where Bentham insisted that he and Gans were clearly on the same side in the debates against the historicist school headed by Savigny in Berlin. Bentham held that both he and Gans stood on the side of reason as against mere appeal to "hallowed" custom represented by Savigny. Gans' invitation from Bentham most likely came about via Gans' friendly acquaintance with the dean of the Paris law faculty, Hyacinthe Blondeau, who had been appointed dean after the "liberal" 1830 July Revolution and who himself was a Benthamite of sorts. See (Gans 1836), pp. 198–214. On the relation between Hegel, Gans and Savigny, see (Pinkard 2000). On the antipathy of French liberals to utilitarianism in general and to Bentham in particular, see (Welch 2012). However, Welch omits the Benthamite connection with regard to Blondeau.

165. See the account in (Furet 1992).

166. (Hegel 1969j), p. 534.

167. Even though Hegel clearly dismissed liberalism in its "atomistic" form, he could fairly be said to be a version of the kind of familiar, rather authoritarian, liberal of the nineteenth century. Liberalism did not conciliate itself with democracy until the twentieth century. On Hegel's brand of nineteenth-century "authoritarian" liberalism, see (Kervégan 2007).

168. (Hegel 1969j), p. 535; (Hegel 1956), p. 453.

169. Although Hegel speaks of this in the *Philosophy of Right,* he also makes the same point in the lectures on the philosophy of history: (Hegel 1969j), p. 539. (Hegel 1956), p. 456.: "The government rests on the world of civil servants, and the personal decision of the monarch constitutes its apex; for a final decision is, as was remarked above, utterly necessary. Yet with firmly established laws, and a determinate organization of the state, what is left to the exclusive decision of the monarch is, with regard to what is substantial, no great matter. It is certainly a very fortunate circumstance for a nation, when a sovereign of noble character falls to its lot; yet in a great state even this is of small moment, since its strength lies in the reason incorporated in it." (Hegel 1956), p. 456.

170. (Hegel 1969j), pp. 526–527; (Hegel 1956), pp. 444–445: "In Germany the Enlightenment was conducted in the interest of theology: in France it immediately took up a position of hostility to the Church. In Germany, with regard to secular relations, everything had already undergone a change for the better. Those pernicious ecclesiastical institutes of celibacy, poverty and laziness had been already abolished; there was no dead weight of enormous wealth attached to the Church, and no constraint put upon the ethical, a constraint which is the source and occasion of vices; there was not that unspeakable injustice which arises from the interference of spiritual power with secular law, nor that other of the divinely anointed legitimacy of Kings, i.e. the doctrine that the arbitrary will of princes, by virtue of their being the Lord's anointed ones, is divine and holy. On the contrary, their will is regarded as deserving of respect only so far as in association with reason, it wisely wills right, justice, and the welfare of the polity. The principle of thought, therefore, had been so far reconciled already; moreover the Protestant world was aware that in the reconciliation which had previously explicitly arisen, there was the principle that would lead to a further development of justice in the sphere of right."

171. (Hegel 1969g), p. 353; (Hegel 1988), p. 1062.

172. Klaus Vieweg has suggested a slightly alternative readings of Hegel's philosophy of history: The "world spirit" should be taken, he argues, as "cosmopolitanism," as reason, whose being-for-itself constitutes knowledge, as what is universal, which exists in the multiplicity and plurality of states, as a global whole of states." For him, the end of history just is the modern state that respects and embodies freedom, except that the "end" (freedom) now goes global. (Vieweg 2012), p. 509.

5. Infinite Ends at Work in History

1. (Hegel 1969a), pp. 22–23; (Hegel 2010), ¶17.

2. (Hegel 1969i); (Hegel and Di Giovanni 2010), p. 515 "It is one of the profoundest and truest insights to be found in the Critique of Reason that the *unity* which constitutes the *essence of the concept* is recognized as the *original synthetic* unity of apperception, the unity of the *"I think,"* or of self-consciousness."

3. In his novel and important work on Hegel (which overlaps with a few of the ideas presented here), Robert Brandom has helpfully distinguished in Hegel's system the distinction between reference-dependence and sense-dependence, even though Hegel himself does not use those terms. Sense-dependence occurs on the side of deontic normative relations among senses, which are the flip side of the alethic modal relations among objects. Conflating the two is the root of the mistaken conclusion that Hegel thinks objects are somehow mind-constituted. (Brandom 2014)

4. See the helpful discussion in (Pippin forthcoming); and (Pippin 2014).

5. "The aim of world history, therefore, is that the spirit should attain knowledge of its genuinely is, that it should make this knowledge objective and actualize this into a present world, and bring itself forth objectively. What is essential here is that this aim is itself something brought forth. Spirit is not a natural entity like an animal, for the animal is only immediately what it is. Spirit is such that it brings itself forth and makes itself what it is. Thus the first embodiment it assumes so that it may be actual is only self-activity. Its essential being is actuosity, not static existence, for it has brought itself forth, it has come to exist for itself, and made itself what it is by its own agency. It can only be said to have a true existence if it has brought itself forth, and its being is process in the absolute sense. . . . The world spirit has an infinite urge and an irresistible impulse to realize these stages of its development; for this structuring and its realization are its concept. World history merely shows how the spirit gradually attains consciousness and the will to truth; it progresses from its early glimmerings to critical points and finally to complete consciousness." (Hegel and Hoffmeister 1994), pp. 74–75; (Hegel 1975), pp. 64–65.

6. It would take far too much space here to do it even half-justice, but Robert Brandom's novel interpretation of Hegel in semantic terms offers another, very different interpretation. As Brandom summarizes his view: "The retrospective, recollective form of reason (the owl of Minerva that flies only at dusk, reason's march through history) constructs a sunny, optimistic, Whiggish perspective that reveals, amid the random, contingent charnel house of our earlier discursive muddling, the emergence of an unbroken record of progress toward truth, understanding, and correct representation of how it is with the real world we turn out all along to have been thinking about and acting in. This is what Hegel means when he talks about 'giving contingency the form of necessity.'" (Brandom 2009), p. 102. The model Brandom puts to use as Hegel's rational reconstruction of history is that of Anglo-American case law, where one judge is bound by the commitments of earlier judges in making her decisions but capable of changing the content in certain prescribed ways. Given this, "Because the future stands to the present as the present does to the past, and there is no final future, hence no final authority, every judge is symmetrically recognized and recognizing." (Brandom 2009), p. 88. As an account of history, this seems far more Whiggish than anything Hegel would have considered. For example, when Rome assumed control of Greece, it did not do so in terms of extending the precedent Greek culture had established. It sacked Corinth and burned it to the ground, even as it did incorporate elements of Greek culture into itself. A slightly better model of history might be the establishment of common law itself: After violently subjecting the Anglo-Saxon

king and his subjects at Hastings, William sent out judges to various parts of his new domain to establish a "common law." There the object was not to rationally extend some old rulings but to displace the old rulings root and branch and replace them with a new authority, one backed up by more than semantic sanctions. Brandom's reading of Hegel's historical mode seriously underplays, if not ignores, the kinds of historical tensions which are so crucial to Hegel's conception of how the "Idea" takes shape in history. This is no doubt because of Brandom's decision to interpret Hegel in terms of the conditions and development of discursive activity (which is, to be sure, an essential component of the Hegelian project): "The tradition I have retrospectively picked out (and given a rationale for) by selectively privileging some ampliative and critical moves as precedential, expressively progressive developments has at its core a concern with how conceptual content, in various senses, can be understood in terms of its role in discursive activity more generally." (Brandom 2009), p. 108.

7. This charge—that Hegel was defending the "ruling classes"—was made in Hegel's own lifetime, and a rebuttal appeared in an entry to an 1824 "Lexicon for the Cultured Classes" which seemed to have had Hegel's own input in it. Against that charge, it said that "to the extent that Hegel's view on the state are known to us through his writings, [the phrase, "the actual is the rational"] was in no way employed *later on* for the benefit of the ruling classes but arose out of the foundations of his philosophy, which everywhere combats *empty* ideals and seeks to reconcile thoughts and actuality in the absolute Idea through, as it were, the Idea itself." Cited and discussed by Friedhelm Nicolin, "Der erste Lexicon-Artikel über Hegel (1824)," in (Nicolin, Sziborsky, and Schneider 1996), p. 212. The 1827 version of the Lexicon article (with only minor changes) is reprinted in (Nicolin 1970), #559, pp. 363–371. See the discussion in (Pinkard 2000).

8. He makes this clear that his interest lies in showing how the non-European civilizations have either never left their natural state and thus have not attained a kind of reflective principled way of thought and that this way of viewing subjectivity has as its consequence some ethical results that, from the point of view of subjectivity as having value in and for itself, are negative. That he thinks that Africans exist in an actual "state of nature" only shows once again how little he understood about African life. Hegel's argument is, roughly, that if Africans do exist in a real, and not hypothetical, Hobbesian state of nature, then the only element binding them can itself only be something like a Hobbesian set of strategies (and, of course, he took the first premise to be true). The core example around which his argument turns is, once again, that of slavery. (Hegel 1969h), p. 129; (Hegel 1956), pp. 98–99: "The doctrine which we draw from this condition of slavery among the negroes, and which constitutes the only side of

the question that has an interest for our inquiry, is that with which we are familiar from the Idea, namely, that the state of nature itself is one of absolute and thorough injustice. Every intermediate grade between this and the actuality of a rational state retains moments and aspects of injustice; therefore we find slavery even in the Greek and Roman states, as we do serfdom down to the latest times. But thus existing in a state, slavery is itself a phase of advance from the merely individualized sensual existence. It is a moment of education, a way of becoming a participant in a higher ethical life and the culture connected with it. Slavery is in and for itself injustice, for the essence of humanity is freedom, but for this man must be matured. The gradual abolition of slavery is therefore wiser and more equitable than its sudden removal *(Aufhebung)*."

9. See (Pippin 2014, Pinkard 2012).

10. Hegel thus does not subscribe to an "additive theory" of rationality, as defined by (Boyle forthcoming). A different but related line of interpretation of Hegel in this regard is that of (Yeomans 2015).

11. (Aristotle 1941b), 1367a 30–34, p. 1356.

12. (Aristotle 1998), Book V, chapter 6.

13. The Greek institutions of slavery simply obscure the fact, as David Brion Davis put it, that the slave is "not a piece of property, nor a half-human instrument, but a man held down by force." (Davis 1966), p. 261.

14. (Aristotle 1941a), 1259b.

15. (Hegel 1969d), §482, pp. 301–302; (Hegel et al. 1971), pp. 239–240: "The Greeks and Romans, Plato and Aristotle, even the Stoics, did not have [the Idea of freedom]. On the contrary, they saw that it is only by birth (as, for example, as an Athenian or Spartan citizen), or by strength of character, education, or philosophy (the sage is free even as a slave and in chains) that the human being is actually free. It was through Christianity that this Idea came into the world. . . . If the knowledge of the Idea—that is, the knowledge that that people the their essence, purpose, and object is that of freedom—is speculative knowledge, then this very Idea itself is the actuality of people, not something which they *have* but which they *are*."

16. The gendering continued to exercise its hold on Hegel himself, and it shows up in Kant before him. Closely linked to the gendered conception is the idea of independence as not being at the beck and call of another. Kant thought this was a natural feature of women and a contingent, although apparently unavoidable, feature of some men: "This quality of being independent, however, requires a distinction between *active* and *passive* citizens, though the concept of a passive citizen seems to contradict the concept of a citizen as such. The following examples can serve to remove this difficulty: an apprentice in the

service of a merchant or artisan; a domestic servant (as distinguished from a civil servant); a minor (*naturaliter uel civiliter*); all women and, in general, anyone whose preservation in existence (his being fed and protected) depends not on his management of his own business but on arrangements made by another (except the state). All these people lack civil personality and their existence is, as it were, only inherence." (Kant and Gregor 1996), p. 126. When Kant includes "all women" here, he seems to be ruling out the very idea that women could escape the predicament of depending "not on [her] management of [her] own business but on arrangements made by another."

17. (Hegel 1969b), §213, p. 368, 369; (Hegel et al. 1991), p. 286–287: "The Idea is the truth, for the truth is this, that objectivity corresponds with the concept. . . . It is because of this judgment that the Idea is at first just the one and universal substance, but its developed, authentic actuality is to be as subject and so as spirit. . . . It is this deeper sense of truth which is at issue when speak, for instance of a *true* state or a *true* work of art. These objects are *true* when they are what they *ought* to be, that is, when their reality corresponds to their concept."

18. (Hegel 1969d), §482, p. 302; (Hegel et al. 1971), p. 240. The specifically philosophical approach to history, as contrasted with all the other ways in which empirically oriented historians might approach the subject matter, turns on Hegel's core idea, that of the intelligibility of the world and of subjectivity within it. Forms of life, shapes of spirit, are, as he puts it, the concepts people have of themselves. As they articulate the "Idea" that holds them together, the antinomies within it begin to appear more clearly (as people are pushed to reflect on what for them has until then counted as the "unconditioned," the absolute), and, as the "Idea" falls apart, those people turn out to be unintelligible to themselves. The sense of their lives threatens to collapse into nothing. Typically at the end of such periods of breakdown, the subjects defending the current "Idea," as committed to contradictions that seem to be both unintelligible and unavoidable, end up babbling. In the movement of Hegel's philosophy, the transition to the next stage is not moving to the presuppositions of the preceding stages but to some way of reconciling the contradictions of those previous stages. These transitions are where the Hegelian *Aufhebung* comes into play. Hegel is thus not offering a "transcendental argument" for these transitions. The later stages are not the presupposition of the former ones. T. W. Adorno's influential view of Hegel is thereby fundamentally mistaken: "There is no question of whether Hegel was a transcendental analytic philosopher like Kant. One could show in detail how Hegel, as Kant's critic, sought to do justice to Kant's intentions by going beyond the *Critique of Pure Reason,* just as Fichte's

Science of knowledge had pushed the limits of Kant's concept of the pure. The Hegelian categories, and especially the category of spirit, fall within the domain of transcendental constituents." (Adorno 1993), pp. 18–19.

19. (Hegel 1969f), p. 249; (Hegel 1988), p. 980.

20. For an account of Hegel's philosophy in light of contemporary literature on the nature of oppression and oppressed groups, see (Anderson 2009).

21. (Hegel and Hoffmeister 1994), p. 108; (Hegel 1975), p. 92.

22. That is, the agents acting in light of the ethical requirements and permissions of an earlier period may be said to be justified in what they are doing, but they are acting in light of facts (those of their limited ethical order) that turn out historically to be false (that this order makes sense, is rational). Roman aristocrats were therefore ethically justified in doing certain things that were based on an ethical order that was itself false, but which we can know to be false only by virtue of where we stand in the historical order. Some light on this is thrown by R. Jay Wallace's discussion in a different context of the conditions under which we might retrospectively judge something to have been a good thing even though we should not say that, even so, the agent was not justified in what she did. (Wallace's example is of somebody promising to drive a friend to the airport but failing to keep the promise, with the result that the friend missed the flight, and the plane crashed, killing everyone on board. It was still wrong to have broken the promise although neither party will regret that the duty taken on by the promise was not fulfilled.) Wallace notes: "Though they do not affect the *justification* of my earlier action, however, the subsequent events . . . might have some bearing on the truth of judgments about what I ought to have done." (Wallace 2013), p. 99. A similar point is made by (Alznauer 2015).

23. (Hegel 1969g), p. 40; (Hegel 1963), p. 21.

24. (Hegel 1969h), p. 329; (Hegel 1956), p. 269: "Socrates is celebrated as a teacher of morality, but we should rather call him the *inventor* of morality."

25. This touches on the contested topic of Hegel's philosophy of religion and what role it plays in his philosophy of history. Hegel clearly thinks that history is the manifestation in some sense of the divine. But what sense? Hegel's conception of divinity is very nonorthodox, consisting in a fusion of Aristotle's god in the *Nicomachean Ethics* (as contemplating eternal truths) and the view in the Gospel of John that in the beginning was the *Logos* (the "word"). Hegel does indeed think that there is a rational structure to the world, and that this rational structure—the world's making sense to rational creatures—is what we really care about when we care about divine things. Religion is fundamentally a comprehensive view committed to the idea that there are goods inherent in the structure of the world, and, so Hegel thinks, also to the idea that these goods show up for rational beings and for which justifications can be given. For him, the

Christian God just is this *Logos* made flesh. Thus, as the way in which *Geist* comes to know itself in time, history manifests not a divine plan but the way in which divinity takes shape in time. Ultimately, this conception strives for a complete theory of all that is, which cannot on its own come from the natural sciences themselves (even though they may manifest this desire to understand everything comprehensively in their own way). Part of Hegel's most audacious view is his claim that it is his philosophy, and not the natural sciences of physics, chemistry, and biology that provide this comprehensive picture of the world as a place that can be made intelligible to thought. This is why ultimately "religion" has to be sublated by philosophy in Hegel's system. Nonetheless, the conception of divinity—as the "higher" or "divine" element in such comprehensive thought—that emerges in modern life is itself historical, and, in Hegel's system, is also something made retrospectively true. It does point to the way in which Hegel tries to combine a more traditionally Christian conception of justice with his insistent modernism. To sketch out that point: The older conception, like the Greek conception, saw justice in terms of an ordering of the cosmos that was reflected also in the human order. As that conception of justice developed in history, it was seen to be sublated into a conception of justice as resting on freedom. The truly just order was one in which "all are free." To the extent that the move to the institutional and practical embodiment of the "all are free" principle has taken the shape it has, it expresses the way in which the *Logos*—or, to stretch matters a bit, the space of reasons—is a development of the divine order itself. This way of drawing the distinction between the "cosmic" order of justice and the "freedom-based" order of justice points back to the way that distinction is drawn in (Taylor 1975). However, in Taylor's view, Hegel's version of the modern freedom-based order is still dependent on a cosmic view of spirit developing itself—a kind of subject writ large, seeking its own purposes—rather than the more overtly hybrid logic-historicist view I have articulated. Taylor's view in effect also locates Hegel as the "ontotheologian" his Heideggerian critics have always made him to be. In any event, it is a separate issue as to whether Hegel has also made his case for such a religious view of history. Hegel's own position sounds suspiciously like the brand of "religious atheism" that is defended in (Dworkin 2013). It also sounds rather like the view that Hegel himself described in the "Preface" to the 1807 *Phenomenology*, where he spoke of the thinness of contemporary religious conceptions: "Now it seems that there is the need for the opposite, that our sense of things is so deeply rooted in the earthly that an equal power is required to elevate it above all that. Spirit has shown itself to be so impoverished that it seems to yearn for its refreshment merely in the meager feeling of divinity, very much like the wanderer in the desert who longs for a simple drink of water. That it now takes so little to satisfy spirit's needs is the full measure of the magnitude of its loss." (Hegel 1969a), p. 17; (Hegel 2010), ¶8. On the issue of where Hegel's philosophy of religion stands in relation to his works, see the analysis in (Lewis 2011).

26. See (Hegel and Hoffmeister 1994), p. 109; (Hegel 1975), p. 92.

27. "Erst das Wissen der Individuen von ihrem Zwecke ist das wahrhaft Sittliche. Es muß das Unbewegte gewußt werden, der unbewegte Bewegende, wie Aristoteles sagt, der das Bewegende ist in den Individuen. Daß es so das Bewegende sei, dazu gehört, daß das Subjekte für sich zur freien Eigentümlichkeit herausgebildet sei." (Hegel and Hoffmeister 1994), p. 91; (Hegel 1975), p. 91: "No truly ethical existence is possible until individuals have become fully conscious of their ends. They must attain knowledge of the unmoved mover, as calls it, of the unmoved motive force by which all individuals are activated. For this force to become effective, the subject must have developed to a condition of free individuality in which it is fully conscious of the eternally unmoved mover, and each individual subject must be free and independent in its own right."

28. For the Heideggerians, who think that Hegel simply has to be an "ontotheologian," this looks like the determining piece of evidence. It looks, that is, as if Hegel is asking for the origin of this normativity and locating it in this unchanging kernel of subjectivity. Hegel's point, however, is different. There is no "origin" of normativity. To be is to be intelligible, and to make that statement itself intelligible requires one to go back to the ground-zero of intelligibility, which would be the thought of what "is," of "pure being." There is no origin to "being." However, that thought already includes its opposite, "nothing," since if anything is true, then being is not nothing, and, with no way to distinguish the two at that level of ultimate abstraction, the *Logic* gets moving. To go deeper into the *Logic* rather than parsing it in the loose way I have done throughout would be another, very different, and very much longer book. When giving his lectures on the philosophy of history, Hegel himself preferred to draw on his *Logic* in this very loose way, and I am at least following his lead here.

29. He notes this in his scribbled marginalia to the *Philosophy of Right:* "In §57 it is mentioned—in the activity of forming—it's heterogeneous. / Man must form himself. It is historical, i.e., belongs in time, into the history prior to freedom—there is history." (Hegel 1969e), p. 124.

30. "We must merely note for the present that the spirit *begins* in a state of infinite potentiality *(Möglichkeit)*—but no more than potentiality—which contains its absolute content *(Gehalt)* as something as what is *in itself,* as the object and goal which it only attains as the end result in which it at last achieves its actuality." (Hegel and Hoffmeister 1994), p. 157; (Hegel 1975); p. 131.

31. (Hegel 1969c), §376, pp. 538–539; (Hegel and Miller 2004), p. 445: "But it is one-sided to regard spirit in this way as only a *becoming* from out of the In-itself only that of being-for-itself. To be sure, nature is the immediate—but even so, as the other of spirit, its existence is a relativity: and so, as the negative, its being is only posited. It is the power of free spirit which sublates this negativity; spirit is no less *before* than *after* nature, it is not merely the metaphysical Idea of it. Spirit, just because it is the goal of Nature, is *prior* to it, nature has proceeded from spirit: not empirically, however, but in such a manner that spirit is already from the very first implicitly present in Nature which is spirit's own presupposition."

32. This is why Hegel puts so much effort into his *Logic.* He thinks that unless he can give a non-question-begging account of why this and not other conceptions of subjectivity are to be given priority has to be answered, and that pushes him, as he rightly saw, into the most abstruse areas of metaphysical theory.

33. See Charles Larmore, (Larmore 2012). (Larmore should not be charged with the use I make of the idea.) For a criticism of the more "factualist" approach to reasons that Larmore seems to pursue, see (Wiland 2012). This idea of a practical reason is illustrated in Hegel's discussion of "the good" in (Hegel 1969i), p. 548; (Hegel and Di Giovanni 2010), p. 733: "In this the presupposition itself is sublated, namely the determination of the good as a merely subjective purpose restricted in content, the necessity of first realizing it by subjective activity, and this activity itself. In the result the mediation itself sublates itself; the result is an *immediacy* which is not the restoration of the presupposition, but is rather the presupposition as sublated. The idea of the concept that is determined in and for itself is thereby posited, no longer just in the active subject but equally as an immediate actuality; and conversely, this actuality is posited as it is in cognition, as an objectivity that truly exists." Like all conceptions allied with a more or less ethical functionalist view of subjectivity, Hegel's conception has at its core the concept of what it means to be a good subject—what function does subjectivity fulfill? Like his great philosophical model, Aristotle, Hegel thinks that this is a feature of our place in the cosmos, and he shares with Aristotle the basic idea that it is reason that is the essential component of being a subject. For Hegel, however, that place in the cosmos is just our place in the space of reasons, concretely and socially conceived. The divine order is nothing else but that: "The speculative is in its innermost unified with the shape of Christ. John already grasped this shape more deeply [than others]. The Logos is God, and the Logos was first." (Hegel 2005), p. 168. However, he also thinks that an adequate account of subjectivity must be social and historical, and unlike his other great philosophical model, Kant, he does not think that the general and

formal category of "rational being" is adequate to characterize what is meant by "rational animal." He also shares with Kant the conviction that self-consciousness—or, put even more abstractly, the peculiar kind of "self-relation" that makes up the subjectivity of a rational animal—is the key to understanding how practical content is generated. His theory is decidedly not a purely constructivist theory in which people as conceived as blank slates on which something like "culture" works—nor, as already noted, is his view simply that of a lazy teleological view in which we posit some kind of an end to life or history and then see how things do or do not measure up to it or contribute to it, nor is it that of constructing a single idea (even that of "freedom" itself) which is simply applied to many instances.

34. (Hegel 1969d), §482, p. 301; (Hegel 1969d), pp. 239. See also the related discussion in (Boyle forthcoming). Boyle's suggestion about the concept of rational animals not being "additive" could be taken as another way of stating Hegel's otherwise obscure point that the "Idea" is not something that people "have" but what they "are."

35. (Hegel 1969a), p. 143; (Hegel 2010), ¶173. "But this other life for which the *genus* as such exists and which is the genus for itself, namely, *self-consciousness,* initially exists in its own eyes merely as this simple essence and, in its own eyes, is an object as the *pure I.*"

36. In his study of Hegel's philosophy of history, Joseph McCarney also notes that the empirical findings of history are important "not merely in bearing out the central doctrine but also as contributing to its derivation in the first place." He does not go into how this works, except to note that if in some future time, as a thought experiment, civil society reverted to a slave society, we would have to give up "Hegel's conception of the historical dialectic." However, Hegel need not accept that such an outcome meant we had to give up what he argued. That a slave society might develop out of a free society could not count as progress, period. This would be a problem only if we thought of the standards of freedom as having some kind of metaphysical causal power in the development of history. That the world might nonetheless go through various bouts of grand irrationality, even for thousands of years, is not ruled out by Hegel's theory. Indeed, he even worried that such a reversion was transpiring in his own time, as McCarney notes. See (McCarney 2000), pp. 208, 213. On Hegel's worries about the backsliding of his own times, see (Pinkard 2000).

37. Kieran Setiya has argued for a similar position to be found in Iris Murdoch's writings. On his interpretation, this applies to all our concepts. For Hegel, this idea of perfecting concepts only applies to the metaphysical—"speculative" in his special sense—concepts. It applies to the basic concepts that have come to

assume an essential place in our making ourselves intelligible to ourselves. See (Setiya 2013).

38. This point ties Hegel into a certain type of pragmatism, which sees meaning as fundamentally normative all the way down and for which arguments about meaning are really arguments about something analogous to a different rule of use, that is, about which would be a better rule. On the rule-use version of this, see (Lance and Hawthorne 1997); and (Kukla and Lance 2009). Something like this view is also pressed by (Brandom 2009).

39. This idea that "being one's own person" and freedom as emerging from that is pursued in a different way by (Menke 2010). Menke speaks of "appropriating" social rules or moral laws as "one's own" and argues that this already supposes the subject as existing in a normative space. In Menke's terms, the "event" in which the subject became a subject is not therefore comprehensible in terms of these concepts of normativity. For Menke, there is and cannot be any good account of how we step out of the nonnormative into the normative world. This also holds for concepts such as "revolution," which signify a break that cannot be understood within the terms that precede the break. See (Menke 2015).

40. It is probably worthwhile to note how Hegel's conception of an infinite end differs from interpretations often put on it, or, for that matter, other philosophies of history that are said to be inspired by Hegel's own. To sketch out one of the other views in its broadest terms: There is a goal to history, and the stages of history are means to this end. Likewise, for such an important end, there are great sacrifices worth making, and perhaps even great sacrifices which may be legitimately imposed in order to achieve that end. Any interpretation falling into that model mistakes Hegel's infinite end for, in effect, a finite end. It would treat the infinite end at work in history as if it were something large and difficult to achieve—such as a passionate desire to become a multi-billionaire—and which, once it is achieved, gives way to a new desire (maybe to become a multi-multi-billionaire or a pop star). The end that history shows to be in fact at work in it has to do with the desire to be at one with oneself—to be *"bei sich,"* which—to translate *"bei sich"* another way—is to be one's own person. Hegel's own argument about that rests on his social conception of subjectivity, specifically, on the need for recognition by subjects to become subjects and to remain subjects. When those forms of recognition fail, people also fail in their subjectivity. They do not fail to have intentions, to speak languages or to act. They do however fail to achieve the purposes, which, under a very specific self-interpretation and social interpretation, they take to be at the heart of what it constitutes "true" subjectivity. They may then see themselves as acting, speaking

creatures caught in nature's indifferent swirl, playthings of the gods, flotsam captured by the flow of history, or merely painfully subject to the arbitrary whims and despotic desires of those more powerful than themselves. They may even resist all of those thoughts, but even in doing so, in trying to reclaim some form of agency for themselves, the fact or at least the possibility of some kind of enervating and devitalizing failure lies before them.

41. In speaking of the role of the *Germanen,* he says: "The German spirit is the spirit of the new world. Its purpose is the realization of absolute truth as the infinite self-determination of freedom—*that* Freedom which has its own absolute form itself as its content. The vocation *(Bestimmung)* of the German peoples is to be the bearers of the Christian principle. The fundamental principle of spiritual freedom, the principle of reconciliation, was introduced into the still unencumbered, uncultured minds of those peoples, and the part assigned them in the service of the world-spirit was that of not merely possessing the concept of genuine freedom as their religious substance but of producing it freely from their subjective self-consciousness." (Hegel 1969h), p. 414; (Hegel 1956), p. 341. He also cites Jesus' biblical statement from Matthew 5:10, which in Luther's translation is: "Selig sind, die um Gerechtigkeit willen verfolgt werden; denn das Himmelreich ist ihr." In the King James version, the reference to justice is not as clear: "Blessed are they which are persecuted for righteousness' *(Gerechtigkeit, justice's)* sake: for theirs is the kingdom of heaven."

42. On the pervasiveness of ancient slavery and the failure of the ancient world to come to terms with it, see M. I. Finley's nice summary of some of his own views: (Finley 1964).

43. (Hegel 1969d), §482 pp. 301–302; (Hegel 1969d), pp. 239–240. He repeats this idea in the lectures: see (Hegel 1969h), p. 31; (Hegel 1956), p. 18. To be sure, Hegel himself sometimes states his own case in such polemical terms that he can be read as endorsing the idea that history's goal is such a finite end, as when he discusses what he calls "world historical individuals." See, for example, (Hegel 1969h), pp. 45–46; (Hegel 1956), pp. 29–30. There are various passages in his works where he says that world history is more or less amoral, by which he means that an account of the key events in world history will rarely have a moral imperative as their explanation. (More likely they will be struggles over power, status, and access to resources.) Here is a typical passage: "Justice and virtue, violence and vice, talents and their [expressions in] deeds, the small passions and the great, guilt and innocence, the splendor of individual and national life, the independence, fortune and misfortune of states and individuals—all of the have their determinate significance and value in the sphere of conscious actuality, in which judgment and justice—albeit imperfect justice—are meted out to them. World history falls outside of these points of view; in it, that

necessary moment of the Idea of the world spirit which constitutes its current stage attains its absolute right, and the people which live at this point, and the deeds of that nation, achieve fulfillment, fortune, and fame." (Hegel 1969e), §345, p. 505; (Hegel 1991), pp. 373–374.

44. (Hegel 1969g), p. 40; (Hegel 1963), p. 21.

45. (Hegel 1969d), §482, p. 301; (Hegel et al. 1971), p. 239.

46. (Hegel 1969h), p. 496; (Hegel 1956), p. 416.

47. (Hegel 1969d), p. 171, §408. (Hegel et al. 1971), p. 130. ("Aus diesem Grunde muß auch das Moralische *vor* dem Sittlichen betrachtet werden, obgleich jenes gewissermaßen nur als eine Krankheit an diesem sich hervortut.")

48. "Similarly, one citizen differs from another, but the salvation of the community is the common business of them all. This community is the constitution; the virtue of the citizen must therefore be relative to the constitution of which he is a member. If, then, there are many forms of government, it is evident that there is not one single virtue of the good citizen which is perfect virtue. But we say that the good man is he who has one single virtue which is perfect virtue. Hence it is evident that the good citizen need not of necessity possess the virtue which makes a good man." (Jowett translation) Aristotle, (Aristotle 1941a)

49. It would be an understatement to say that Hegel's account as laid out in the 1820 *Philosophy of Right* has provoked rival accounts of just what that account is. It is clear that in some sense there is a sequence from rights to morality to ethical life, but exactly what that sequence is and how the elements relate to each other is a matter of no small dispute. Entering into it, much less attempting to resolve it, is beyond the bound of this work.

50. (Hegel 1969b) §6, p. 49; (Hegel et al. 1991), p. 30.

51. (Finley 1964); (Finley 1980).

52. See the helpful comparisons of Hegel's views and those of the Confederacy in (Westphal 2016).

53. See (Baptist 2014).

54. This idea of "necessary, so make the best of it" is drawn off Finley's nice summation of that tradition: (Finley 1964).

55. (Hegel and Ilting 1973): "there can be a historically grounded right which can be rejected by philosophy as irrational. For example, one might justify slavery in the Indies historically . . . but notwithstanding this justification, reason has to remain firm that the slavery of the negroes is completely wrong, that it is an institution in contradiction to true human and divine rights, and it is to be rejected."

56. The idea that there could be a modern moral order based on slavery and the subjugation of people by virtue of race was, so Hegel clearly thought, an absurdity. The attempt of the Confederacy in the United States to draft, implement

and defend such an order—an effort in which it was decisively defeated—
would have struck him as yet another example of a false start in history. Yet as
some recent scholarship has argued, slavery was not merely a relic of premodern past still living on in the nineteenth century but a key factor in the rise of
modern financial institutions and the wealth-creating machinery of the
modern state. On the way in which modernity and the slave system of the
south intersected, see (Baptist 2014). See also (Rothman 2005). On the general
issue of Hegel's attitude to slavery as a combination of historical and philosophical phenomena, see the discussion in (Alznauer 2015). Alznauer gives a nuanced
interpretation of how Hegel can argue for the relative historical justification of
slavery and still claim that, as Hegel himself puts it, "it is in the nature of the
case that the slave has an absolute right to free himself." (Hegel 1969e), §66,
Zusatz, p. 144; (Hegel 1991), p. 97.

57. (Hegel 1969e), §258, Zusatz, p. 403; (Hegel 1991), p. 279: "The state is in and for
itself the ethical whole, the actualization of freedom, and it is the absolute end
of reason that freedom should be actual." (I take "absolute end" and "infinite
end" here to be interchangeable.)

58. A bit of terminology is in order to grasp Hegel's point. Hegel understood his
own views to be opposed to patriarchal rule in families, but he understood
"patriarchy" in an older sense, namely, as that of unbridled autocratic rule by
the father. However, in the more modern sense of patriarchy as rule by males,
it is clear that Hegel in fact argued for the patriarchal family. Obviously one of
the issues for interpreting Hegel and his commitments is to tease out whether
his views against patriarchy as autocratic rule also push in the direction of
opposition to all forms of patriarchy in the contemporary and broader sense.
Although she does not explicitly raise these issues about the family, Sybol
Anderson explores this aspect of Hegel's theory. See (Anderson 2009).

59. On the intricacies of reclaiming Hegel's views for a form of cosmopolitanism,
see (Moland 2011). See also the discussion in (Buchwalter 2012).

60. Hegel's view is thus not at odds with but has a different focus from that pro-
posed by Joshua Cohen in his well-known piece, "The Arc of the Moral
Universe," in (Cohen 2010). Cohen wishes to show how it is possible that "ethical explanations," as he calls them, can have a legitimate place in historical
explanation. Hegel might well agree that they do, but that is not his concern in
his own philosophy of history. Cohen's piece does fit nicely into the idea that
"what drives human history is the human ambition to alter one's condition to
match one's hopes" to be found in (McNeill and McNeill 2003). In referring to
the way world history might be treated in an aesthetic fashion, Hegel himself
notes: "This could only be done poetically if the inner architect *(Werkmeister)* of
history, the eternal and absolute Idea, which realizes itself in humanity, either

came into appearance as a directing, active, and executive individual, or else asserted itself as merely a hidden ever-operative necessity. . . . In the second case, the part of particular heroes would have to be played by the different national spirits, and their conflict would be the theatre in which the pageant of history would unfold and move forward in continuous development . . . if an attempt were made to grasp the national spirits in their universality and make them act in that fundamental character, this too would only give us a similar series, and, besides, the individuals in it would only have, like Indian incarnations, a show of existence, a fiction that would have to grow pale in face of the truth of the world-spirit realized in the actual course of history." (Hegel 1969f), p. 356; (Hegel 1988), pp. 1064–65.

61. (Hegel and Hoffmeister 1994), p. 34; (Hegel 1975), p. 30.
62. He also did not seem to think that this was a problem that had been solved. In his last lecture on the topic before his death in 1831, he noted (remarking on the French Revolution of 1830): "Each particularization appears as a privilege, but there is supposed to be equality. In terms of this principle, no government is possible. This collision, this knot of this problem stands before history, and it is history which has to loosen the knot." (Hegel 2005), p. 231.

BIBLIOGRAPHY

Adorno, Theodor W. 1993. *Hegel: three studies, Studies in contemporary German social thought.* Cambridge, Mass.: MIT Press.

Adorno, Theodor W., and Rolf Tiedemann. 2006. *History and freedom: lectures 1964–1965.* Cambridge, UK; Malden, MA: Polity.

Allison, Henry E. 1990. *Kant's Theory of Freedom.* Cambridge England; New York: Cambridge University Press.

Alznauer, Mark. 2015. *Hegel's theory of responsibility.* Cambridge, England: Cambridge University Press.

Anderson, Sybol Cook. 2009. *Hegel's theory of recognition: from oppression to ethical liberal modernity, Continuum studies in philosophy.* London; New York: Continuum.

Appiah, Kwame Anthony. 1998. "Africa: The Hidden History." *New York Review of Books*, December 17, 1998.

Aristotle. 1941a. "Politics." In *The basic works of Aristotle*, edited by Richard McKeon. New York: Random House.

Aristotle. 1941b. "Rhetoric." In *The basic works of Aristotle*, edited by Richard McKeon, 1317–1451. New York,: Random House.

Aristotle. 1998. *The Nicomachean Ethics.* Translated by W. D.; Urmson Ross, J. O.; Ackrill, J. L., *The World's classics.* New York; Oxford: Oxford University Press.

Baptist, Edward E. 2014. *The half has never been told: slavery and the making of American capitalism.* New York: Basic Books, a member of the Perseus Books Group.

Bayly, C. A. 2004. *The Birth of the Modern World, 1780–1914: Global Connections and Comparisons, The Blackwell history of the world.* Malden, MA: Blackwell Pub.

Beard, Mary. 2007. *The Roman Triumph*. Cambridge, Mass.: Belknap Press of Harvard University Press.

Beard, Mary. 2013. "Alexander: How Great?" In *Confronting the classics: traditions, adventures, and innovations*, 42–53. New York: Liveright Publishing Corporation, a division of W. W. Norton & Company.

Beard, Mary. 2015. *SPQR: a history of ancient Rome*. First edition. ed. New York: Liveright Publishing Corporation.

Beiser, Frederick. 2011. "Hegel and Ranke: A Re-Examination." In *A companion to Hegel*, edited by Stephen Houlgate and Michael Baur, 332–350. Chichester, West Sussex; Malden, MA: Wiley-Blackwell.

Beiser, Frederick C. 2005. *Hegel*. 1st ed, *Routledge philosophers*. New York; London: Routledge.

Bernasconi, Robert. 1998. "Hegel at the Court of the Ashanti"." In *Hegel After Derrida*, edited by Stuart Barnett, 41–63. London; New York: Routledge.

Bernasconi, Robert. 2002. "With what must the history of philosophy begin? Hegel's role in the debate on the place of India within the history of philosophy." In *Hegel's History of Philosophy: New Interpretations*, edited by David A. Duquette. New York: SUNY Press.

Blanning, T. C. W. 2007. *The Pursuit of Glory: Europe, 1648–1815*. 1st American ed, *The Penguin history of Europe*. New York: Viking.

Bonetto, Sandra. 2006. "Race and Racism in Hegel—An Analysis." *Minerva—An Internet Journal of Philosophy* 10:35–64.

Bouton, Christophe. 2004. *Le procès de l'histoire: fondements et postérité de l'idéalisme historique de Hegel, Bibliothèque d'histoire de la philosophie Nouvelle série,*. Paris: Libr. philosophique J. Vrin.

Bowman, Brady. 2013. *Hegel and the Metaphysics of Absolute Negativity, Modern European philosophy*. Cambridge; New York: Cambridge University Press.

Boyle, Matthew. 2009. "Two Kinds of Self-Knowledge." *Philosophy and Phenomenological Research* 78 (1): 133–164.

Boyle, Matthew. 2015. "Additive Theories of Rationality: A Critique." *European Journal of Philosophy* 23 (4).

Brandom, Robert. 2009. *Reason in Philosophy: Animating Ideas*. Cambridge, Mass.: Belknap Press of Harvard University Press.

Brandom, Robert. 2014. "Some Hegelian Ideas of Note for Contemporary Analytic Philosophy." *Hegel Bulletin of the Hegel Society of Great Britain* 35 (1):1–15.

Brooks, Thom. 2013. *Hegel's political philosophy: a systematic reading of the Philosophy of right*. Second edition. ed. Edinburgh: Edinburgh University Press.

Buchwalter, Andrew. 2012. *Dialectics, Politics, and the Contemporary value of Hegel's Practical Philosophy, Routledge studies in nineteenth century philosophy*. New York: Routledge.

Burbank, Jane, and Frederick Cooper. 2010. *Empires in World History: Power and the Politics of Difference*. Princeton, N.J.: Princeton University Press.

Butterfield, Herbert. 1951. *The Whig Interpretation of History*. [1st American ed. New York: Scribner.

Chalybäus, Heinrich Moritz, and Alfred Edersheim. 1854. "Historical development of speculative philosophy, from Kant to Hegel From the German of Dr. H.M. Chalybäus." In. Edinburgh; London: T. & T. Clark; Hamilton, Adams. http://purl.oclc.org/DLF/benchrepro0212

http://catalog.hathitrust.org/api/volumes/oclc/68138310.html.

Cline, Eric H. 2014. *1177 B.C.: the year civilization collapsed, Turning points in ancient history*. Princeton: Princeton University Press.

Cohen, Hermann. 1995. *Religion of reason out of the sources of Judaism, Texts and translations series*. Atlanta, Ga.: Scholars Press.

Cohen, Joshua. 2010. *The arc of the moral universe and other essays*. Cambridge, Mass.: Harvard University Press.

Crawford, Oliver. 2014. https://www.academia.edu/4985405/Hegel_and_the_Orient.

Dale, Eric Michael. 2014. *Hegel, the End of History, and the Future*. New York: Cambridge University Press.

Davis, David Brion. 1966. *The problem of slavery in Western culture*. Ithaca, N.Y.,: Cornell University Press.

Deligiorgi, Katerina. 2010. "Doing without Agency: Hegel's social theory of agency." In *Hegel on Action*, edited by Arto Laitinen and Constantine Sandis. Houndmills, Basingstoke, Hampshire; New York: Palgrave Macmillan.

Deligiorgi, Katerina. 2012. "Actions as Events and Vice Versa: Kant, Hegel and the Concept of History." *Internationales Jahrbuch des deutschen Idealismus* 10:175–197.

Dworkin, Ronald. 2013. *Religion without God*. Cambridge, Massachusetts: Harvard University Press.

Eldridge, Richard Thomas. 1997. *Leading a human life: Wittgenstein, intentionality, and romanticism*. Chicago: University of Chicago Press.

Fairbank, John King, and Merle Goldman. 2006. *China: a new history*. 2nd enl. ed. Cambridge, Mass.: Belknap Press of Harvard University Press.

Fichte, Johann Gottlieb, and Immanuel Hermann Fichte. 1965. *Johann Gottlieb Fichte's Sämmtliche werke*. 11 vols. Berlin: de Gruyter.

Fichte, Johann Gottlieb, and Peter Preuss. 1987. *The vocation of man*. Indianapolis: Hackett Pub. Co.

Finley, M. I. 1964. "Between Slavery and Freedom." *Comparative Studies in Society and History* 6 (3):233–249.

Finley, M. I. 1977. *The Ancient Greeks, A Pelican book*. New York: Penguin.

Finley, M. I. 1980. *Ancient slavery and modern ideology*. New York: Viking Press.

Finley, M. I. 1983. *Politics in the ancient world, The Wiles lectures*. Cambridge Cambridgeshire; New York: Cambridge University Press.

French, R. K. 1994. *Ancient natural history: histories of nature, Sciences of antiquity*. London; New York: Routledge.

Fulbrook, Mary. 2004. *A concise history of Germany*. 2nd ed, *Cambridge concise histories*. Cambridge; New York: Cambridge University Press.

Furet, François. 1992. *Revolutionary France, 1770–1880, History of France*. Oxford, UK; Cambridge, USA: Blackwell.

Gans, Eduard. 1836. *Rückblicke auf Personen und Zustände, von Eduard Gans*. Berlin: Veit.

Gay, Peter. 1974. *Style in history*. New York: Basic Books.

Geuss, Raymond. 2014. *A world without why*. Princeton, NJ: Princeton University Press.

Green, Peter. 2012. "He Found the Real Alexander." *The New York Review of Books*, November 22, 2012.

Hahn, Songsuk Susan. 2007. *Contradiction in motion: Hegel's organic concept of life and value*. Ithaca: Cornell University Press.

Halbfass, Wilhelm. 1988. *India and Europe: an essay in understanding*. Albany, N.Y.: State University of New York Press.

Hegel, Georg Wilhelm F. 1969a. *Phänomenologie des Geistes*. Edited by Eva Moldenhauer and Karl Markus Michel. 20 vols. Vol. 3, *Theorie-Werkausgabe*. Frankfurt a. M.: Suhrkamp.

Hegel, Georg Wilhelm F. 1999. *Berliner Schriften*. Edited by Eva Moldenhauer and Karl Markus Michel. 20 vols. Vol. 11, *Theorie-Werkausgabe*. Frankfurt a.M.: Suhrkamp.

Hegel, Georg Wilhelm F. 2010. "*Phenomenology of Spirit* translated by Terry Pinkard." In. http://dl.dropbox.com/u/21288399/Phenomenology of Spirit in English and German.pdf.

Hegel, Georg Wilhelm Friedrich. 1956. *The Philosophy of History*. New York: Dover Publications.

Hegel, Georg Wilhelm Friedrich. 1963. *Lectures on the History of Philosophy*. 3 vols. London, New York: Routledge and K. Paul; Humanities Press.

Hegel, Georg Wilhelm Friedrich. 1969b. *Enzyklopädie der philosophischen Wissenschaften I*. Edited by Eva Moldenhauer and Karl Markus Michel. 20 vols. Vol. 8, *Theorie-Werkausgabe*. Frankfurt a. M.: Suhrkamp.

Hegel, Georg Wilhelm Friedrich. 1969c. *Enzyklopädie der philosophischen Wissenschaften II*. Edited by Eva; Michel Moldenhauer, Karl Markus. 20 vols. Vol. 9, *Theorie-Werkausgabe*. Frankfurt a. M.: Suhrkamp.

Hegel, Georg Wilhelm Friedrich. 1969d. *Enzyklopädie der philosophischen Wissenschaften III*. Edited by Eva Moldenhauer and Karl Markus Michel. 20 vols. Vol. 10, *Theorie-Werkausgabe*. Frankfurt a. M.: Suhrkamp.

Hegel, Georg Wilhelm Friedrich. 1969e. *Grundlinien der Philosophie des Rechts*. Edited by Eva Moldenhauer and Karl Markus Michel. 20 vols. Vol. 7, *Theorie-Werkausgabe*. Frankfurt a. M.: Suhrkamp.

Hegel, Georg Wilhelm Friedrich. 1969f. *Nürnberger und Heidelberger Schriften 1808–1817*. Edited by Eva Moldenhauer and Karl Markus Michel. 20 vols. Vol. 4, *Theorie-Werkausgabe*. Frankfurt a. M.: Suhrkamp.

Hegel, Georg Wilhelm Friedrich. 1969g. *Vorlesungen über die Ästhetik I*. Edited by Eva Moldenhauer and Karl Markus Michel. 20 vols. Vol. 13, *Theorie-Werkausgabe*. Frankfurt a. M.: Suhrkamp.

Hegel, Georg Wilhelm Friedrich. 1969h. *Vorlesungen über die Ästhetik II*. Edited by Eva Moldenhauer and Karl Markus Michel. 20 vols. Vol. 14, *Theorie-Werkausgabe*. Frankfurt a. M.: Suhrkamp.

Hegel, Georg Wilhelm Friedrich. 1969i. *Vorlesungen über die Ästhetik III*. Edited by Eva Moldenhauer and Karl Markus Michel. 20 vols. Vol. 15, *Theorie-Werkausgabe*. Frankfurt a. M.: Suhrkamp.

Hegel, Georg Wilhelm Friedrich. 1969j. *Vorlesungen über die Geschichte der Philosophie I*. Edited by Eva Moldenhauer and Karl Markus Michel. 20 vols. Vol. 18, *Theorie-Werkausgabe*. Frankfurt a. M.: Suhrkamp.

Hegel, Georg Wilhelm Friedrich. 1969k. *Vorlesungen über die Geschichte der Philosophie II*. Edited by Eva Moldenhauer and Karl Markus Michel. 20 vols. Vol. 19, *Theorie-Werkausgabe*. Frankfurt am Main: Suhrkamp.

Hegel, Georg Wilhelm Friedrich. 1969l. *Vorlesungen über die Philosophie der Geschichte*. Edited by Eva Moldenhauer and Karl Markus Michel. 20 vols. Vol. 12, *Theorie-Werkausgabe*. Frankfurt a. M.: Suhrkamp.

Hegel, Georg Wilhelm Friedrich. 1969m. *Wissenschaft der Logik I*. Edited by Eva Moldenhauer and Karl Markus Michel. 20 vols. Vol. 5, *Theorie-Werkausgabe*. Frankfurt a. M.: Suhrkamp.

Hegel, Georg Wilhelm Friedrich. 1969n. *Wissenschaft der Logik II*. Edited by Eva Moldenhauer and Karl Markus Michel. 20 vols. Vol. 6, *Theorie-Werkausgabe*. Frankfurt a. M.: Suhrkamp.

Hegel, Georg Wilhelm Friedrich. 1975. *Lectures on the Philosophy of World History: Introduction, Reason in History*. Edited by Johannes Hoffmeister, *Cambridge studies in the history and theory of politics*. Cambridge Eng.; New York: Cambridge University Press.

Hegel, Georg Wilhelm Friedrich. 1987. *Introduction to the lectures on the history of philosophy*. Translated by T. M. Knox and A. V. Miller. Oxford [Oxfordshire]; New York: Clarendon Press; Oxford University Press.

Hegel, Georg Wilhelm Friedrich. 1988. *Aesthetics: lectures on fine art*. Translated by T. M. Knox. 2 vols. Oxford: Clarendon Press.

Hegel, Georg Wilhelm Friedrich. 1991. *Elements of the philosophy of right.* Translated by Hugh Barr Nisbet. Edited by Allen W. Wood, *Cambridge texts in the history of political thought.* Cambridge [England]; New York: Cambridge University Press.

Hegel, Georg Wilhelm Friedrich. 1996. *Vorlesungen über die Philosophie der Weltgeschichte: Berlin 1822/1823.* Edited by Karl-Heinz Ilting, Hoo Nam Seelmann and Karl Brehmer, *Vorlesungen / Georg Wilhelm Friedrich Hegel.* Hamburg: F. Meiner Verlag.

Hegel, Georg Wilhelm Friedrich. 2005. *Die Philosophie der Geschichte: Vorlesungsmitschrift Heimann (Winter 1830/1831).* Edited by Klaus Vieweg. Munich: Fink Verlag.

Hegel, Georg Wilhelm Friedrich, Myriam Bienenstock, and Norbert Waszek. 2007. *La philosophie de l'histoire édition réalisée sous la direction de Myriam Bienenstock traduction française de Myriam Bienenstock, Christophe Bouton, Jean-Michel Buée... [et al.] appareil critique de Norbert Waszek, La pochothèque.* Paris: Librairie générale française.

Hegel, Georg Wilhelm Friedrich, Robert F. Brown, Peter Crafts Hodgson, and Georg Wilhelm Friedrich Hegel. 2011. *Lectures on the Philosophy of World History: Volume I: Manuscripts of the Introduction and the Lectures of 1822–23, The Hegel lectures series.* Oxford England: Oxford University Press.

Hegel, Georg Wilhelm Friedrich, Clark Butler, and Christiane Seiler. 1984. *Hegel, the letters.* Bloomington: Indiana University Press.

Hegel, Georg Wilhelm Friedrich, and George Di Giovanni. 2010. *The science of logic, Cambridge Hegel translations.* Cambridge; New York: Cambridge University Press.

Hegel, Georg Wilhelm Friedrich, Laurence Winant Dickey, and H. B. Nisbet. 1999. *G.W.F. Hegel—Political Writings, Cambridge texts in the history of political thought.* New York: Cambridge University Press.

Hegel, Georg Wilhelm Friedrich, Théodore F. Geraets, W. A. Suchting, and H. S. Harris. 1991. *The encyclopaedia logic, with the Zusätze: Part I of the Encyclopaedia of philosophical sciences with the Zusätze.* Indianapolis: Hackett.

Hegel, Georg Wilhelm Friedrich, and Peter Crafts Hodgson. 1984. *Lectures on the philosophy of religion: Volume III: Determinate Religion.* 3 vols. Berkeley: University of California Press.

Hegel, Georg Wilhelm Friedrich, and Johannes Hoffmeister. 1956. *Berliner Schriften, 1818–1831.* Vol. 11, *His Sämtliche Werke, neue kritische Ausgabe, Bd 11.* Hamburg,: F. Meiner.

Hegel, Georg Wilhelm Friedrich, and Johannes Hoffmeister. 1961. *Briefe von und an Hegel.* [2. unveränderte Aufl.] ed. 4 vols. Hamburg,: Felix Meiner.

Hegel, Georg Wilhelm Friedrich, and Johannes Hoffmeister. 1994. *Vorlesungen über die Philosophie der Weltgeschichte: Band I: Die Vernunft in der Geschichte.* 4 vols. Vol. Band 1: Die Vernunft in der Geschichte, *Philosophische Bibliothek.* Hamburg: F. Meiner.

Hegel, Georg Wilhelm Friedrich, and Karl-Heinz Ilting. 1973. *Vorlesungen über Rechtsphilosophie, 1818–1831: Philosophie des Rechts nach der Vorlesungsnachschrift K.G. v. Griesheims 1824/25*. Edited by Karl-Heinz Ilting. Vol. iv. Stuttgart-Bad Cannstatt: Frommann-Holzboog.

Hegel, Georg Wilhelm Friedrich, and Georg Lasson. 1923. *Vorlesungen über die Philosophie der Weltgeschichte: III: Die griechische und die römische Welt*. Vol. III: Die griechische und die römische Welt, *Georg Wilhelm Friedrich Hegel Sämtliche Werke*. Leipzig: F. Meiner.

Hegel, Georg Wilhelm Friedrich, and Georg Lasson. 1968. *Vorlesungen über die Philosophie der Weltgeschichte: IV: Die germanische Welt*. 4 vols. Vol. Band 4: Die germanische Welt, *Philosophische Bibliothek, Bd 171c–171d*. Hamburg: F. Meiner.

Hegel, Georg Wilhelm Friedrich, and Arnold V. Miller. 2004. *Hegel's philosophy of nature: being part two of the Encyclopedia of the philosophical sciences (1830), translated from Nicolin and Pöggeler's edition (1959), and from the Zusätze in Michelet's text (1847)*. Oxford / New York: Clarendon Press; Oxford University Press.

Hegel, Georg Wilhelm Friedrich, William Wallace, Arnold V. Miller, and Ludwig Boumann. 1971. *Hegel's Philosophy of Mind: being Part Three of the 'Encyclopaedia of the Philosophical Sciences' (1830)*. Oxford: Clarendon Press.

Hobsbawm, E. J. 1996. *The age of revolution 1789–1848*. 1st Vintage Books ed. New York: Vintage Books.

Hodgson, Peter Crafts. 2012. *Shapes of Freedom: Hegel's Philosophy of World History in Theological Perspective*. 1st ed. Oxford: Oxford University Press.

Horstmann, Rolf-Peter. 2006. "Substance, subject and infinity: a case study of the role of logic in Hegel's system"." In *Hegel: New Directions*, edited by Katerina Deligiorgi, 69–84. Chesham: Acumen.

Houlgate, Stephen. 1991. *Freedom, truth and history: an introduction to Hegel's philosophy*. London: Routledge.

Houlgate, Stephen. 2003. "G. W. F. Hegel: The Phenomenology of Spirit"." In *The Blackwell guide to continental philosophy*, edited by Robert C. Solomon and David L. Sherman, 8–29. Malden, MA: Blackwell Pub.

Houlgate, Stephen. 2006. *The opening of Hegel's logic: from being to infinity, Purdue University Press series in the history of philosophy*. West Lafayette, Ind.: Purdue University Press.

Jaeggi, Rahel. 2014. *Kritik von Lebensformen*. 1. Aufl. ed, *Suhrkamp Taschenbuch Wissenschaft*. Berlin: Suhrkamp.

Kant, Immanuel. 1929. *Immanuel Kant's Critique of pure reason*. Translated by Norman Kemp Smith. London: Macmillan.

Kant, Immanuel. 1960. *Religion within the limits of reason alone, Harper torchbooks. The Cloister Library,*. New York,: Harper.

Kant, Immanuel, and Mary J. Gregor. 1996. *The metaphysics of morals, Cambridge texts in the history of philosophy.* Cambridge; New York: Cambridge University Press.

Kervégan, Jean-François. 2007. *L'effectif et le rationnel: Hegel et l'esprit objectif, BibliothÁeque d'histoire de la philosophie Temps modernes.* Paris: J. Vrin.

Khurana, Thomas, ed. 2013. *The Freedom of Life.* Berlin: August Verlag.

Knowles, Dudley, and Michael Carpenter. 2010/2011. "Hegel as Ornithologist." *The Owl of Minerva* 42 (1/2):225–227.

Krebs, Christopher B. 2011. *A most dangerous book: Tacitus's Germania from the Roman Empire to the Third Reich.* 1st ed. New York: W.W. Norton & Co.

Kreines, James. 2006. "Hegel's Metaphysics: Changing the Debate." *Philosophy Compass* 1 (5):466–480.

Kreines, James. 2008a. "The Logic of Life: Hegel's Philosophical Defense of Teleological Explanation of Living Beings"." In *The Cambridge Companion to Hegel and Nineteenth-Century Philosophy, Beiser, Frederick C. (ed).* Cambridge: Cambridge University Press.

Kreines, James. 2008b. "Metaphysics without Pre-Critical Monism: Hegel on Lower-Level Natural Kinds and the Structure of Reality." *Bulletin of the Hegel Society of Great Britain* 57–58:48–70.

Kreines, James. 2015. *Reason in the world: Hegel's metaphysics and its philosophical appeal.* Oxford: Oxford University Press.

Krieger, Leonard. 1977. *Ranke: the meaning of history.* Chicago: University of Chicago Press.

Kukla, Rebecca, and Mark Norris Lance. 2009. *'Yo!' and 'Lo!': The Pragmatic Topography of the Space of Reasons.* Cambridge, Mass.; London: Harvard University Press.

Lance, Mark Norris, and John Hawthorne. 1997. *The grammar of meaning: normativy and semantic discourse, Cambridge studies in philosophy.* Cambridge: Cambridge University Press.

Larmore, Charles E. 2012. *Vernunft und Subjektivität: Frankfurter Vorlesungen.* 1. Aufl. ed, *Suhrkamp Taschenbuch Wissenschaft.* Berlin: Suhrkamp.

Lauer, Quentin, and Georg Wilhelm Friedrich Hegel. 1983. *Hegel's idea of philosophy with a new translation of Hegel's Introduction to the history of philosophy.* 2nd ed. New York: Fordham University Press.

Lavin, Douglas. 2004. "Other Wills: the second-person in ethics." *Philosophical Explorations* 17 (3):279–288.

Le Goff, Jacques. 2005. *The birth of Europe, The making of Europe.* Malden, MA: Blackwell.

Lewis, Thomas A. 2011. *Religion, modernity, and politics in Hegel.* Oxford; New York: Oxford University Press.

Longuenesse, Béatrice. 2012. "Kant and Hegel on the Moral Self"." In *Self, world, and art: metaphysical topics in Kant and Hegel*, edited by Dina Emundts, 89–113. Berlin: Walter de Gruyter.

Lopez, Robert Sabatino. 1967. *The birth of Europe*. New York,: M. Evans; distributed in association with Lippincott.

Marchand, Suzanne L. 2009. *German orientalism in the age of empire: religion, race, and scholarship, Publications of the German Historical Institute*. Washington, D.C.; New York: German Historical Institute; Cambridge University Press.

McCarney, Joe. 2000. *Routledge philosophy guidebook to Hegel on history, Routledge philosophy guidebooks*. London; New York: Routledge.

McDowell, John Henry. 2009. *Having the World in View: Essays on Kant, Hegel, and Sellars*. Cambridge, Mass.: Harvard University Press.

McNeill, John Robert, and William Hardy McNeill. 2003. *The human web: a bird's-eye view of world history*. 1st ed. New York: W.W. Norton.

Menke, Christoph. 2010. "Autonomie und Befreiung." *Deutsche Zeitschrift für Philosophie* 58 (5):675–694.

Menke, Christoph. 2015. "Die Möglichkeit der Revolution." *Merkur—Deutsche Zeitschrift für europäisches Denken* 69 (July 2015).

Moland, Lydia L. 2011. *Hegel on political identity: patriotism, nationality, cosmopolitanism, Topics in historical philosophy*. Evanston, Ill.: Northwestern University Press.

Moore, A. W. 2012. *The Evolution of Modern Metaphysics: Making Sense of Things, The evolution of modern philosophy*. New York: Cambridge University Press.

Moyar, Dean. 2010. *Hegel's conscience*. New York: Oxford University Press.

Nicolin, Friedhelm, Lucia Sziborsky, and Helmut Schneider. 1996. *Auf Hegels Spuren: Beiträge zur Hegel-Forschung, Hegel-Deutungen*. Hamburg: F. Meiner.

Nicolin, Günther. 1970. *Hegel in Berichten seiner Zeitgenossen, Philosophische Bibliothek*. Hamburg,: F. Meiner.

Novakovic, Andreja. 2015. "Gewohnheit des Sittlichen bei Hegel"." In *Momente der Freiheit*, edited by Julia Christ and Titus Stahl. Frankfurt a.M.: Klostermann.

O'Brien, Dennis. 1975. *Hegel on reason and history: a contemporary interpretation*. Chicago: University of Chicago Press.

Osborne, Robin. 2004. *Greek history, Classical foundations*. London; New York: Routledge.

Padgett-Walsh, Katherine. 2010. "Reasons Internalism, Hegelian Resources." *The Journal of Value Inquiry* 44 (2).

Padgett-Walsh, Katherine. forthcoming. "A Hegelian Critique of Desire-Based Reasons." *Idealistic Studies: An Interdisciplinary Journal of Philosophy* 45 (1).

Pinkard, Terry. 1992. "L'Internalisme Historique et la Légitimité des Institutions Sociales"." In *Cahiers de philosophie politique et juridique* edited by Otfried Höffe. Caen, France.

Pinkard, Terry. 2007. "Symbolic, Classical and Romantic Art." In *Hegel and the Arts*, edited by Stephen Houlgate, 3–28. Evanston, IL.: Northwestern University Press.

Pinkard, Terry. 2008. "Autorität und Kunst-Religion." In *Hegels Phänomenologie des Geistes: ein kooperativer Kommentar zu einem Schlüsselwerk der Moderne*, edited by Klaus Vieweg and Wolfgang Welsch, 540–561. Frankfurt am Main: Suhrkamp.

Pinkard, Terry. 2012. *Hegel's Naturalism: Mind, Nature, and the Final Ends of Life*: Oxford University Press.

Pinkard, Terry P. 1988. *Hegel's dialectic: the explanation of possibility*. Philadelphia: Temple University Press.

Pinkard, Terry P. 1994. *Hegel's Phenomenology: the sociality of reason*. Cambridge: Cambridge University Press.

Pinkard, Terry P. 2000. *Hegel: a biography*. Cambridge: Cambridge University Press.

Pippin, Robert. 2014a. "Die Logik der Negation bei Hegel." In *Hegel—200 Jahre Wissenschaft der Logik*, edited by Claudia Wirsing, Koch A. F. Koch, F. Schick and Klaus Vieweg, 480. Hamburg, Germany: Felix Meiner.

Pippin, Robert. 2014b. "The Significance of Self-Consciousness in Idealist Theories of Logic." *Proceedings of the Aristotelian Society* cxiv, part 2:145–166.

Pippin, Robert. forthcoming. "Hegel on Logic as Metaphysics"." In *Oxford Handbook on Hegel's Philosophy*, edited by Dean Moyar. New York: Oxford University Press.

Pippin, Robert B. 1991. *Modernism as a philosophical problem: on the dissatisfactions of European high culture*. Cambridge, Mass; Oxford: Blackwell.

Pippin, Robert B. 1997. *Idealism as modernism: Hegelian variations, Modern European philosophy*. Cambridge: Cambridge University Press.

Pippin, Robert B. 2005. "Concept and Intuition: On Distinguishability and Separability." *Hegel-Studien* 40.

Pippin, Robert B. 2008. *Hegel's practical philosophy: rational agency as ethical life*. Cambridge: Cambridge University Press.

Pippin, Robert B. 2010a. *Hegel on Self-Consciousness: Desire and Death in Hegel's Phenomenology of Spirit*. Princeton: Princeton University Press.

Pippin, Robert B. 2010b. *Hollywood westerns and American myth: the importance of Howard Hawks and John Ford for political philosophy, The Castle lectures in ethics, politics, and economics*. New Haven [Conn.]: Yale University Press.

Pippin, Robert B. 2014c. *After the beautiful: Hegel and the philosophy of pictorial modernism*. Chicago; London: The University of Chicago Press.

Polybius, W. R. Paton, F. W. Walbank, ·Christian Habicht, Polybius, and Polybius. 2010. *The Histories*. Second Edition / ed, *Loeb Classical Library*. Cambridge, Massachusetts: Harvard University Press.

Quante, Michael. 2004. *Hegel's concept of action, Modern European philosophy*. Cambridge, U.K.; New York: Cambridge University Press.

Rand, Sebastian. 2016. "The Philosophy of Nature"." In *Oxford Handbook on Hegel's Philosophy*, edited by Dean Moyar. New York: Oxford.

Ranke, Leopold von, Walther Peter Fuchs, and Theodor Schieder. 1964. *Aus Werk und Nachlass*. München: Historische Kommission bei der Bayerischen Akademie der Wissenschaften.

Rebentisch, Juliane. 2012. *Die Kunst der Freiheit: zur Dialektik demokratischer Existenz*. 1. Auflage, Originalausgabe. ed, *Suhrkamp Taschenbuch Wissenschaft*. Berlin: Suhrkamp.

Redding, Paul. 2014. "The Role of Logic 'Commonly So Called' in Hegel's Science of Logic." *British Journal for the History of Philosophy* 22 (2):281–301. doi: 10.1080/09608788.2014.891196.

Richardson, Henry S. 2002. *Democratic autonomy: public reasoning about the ends of policy, Oxford political theory*. New York: Oxford University Press.

Rödl, Sebastian. 2007. *Self-consciousness*. Cambridge, Mass.; London: Harvard University Press.

Rödl, Sebastian. 2010. "The Form of the Will"." In *Desire, Practical Reason, and the Good*, edited by Sergio Tenenbaum, 138–160. New York: Oxford University Press.

Romm, James S. 1989. "Aristotle's Elephant and the Myth of Alexander's Scientific Patronage." *The American Journal of Philology* 110 (No. 4):566–575.

Rorty, Amélie, and James Schmidt. 2009. *Kant's Idea for a universal history with a cosmopolitan aim: a critical guide, Cambridge critical guides*. Cambridge, UK; New York: Cambridge University Press.

Rosen, Michael. 2011. "Freedom in History"." In *Freiheit: Stuttgarter Hegel-Kongress 2011*, edited by Gunnar Hindrichs and Axel Honneth, 535–51. Frankfurt a. M.: Klostermann.

Rothman, Adam. 2005. *Slave country: American expansion and the origins of the Deep South*. Cambridge, Mass.: Harvard University Press.

Rousseau, Jean-Jacques. 1968. *The social contract, Penguin classics, L201*. Baltimore: Penguin Books.

Rousseau, Jean-Jacques, and Willmoore Kendall. 1985. *The government of Poland*. Indianapolis, Ind.: Hackett Pub. Co.

Rutter, Benjamin. 2011. *Hegel on the Modern Arts*. Cambridge: Cambridge University Press.

Sedgwick, Sally. 2015. "Philosophy of History"." In *The Oxford handbook of German philosophy in the nineteenth century*, edited by Michael N. Forster and Kristin Gjesdal, 436–452. New York; Oxford: Oxford University Press.

Sedgwick, Sally S. 2012. *Hegel's critique of Kant: from dichotomy to identity.* Oxford: Oxford University Press.

Sellars, Wilfrid. 1963. *Science, Perception and Reality, International library of philosophy and scientific method.* New York: Humanities Press.

Sen, Amartya. 2005. *The argumentative Indian: writings on Indian history, culture, and identity.* 1st American ed. New York: Farrar, Straus and Giroux.

Setiya, Kieran. May 2013. "Murdoch on the Sovereignty of Good." *Philosopher's Imprint* 13 (9):1–21.

Smith, Anthony D. 1991. *National identity, Ethnonationalism in comparative perspective.* Reno: University of Nevada Press.

Smith, Anthony D. 1998. *Nationalism and modernism: a critical survey of recent theories of nations and nationalism.* London; New York: Routledge.

Sparby, Terje. 2014. "The Open Closure of Hegel's Method and System: A Critique of Terry Pinkard's Naturalized Hegel"." *Clio* 22 (1):1–32.

Stekeler-Weithofer, Pirmin. 2001. "Vorsehung und Entwicklung in Hegels Geschichtsphilosophie"." In *Weltgeschichte–das Weltgericht? Stuttgarter Hegel Kongress 1999*, edited by Rüdiger Bubner and Walter Mesch, 141–168. Stuttgart: Klett-Cotta.

Taiwo, Olufemi. 1998. "Exorcising Hegel's Ghost: Africa's Challenge to Philosophy." *African Studies Quarterly* 1 (4):1–16.

Taylor, Charles. 1975. *Hegel.* Cambridge Eng.; New York: Cambridge University Press.

Testa, Italo. 2009. "Second Nature and Recognition: Hegel and the Social Space." *Critical Horizons: A Journal of Philosophy and Social Theory* 10 (3):341–70.

Testa, Italo. 2013. "Hegel's Naturalism or Soul and Body in the Encyclopedia"." In *Essays on Hegel's philosophy of subjective spirit*, edited by David S. Stern, 19–36. Albany: State University of New York Press.

Thomas, Keith. 2009. *The ends of life: roads to fulfilment in early modern England.* Oxford; New York: Oxford University Press.

Thompson, Michael. 2004. "What Is It to Wrong Someone? A Puzzle about Justice"." In *Reason and Value: Themes from the Moral Philosophy of Joseph Raz* edited by R. Jay Wallace, et al., 333–384. Oxford; New York: Oxford University Press.

Thompson, Michael. 2008. *Life and action: elementary structures of practice and practical thought.* Cambridge, Mass.: Harvard University Press.

Thompson, Michael. 2013. "Forms of nature: 'first', 'second', 'living', 'rational' and 'phronetic'." In *Freiheit: Stuttgarter Hegel-Kongress 2011*, edited by Gunnar Hindrichs and Axel Honneth, 701–735. Frankfurt am Main: Vittorio Klostermann.

Tinland, Olivier. 2013. *L'idéalisme hégélien.* Paris: CNRS éditions.

Toews, John Edward. 2004. *Becoming historical: cultural reformation and public memory in early nineteenth-century Berlin.* Cambridge, UK; New York: Cambridge University Press.

Vieweg, Klaus. 2012. *Das Denken der Freiheit: Hegels Grundlinien der Philosophie des Rechts*. München: Wilhelm Fink.

Viyagappa, Ignatius. 1980. *G.W.F. Hegel's concept of Indian philosophy, Documenta missionalia*. Roma: Università Gregoriana.

Wallace, R. Jay. 2005. "Moral Psychology." In *The Oxford Handbook of Contemporary Philosophy*, edited by Frank Jackson and Michael Smith, 86–113. Oxford: New York: Oxford University Press.

Wallace, R. Jay. 2013. *The view from here: on affirmation, attachment, and the limits of regret*. Oxford; New York: Oxford University Press.

Wang, Hui. 2014. *China from empire to nation-state*. Cambridge: Harvard University Press.

Weiss, Leonhard. 2012. *Hegels Geschichtsphilosophie und das moderne Europa*. Wien: Lit Verlag. Based on author's thesis (doctoral).

Welch, Cheryl. 2012. " 'Anti-Benthamism': Utilitarianism and the French Liberal Tradition"." In *French Liberalism from Montesquieu to the Present Day*, edited by Raf Geenens and Helena Rosenblatt, 134–151. New York: Cambridge University Press.

Westphal, Kenneth R. 2016. "Hegel's Natural Law Constructivism: Progress in Principle and in Practice"." In *Hegel's Practical Philosophy: On the Normative Significance of Method and System*, edited by Thom Brooks and Sebastian Stein. Oxford: Oxford University Press.

Wiland, Eric. 2012. *Reasons, Continuum ethics series*. London; New York: Continuum International Pub.

Wilkins, Burleigh Taylor. 1974. *Hegel's philosophy of history*. Ithaca,: Cornell University Press.

Winfield, Richard Dien. 2013. *Hegel's phenomenology of spirit: a critical rethinking in seventeen lectures*. Lanham: Rowman & Littlefield Publishers, Inc.

Wittgenstein, Ludwig. 1963. *Tractatus logico-philosophicus. The German text of Logisch-philosophische Abhandlung, International library of philosophy and scientific method*. London, New York,: Routledge & Kegan Paul;Humanities Press.

Wood, Allen W. 1990. *Hegel's ethical thought*. Cambridge [England]; New York: Cambridge University Press.

Woolf, Greg. 2012. *Rome: an empire's story*. New York: Oxford University Press.

Yeomans, Christopher. 2015. *The expansion of autonomy: Hegel's pluralistic philosophy of action*. New York, N.Y.: Oxford University Press.

Ziolkowski, Theodore. 2004. *Clio the Romantic muse: historicizing the faculties in Germany*. Ithaca: Cornell University Press.

ACKNOWLEDGMENTS

Several people read over the manuscript and gave me valuable advice on all the mistakes I made and gave me encouragement for the parts they thought I got right. I hope I have been able to follow their advice. My thanks go to Katarina Deligiorgi, Dean Moyar, Robert Pippin, and Sally Sedgwick.

INDEX

Satisfaction *(Befriedigung)*, 101–102
Schiller, Friedrich, 122
Schlegel, Friedrich, 202n35
Science of Logic (Hegel), 30; conception of subjectivity in, 90–91, 140–144; Greece and Rome in, 80–87; human subjectivity in, 12–19; introduction to, 3–5; judgments in, 13; logic in, 20; shadows in, 20, 45, 183n47; spirit in, 19–22
Science of science, 5
Selbstzweck (end unto itself), 10, 175n9, 182n46
Self-awareness, reflection in, 11
Self-certainty, meaning and, 22–23
Self-consciousness, 7–8; in ancient Greece, 68–79; of animals, 7–10; authority in, 20–29; concept of, 11; conflict and, 23–24; as consciousness of consciousness, 29; consumer goods and, 88; desire in, 20–21; in early Roman society, 89–94; freedom in, 29–38; of humans, 10–12; justice and, 26–27; Kant on, 11; of life, 11; in modern world, 157–163; order of thought in, 20–29, 33, 36–37; other and, 22–29; passion in, 14, 30–35, 40; self-presence and, 22; self-relation and, 8, 10; space of reasons and, 44; spirit and, 19–22; subjectivity in, 29–38; universal and, 8, 29, 44, 186n67; will in, 29–38
Self-identity, 1–3; essentialism on, 1
Self-interpreting animals, 45, 166

Self-knowledge, 150–157; of action, 21–22; of subject, 19
Self-presence, self-consciousness and, 22
Self-reflection, 60, 142
Self-relation: of animals, 6; self-consciousness and, 8, 10
Self-sufficiency: in ancient Greece, 72–79; in European formation, 109–110; slavery in, 68–79
Self-understanding, 83–87
Self-unity *(bei sich selbst)*, 36, 92
Sen, Amartya, 61
Sense-certainty, 22–23, 184n58
Sensibility, 122
Servitude, mastery and, 24–29, 44–45
Shadowboxing, 32, 188n79
Shadows, 20
Shakespeare, William, 110–111
Shape of life, Idea and, 20
Sitte (traditional mores), 57, 221n123
Sittlichkeit (ethical life), 57, 122–123, 158
Slave, master and, 24–28
Slavery, 65; in America, 162–163; Christian freedom from, 92–94; in Greece, 68–79; in idea of freedom, 145–146; natural slave, 74–76, 145, 156, 163; normative and, 40–41; in Rome, 86–87
Smith, Adam, 50, 95, 115, 212n51
Sociopath, Greek hero as, 74
Song dynasty, 59, 200n23
Soul, beautiful, 132–133, 226n156
Sovereign, 36–38, 57, 60, 118–121; Hegel and, 36